mutiny

at fort jackson

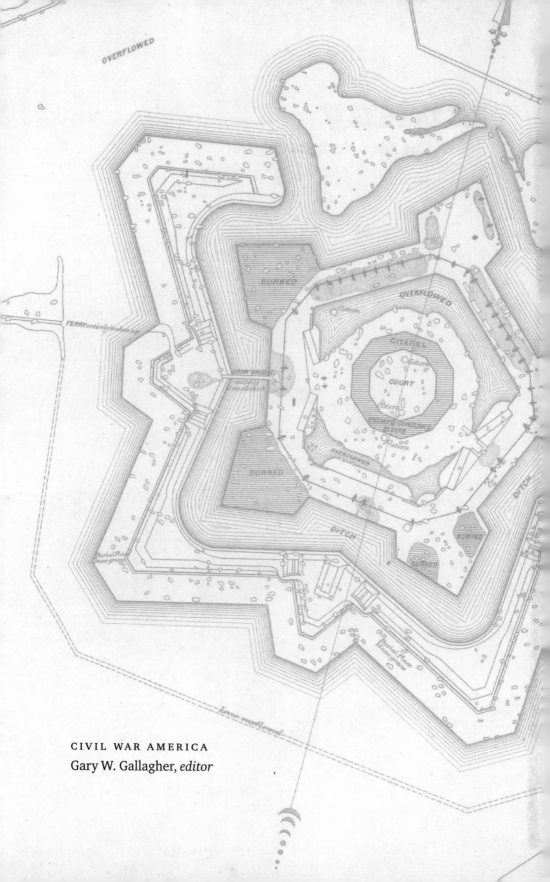

CIVIL WAR AMERICA
Gary W. Gallagher, *editor*

mutiny
at fort jackson

THE UNTOLD STORY OF THE FALL OF NEW ORLEANS

Michael D. Pierson

The University of North Carolina Press

CHAPEL HILL

© 2008 The University of North Carolina Press
All rights reserved
Manufactured in the United States of America

Designed by Courtney Leigh Baker
Set in Charter and Egiziano
by Keystone Typesetting, Inc.

The paper in this book meets the guidelines for permanence
and durability of the Committee on Production Guidelines for
Book Longevity of the Council on Library Resources.

The University of North Carolina Press has been a member of
the Green Press Initiative since 2003.

Library of Congress Cataloging-in-Publication Data
Pierson, Michael D.
Mutiny at Fort Jackson : the untold story of the fall of New
Orleans / Michael D. Pierson.
p. cm. — (Civil War America)
Includes bibliographical references and index.
ISBN 978-0-8078-3228-8 (cloth: alk. paper)
1. Fort Jackson (La.)—History. 2. New Orleans (La.)—
History—Civil War, 1861–1865. 3. Mutiny—Louisiana—New
Orleans—History—19th century. 4. Soldiers—Louisiana—New
Orleans—Social conditions—19th century. 5. Unionists
(United States Civil War)—Louisiana—New Orleans.
6. Confederate States of America. Army—History. 7. New
Orleans (La.)—History—Civil War, 1861–1865—Social
aspects. 8. United States—History—Civil War, 1861–1865—
Social aspects. 9. United States—History—Civil War, 1861–
1865—Participation, German American. 10. United States—
History—Civil War, 1861–1865—Participation, Irish American.
I. Title.
F379.N557P54 2008
973.7'31—dc22   2008018132

A Caravan book. For more information, visit
www.caravanbooks.org.

12 11 10 09 08   5 4 3 2 1

contents

map and illustrations

acknowledgments

In the course of writing this book, I have enjoyed the help and encouragement of a great many people. They may not have saved me from all of my errors, but they have certainly made this a better work of history than it would have been without their help.

Essential support has come from institutions. I am grateful to several groups for funding the archival research trips that underlie this work. In particular, I am indebted to the Lowell National Historical Park for making me its Scholar in the City in 2003 and to the Andersonville National Historical Site for one of its Prisoner of War Research Grants. I have also benefited from two travel grants from the University of Massachusetts, Lowell, including an award from the College of Fine Arts, Humanities, and Social Sciences and a Joseph P. Healey Research Grant. I have also enjoyed support from two fine History Department chairmen while working on this book; Charles Carroll and Joseph Lipchitz not only have come through with financial support but also have created a relaxed department culture that enables people to concentrate on their teaching and research.

The University of Massachusetts, Lowell, has also supported the research for this book through two Faculty-Student Collaborative Research Seed Grants. These grants enabled me to work with two wonderful undergraduates, Megan Williams and Katherine Smith. Both did extensive and demanding research in the newspapers of the period, and citations to periodicals throughout this book usually reflect their work. I appreciate their careful scholarship and enthusiasm. My thanks also to Marvin Stick, Robert Tuholski, and the other members of the Teaching and Learning Grant Task Force for approving my applications.

I would like to thank the Massachusetts Historical Society for graciously allowing me to use material here that previously appeared in the *Massachusetts Historical Review*.

This work could not have been completed without the hard work of librarians and archivists at the many institutions listed in the bibliography. Pamela D. Arceneaux and Siva M. Blake at the Historic New Orleans Collection and Jamie Kingman Rice and William David Barry of the Maine Historical Society were especially helpful and welcoming. The staff members of the Louisiana State University library and the American Antiquarian Society also made my time at their archives not only rewarding but unusually pleasant. Arthur House of the National Archives provided necessary long-distance assistance on a specific project, and I appreciate his help. I would also like to thank Deborah Friedman and Rose Paton of UML's O'Leary Library for their friendly assistance.

Stephen V. Ash and Victoria Bynum have generously read the entire manuscript, and they made many suggestions for how to make it a better book. My thanks to both of them. Gary Gallagher, the editor of the Civil War America series, likewise offered a valuable reading of the manuscript. Crandall Shifflett and Michael Fitzgerald also read parts of this project in its earlier phases, and their enthusiasm helped move it along. Friendly discussions with Stacey Robertson, Frank Towers, Ron and Mary Zboray, and Fred Blue made this project that much more fun.

One of my joys over the past few years in Lowell has been becoming active in a variety of local historical organizations, including the Lowell Historical Society, the Gilman E. Sleeper Camp #60 of the Sons of Union Veterans of the Civil War, and the Friends of Major General Benjamin F. Butler. Through these organizations, I have had the chance to talk about this project and, more important, share in the enthusiasm for history that fills these meetings. There is not room here to thank all of these people by name, but special thanks to Cynthia and Ellsworth Brown, Benjamin Emerick, Philip Belanger, Denise Cailler, Tom Langan, Martha Mayo, and Marie Sweeney.

My mother, Jane Church Pierson, has been a joy to visit and talk with for the whole long time that it has taken to write this book. Moving to Massachusetts has made it possible to once again regularly see my brother, Eric; his wife, Beverley; and their charming son, Ethan. This book is dedicated to their other son, Jordan, who is much missed.

Laura Barefield has shared my life throughout the long years of this book's production. At times, her assistance has been direct and material, at other times subtle and quiet, but always it has been invaluable. I'm looking forward to our post–Fort Jackson life together with eager anticipation.

massacre on the levee

On the morning of April 25, 1862, a U.S. fleet steamed toward New Orleans. Quickly brushing aside Confederate batteries just below the city, the warships approached the largest city in the South just before noon. The sailors strove to catch a glimpse of the city, but smoke from a hundred fires filled the air as Confederates burned anything that might be of value to the United States. Some Confederate patriots set ships alight and cast them adrift on the river, while others scuttled the massive dry docks on the west bank or consigned cotton to the flames. Angry men burst open barrels of sugar and molasses and poured their contents into the gutters.

But Confederate sympathizers were not alone in witnessing the fleet's arrival. Despite "a terrible rain squall," many other people lined the levees and wharves to welcome the Federal fleet to the Crescent City.[1] The deck log of the USS *Brooklyn* notes, "While steaming up the lower part of the city we were cheered by the crowd assembled on the levee." Other men in the fleet reported on the favorable reception they received from the people of

Sketch of New Orleans on the day Farragut's fleet arrived by William Waud, an eyewitness. (The Historic New Orleans Collection)

New Orleans. When the fleet anchored off the city's wharves shortly after noon, Thomas Harris, a Federal crewman on the *Mississippi*, saw that "great excitement was visible. All secesh [secession] flags were pulled down, and the stars and stripes were run up on the Custom House." The sight of the U.S. flag flying from the ships' rigging, he wrote, "called forth some loud huzzas from those who had seen it before, and with joy they hailed it now." Samuel Massa, a clerk on the *Cayuga*, recorded in his diary that at 1 P.M. "a good many men and women came out and cheered us and one woman hoisted the stars and stripes on the Algiers side." Local resident G. M. Shipper later recalled flying the "old, red, white and blue, from [his] house No 205 Lafayette Street, on the morning of the day the Federal fleet came into New Orleans." Reports of the pro-Union demonstrations made their way into Captain David Farragut's report that night to the Navy Department. Men from the fleet had raised the U.S. flag over the former Mint building, he wrote, "and the people cheered it."[2]

Confederates could not bear such displays of Union patriotism. G. M. Shipper, who had hung Old Glory from his house, was hauled off to prison for his indiscretion, where he waited until U.S. general Thomas Williams could spring him from his cell. The flag-waving Americans at the levee faired much worse. Bradley S. Osbon, a reporter for the *New York Herald*, described what happened next: "People were rushing to and fro. *Some of them cheered for the Union, when they were fired upon by the crowd.*" Other eyewitnesses filled in details; the log of the USS *Richmond* notes that the civilians were attacked by "a troop of horsemen [who] came riding up one of the streets and fired a volley into the men, women, and children." Another ship's log includes the news that "a volly [*sic*] of musketry [was] discharged among them by some soldiers standing near[.] A number was seen to fall." This slaughter appears to have cleared the levee of Unionists. Samuel Massa reported that by 4:00 P.M. the Unionist civilians had been replaced by "a different crowd to those we first saw, these black-guarding our men and flag of truce, cursed at officers and men sent ashore, calling them damned Yankee abolitionists." One man, he wrote, "got knocked down kicked and beaten for trying to stop his comrades from calling our boats crews names."[3]

We are not accustomed to reading about the massacre of civilians in the American Civil War. Nor do we commonly read about white southerners who welcomed the U.S. military into Dixie. But this slaughter of Unionist men, women, and children occurred in full view of the general public, reporters, and the crews of a dozen U.S. warships. How many people died remains a mystery, shielded by Confederate control of the crime site until evidence could be removed. The pro-Confederate *New Orleans Bee* minimized the incident, saying only that one man had fired a pistol at "some reckless men" near the French market who had given "proofs of jubilation." The single pistol shot theory, however, was undermined by the *Bee*'s admission that the victim later died at a police station after being "mortally wounded and stabbed in two or three places." Other Confederate sources put the number of civilians killed at under five.[4]

Other people thought that the number of civilians killed and wounded that day was much higher. A correspondent for the *Journal of Commerce* (New York) provided the highest estimate, saying that as many as seventy-five people had been killed and many more wounded. Commander George F. Emmons of the USS *Hatteras*, however, may have recorded the most accurate estimate of the number of fatalities on the levee. Stationed some distance away from New Orleans in Louisiana's Berwick Bay, Emmons talked to a Confederate prisoner who claimed to have been in the city on the day of the shootings. The prisoner said that "some 15 or 20 Germans were shot down on the levee" by Confederates angry about "some Union expressions on the part of some of the foreign population of New Orleans."[5] This witness's inclusion of the German origins of the Unionists makes sense in light of what we will see of ethnic tensions in Confederate New Orleans and adds credibility to this report.

Captain David Farragut acted to protect the city's Unionist community when he negotiated with the mayor for the surrender of the city. Farragut's letter demanding surrender included a final warning: "I particularly demand that no person shall be molested in person or property, for sentiments of loyalty to their government. I shall speedily and severely punish any person or persons who shall commit such outrages as were witnessed yesterday—armed men firing upon helpless women and children for giving expression to their pleasure at witnessing the old flag." In response, Mayor John F. Monroe did not deny the massacre; instead, he justified it. The people of New Orleans, he wrote, "do not allow themselves to be insulted by the interference of such as have rendered themselves odious and contemptible by their dastardly desertion of our cause."[6] The Unionists, apparently, had deserved their deaths because they had insulted the Confederate people of New Orleans. With neither Farragut nor Monroe likely to back down, Confederate and Unionist factions in New Orleans were set for a confrontation of uncertain duration.

Histories of the Civil War usually present New Orleans as among the most vehement of Confederate cities. Those of us who grew up on Civil War stories know all about New Orleans's hostility toward its "invaders" and "occupiers." Authors have told their readers all about the angry mob that beset the two Union officers who landed under a flag of truce that afternoon and marched to the city hall with Farragut's letter. We know the story of William Mumford, a bit of a scoundrel, who dared to pull down and destroy a U.S. flag before a cheering crowd, only to be hanged for his actions by the vengeful U.S. commander Benjamin F. Butler. From that point forward, General Butler stands in as the story's villain, a cruel man who rules the city with an iron fist. After killing Mumford, he busily jails Confederate dignitaries and then famously insults the city's women. He is a thief, a war profiteer, and a singularly unsuccessful general. In an interesting linguistic choice, historians always say that Butler and his forces "occupied" New Orleans. They have never used a more neutral, descriptive phrase, such as "regained control of New Orleans for the United States," or even seen the event from the Unionist perspective and called it a "liberation." Recently, academic historians have added to this standard story the fact that African Americans, both free and enslaved, welcomed the U.S. forces. Nevertheless, they portray whites in Civil War New Orleans as devoted to the Confederacy.

Who, then, waved Union flags at Farragut's approaching fleet? Why did they prefer the United States to the Confederacy? Along the path to answering these questions, we will need to visit some cruel places and examine the hardships of war and urban life in nineteenth-century America. We will go to Fort Jackson, far downriver from the Crescent City. Here, several hundred Confederate soldiers staged the largest mutiny in the Civil War. Their story is sometimes tragic and always shrouded in mystery, but it is also not without its moments of hope. Along our journey between the streets of New Orleans and the casemates of Fort Jackson, we will read long-unread sources and hear voices that have been kept silent since the war itself. We will gain, for our troubling visits to places of hardship, a new understanding of the New Orleans we thought we knew. Better yet, we will understand why the United States proved to be the nation of choice for so many of the world's people in the nineteenth century. We will see, rising out of pain and fear, the promise of America.

fort jackson and the defense of new orleans

Confederate general Mansfield Lovell, charged with the defense of New Orleans, relied on Forts Jackson and St. Philip. These two forts stood facing each other on either side of the Mississippi about sixty-five miles downriver of New Orleans. They were large brick structures, and their immediate commander, Brigadier General Johnson K. Duncan, did much to strengthen them over the course of the first year of the war. By the time the U.S. attack came in April 1862, Major General Lovell had placed more than 630 men and 75 heavy cannon in Fort Jackson. Fort St. Philip's garrison and armament were only slightly smaller than those of Fort Jackson.

So it was a considerable blow to Confederate hopes when, after less than two weeks of fighting, the troops stationed at Fort Jackson mutinied against their officers on the night of April 28. The Confederate soldiers in Fort St. Philip may have sympathized with the mutineers, but even without them the revolt in Fort Jackson was the largest mutiny in the Civil War.

Despite the mutiny's size and strategic importance, historians have not examined it in any detail. Thus the mutinous Confederates are still something of a mystery. Our search for their motives will lead us to New Orleans and beyond. Along the way, we will reveal unpleasant truths about our Civil War but also uncover the hopes of the ordinary men and women who chose to embrace the United States as their best hope for happiness. A short history of the Union military campaign to recapture New Orleans will both clarify the importance of the Fort Jackson mutiny and offer us some ideas about why the revolt occurred.[1]

The Union campaign to regain New Orleans started in the spring of 1862, when the Civil War was one year old. While General Lovell marshaled his forces to defend Louisiana, the United States gathered about fifteen thousand soldiers and a large fleet of warships, mortar boats, troop transports, and supply ships for its offensive. By March, the Union force was assembling on Ship Island, off the Mississippi coast.

Most Union soldiers ended up spending many weeks on Ship Island, and their letters home mix news of adventure with boredom and annoyances. Their efforts to find fun or diversion in between drills taxed the ingenuity of the soldiers caught on what one private called "this barren bed of sand."[2] On both the cramped troop ships and Ship Island, Union soldiers endured something of the boredom that their Confederate counterparts were experiencing in Fort Jackson (though over a shorter period), and their ability to tolerate their troubles may be relevant to the issue of whether the hardships of life in isolated Fort Jackson might have been the cause of the mutiny there.

Certainly, Ship Island was no paradise. Homer Sprague of Connecticut complained about an omnipresent "small fly" and the water, which, though abundant, "had a very laxative effect." The island's fine white sand got everywhere, spread by the Gulf winds. Vermont's Jonathan Allen complained that the soldiers on Ship Island had "sand to eat, drink and wear." Alfie Parmenter and other members of the 13th Connecticut's band had a more troubling experience while floating logs back to their camp. At first, they delighted in a school of porpoises swimming by them at a "great rate." Wonder gave way to panic, however, when they realized why the porpoises swam so quickly: "While watching them we saw at about 200 ft from us and coming at right angles with our course the black fin of a shark scooting through the water at lightening speed." They all got out of the water safely,

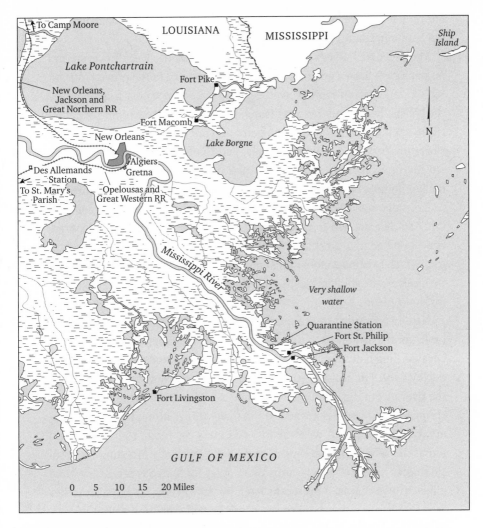

Southeastern Louisiana, 1862

Source: Adapted from *The Official Military Atlas of the Civil War*

(New York: Fairfax Press, 1983), plate CLVI.

but they may have concurred with Jerry Flint of the 4th Wisconsin, who dubbed Ship Island an "accursed Sand bank."[3]

Many Union soldiers managed to entertain themselves, however, and perhaps even have a good time. The exotic flora and fauna proved intriguing. Private Melvan Tibbetts was especially curious. "There is a large bird the Pelican here it sails over the water after fish," he wrote home to Maine. He also found a four-foot-long alligator and put it in a box, presumably for closer observation. Lemons, oranges, and the island's flowers were noteworthy as well. John Goodhue, a private from Salem, Massachusetts, mailed home a box of seashells to his mother and sister, accompanied by remarks about the severe thunderstorms and tornadoes he had seen. Another soldier seemed to enjoy reporting home that he had seen "a huge anaconda hanging over the limb of a tree." (He also "helped kill an alligator," which became a more or less popular sport.) Generally able to amuse themselves, the soldiers eventually reboarded their transports and headed for New Orleans.[4]

Nature continued to dominate the thoughts and letters of men of all ranks as the Union expedition entered the Mississippi. Officers fretted because mud had silted up the passes into the river and delayed the fleet's deployment. For enlisted soldiers and sailors, the slow work of entering the river meant that they had more time to look around them. Packed into cramped quarters, they turned to the living things around them for scenery, for something to write about, and even for food. The northerners found the semitropical creatures and plants especially diverting. Wisconsin soldier Newton Culver's entire diary entry for March 17 reads: "saw ded alligater pleasant day." Six weeks later, he "saw liveing alligator." Another man thought to write about the raccoons he had seen (and eaten), as well as the birds that had sung next to the big ships. A sailor talked of the joys of drinking Mississippi River water—"cold as ice + good tasting too but looks *rather muddy*." Later in the campaign, Melvan Tibbetts sent home a box filled with sand, shells, driftwood, and figs so that his family could sense life in Louisiana.[5] But nature also provided annoyances. A Connecticut soldier on a foraging expedition along the riverbank reported himself "badly wounded" by a chameleon he had tried to get into a bottle. (He seems to have been joking about the extent of his wounds.) Insects plagued everyone. The correspondent for the *New York Times* reported on mosquitoes "of Brobdignagian proportions and midges of lilliputian make."[6]

Fort Jackson and the Defense of New Orleans

But on balance the ships' crews and the soldiers appreciated the sights around them, at times writing letters that could have come from sightseeing tourists. Their ability to entertain themselves for weeks on end helped them resist the most pernicious effects of boredom.

By mid-April the Union force reached its attack positions just below the two main Confederate forts, Jackson and St. Philip. Before getting into position, Commander David Dixon Porter ordered his men to tie branches to his ship's masts so as to camouflage them behind a row of trees. The *New York Times* reporter—he of the Lilliputian midges—remarked optimistically that "Burnam woods come to Dunsinane." Preparing for battle, the men in the fleet were heartened by the "good omen" of "a very large white eagle" that soared over the fleet.[7] Starting on April 18, nineteen mortar schooners under Commander Porter began raining shells into Fort Jackson, the nearer of the two Confederate forts. The mortars continued firing for a week, and the bombardment proved quite a sight. "The River seemed as if on fire for the firing was kept up night and Day," a Connecticut man wrote after three days of mortar shelling. When the wooden parts of Fort Jackson burned in a "large conflagration," Union soldiers and sailors watched the spectacle from their ships and cheered. Especially at the start of the week, their hopes ran high that they would be able to blast the Confederates out of the forts at almost no cost to themselves. Porter and his crews watched the trajectory of their shells as the fiery fuses crossed the night sky. Everett T. Manter, the commander of one of the mortar boats, climbed to the top of a mast and wrote to his brother-in-law, Eben Sherman. "I shall never forget the scene should I live to the age of Noah (and he was pretty old I believe). . . . The shell[s] could be seen from the time they left the mortor [*sic*] untill [*sic*] they exploded." They "looked like falling stars."[8]

The beauty of the bombardment aside, troubling signs arose. Indeed, the lucky eagle apparently did the mortars little good. The work exhausted the gun crews. The guns' recoils also threatened to give crewmen concussions and shook to pieces the ships' decorative woodwork. The masts shuddered under the recoils and caused dead leaves to fall from the camouflage. In the water, "large quantities of dead fish [floated] past our vessels," killed upstream by mortar shells gone astray. Death, you could argue, was everywhere, in the air and in the water. But the Union men refused to see it as foreshadowing their future. Even the *New York Herald* correspondent who had turned a white eagle into good luck saw the dead fish as just so

William Waud's depiction of the Federal mortar bombardment of Fort Jackson,
which is barely visible on the horizon to the right of the plumes of smoke.
(The Historic New Orleans Collection)

many dead fish. But the occasional Confederate return fire filled the air
with real danger. Soldiers and sailors usually greeted the incoming shells
with apparent indifference, but some found them unnerving. "The sound of
approaching hostile shot is by no means agreeable," an assistant surgeon on
a mortar schooner wrote to his family, "& is apt to produce an intense desire
to become smaller."[9] Nor did this return fire stop. Fort Jackson appeared to
be largely intact even after a week of steady mortar barrage.

The Confederate commanders certainly wanted everyone to think their
forts were in good shape. Telegraphic dispatches from the forts' commander, Johnson Duncan, brimmed with confidence. After five days of
combat, the commander reported "but little damage to us so far." A day
later, he updated General Lovell. "We are all cheerful," he wrote, "and have
an abiding faith in our ultimate success." The soldiers' health continued to
be good, he added, and the troops of the garrison "are generally in better
spirits than even in more quiet times." A letter from a young officer in
the fort also found its way into print, no doubt cheering its Confederate
readers with its report of troops "in the highest state of discipline, and
[who] sustained the incessant fire with cheerful courage and patience."

Fort Jackson and the Defense of New Orleans

These reports may not have been true—General Duncan examined all "private dispatches" to make sure that only encouraging reports emerged from Forts Jackson and St. Philip—but even after a week of shelling the forts presented a formidable appearance to the outside world.[10]

After concluding that Porter's mortars would not be able to reduce the rebel forts alone, David Farragut decided to take action with his other warships. Earlier in the week, his men had cut through the massive chain that the Confederates had placed across the river to block ships from steaming past the forts. The river now clear, Farragut ordered his warships upriver on the night of April 24, hoping to get between the forts and New Orleans. Other historians have described the resulting battle with accuracy and in great detail, so it is not necessary here to record the night's events at length. All but four of Farragut's seventeen ships made it past the forts, and only one vessel was sunk. In the course of the battle, the Federal navy destroyed the small Confederate fleet. In all, U.S. casualties for the entire campaign numbered 39 killed and 171 wounded. In every way, the passing of the forts was a success for Farragut. As one soldier on a transport ship below the forts wrote, "The battle of fort Jackson was a grand sight."[11]

Historians usually present Farragut's passing of the forts as the point at which the Union won the New Orleans campaign. That is understandable but not quite accurate. It is true that from this point on, Union ships fought no more large battles before entering New Orleans. On land, Major General Benjamin Butler's Union infantry began the process of moving through the swamps in back of Fort St. Philip to surround the Confederate garrisons. This was no easy task—soldiers reported sleepless nights, long miles of rowing shallow-draft boats, and finally two miles of "wading all the way mud and water up under our arms all the way[.] [W]e were pretty tough looking boys." For all the difficulty nature presented, however, they encountered no Confederate resistance.[12] On the river, things appeared even more promising. Farragut cruised up the river from Forts Jackson and St. Philip to New Orleans almost at his leisure. He and his men encountered resistance from only two small Confederate batteries south of the city, and Farragut described his success there as "a dash and a victory." One veteran of the campaign wrote home that "none of those [forts] above Forts Jackson and St. Philip detained the fleet over 15 minutes. The rebels fled at first fire."[13]

Even many of the people living along the river above Fort Jackson

Union sailor Daniel D. T. Nestell's sketch of Farragut's fleet fighting past the Confederate forts. (Special Collections and Archives Division, Nimitz Library, U.S. Naval Academy)

seemed pleased to see the Union fleet. The enslaved laborers on the rice and sugar plantations welcomed the U.S. fleet. Union sailors mostly seemed amused by their demonstrations. Oscar Smith, a marine on the USS *Hartford*, wrote that the blacks "welcome us," but he minimized the significance of the act: "A venerable old darkey gave his hat a great flourish and called for 'Three cheers for Abraham,' which set the ship in a roar of laughter."[14] But the more astute crewmen made connections between slavery's abuses, the Union arrival, and the allegiances of this part of the Confederacy's population. Frank Peck, a major in the 12th Connecticut, had been a racial conservative before the war, but he now realized that slaves would be his friends. "The darkies are jubilant—except occasionally where we can see an overseer standing by—one with a big whip in his hand—then they give us only sly looks over the shoulder without stopping their work for an instant," he wrote. Frank Harding, who would later serve as an officer in a black regiment, overheard a slave who explained that the slaves "were glad that the old flag had come back and that their masters wouldnt [*sic*] *dare* to use them so bad." For an antislavery man like Harding, the slave's words made him laugh "more that day than I shall for a year to come." Most members of the fleet enjoyed the welcome they received from African Americans. As a surgeon on the USS *Mississippi* remembered it thirty years later, "The negroes were wild with delight, evidently thinking that their millennium had come, and so it had."[15] Recently, historians have traced the slow end of slavery in Louisiana and recognized that the millennium did not come immediately, but certainly the beginnings of a cautious, multirace alliance were visible on the banks of the river when Farragut steamed north.[16]

Fort Jackson and the Defense of New Orleans

Less well known is the reaction of whites along the Mississippi. One would expect that whites living along the river would have glowered at the passing fleet. Some did. Men in the fleet noted that "white masters and mistresses scowled defiance, or turned their backs in impotent scorn and rage." Another wrote of the joys of trading with blacks and "rattling the seceshers" as they journeyed up the river.[17] But they also met whites who seemed glad to see them. Such Unionists were a minority of the riverside population, perhaps even a small minority. Newspaper correspondents with the fleet used phrases such as "in a few instances" and "occasionally" to describe the frequency with which they met white Unionists. The *New York Herald*'s naval reporter saw that "for some miles *the houses on each bank [were] decorated with white flags, and in several instances tattered and torn American ensigns waved over* fishing luggers and houses. We were greeted by the waving of handkerchiefs, and the people seemed glad to see us."[18] The fact that any whites warmly greeted the U.S. Navy speaks to our need to recognize that Louisiana whites were not unanimously Confederate. Even if only "some waved handkerchiefs" while "others stood dumb," as one soldier recorded the ratio of Unionists to Confederates on the riverbank, the presence of "some" Unionists suggests that historians need to look more closely at the relationship between the collapse of the Confederate military around New Orleans and the divided loyalties of the region's white population.[19]

Despite the ease with which Farragut's ships and Butler's infantry moved in the aftermath of Farragut's bold attack, there is little reason to see the Union military position at this point as secure, let alone triumphant. Although Farragut's fleet commanded New Orleans from the vantage point of the flooded Mississippi, he could not yet occupy the city. His warships could muscle past the forts, but the crowded, slow, and thin-walled troop ships surely could not do so, and they languished below the forts. The same could be said for his supply ships. As Farragut sat off the city wharf in late April, he must have realized that he was a long way from accomplishing his main goal of controlling the city. He could demand New Orleans's surrender, but when it was refused, he could not take possession because Butler's infantry remained below the forts. There most of them would remain as long as the forts held out; a handful of Butler's troops only reached the Quarantine Station above the forts after taking the few light draft vessels in the fleet and making a final two-mile hike through waist-

Major General Benjamin Butler was able to get about two regiments of Union infantry close to the Confederate forts on the day before the mutiny occurred. Only two hundred soldiers, however, made it to the Fort Jackson side of the river. This drawing by Daniel Nestell shows how hard the troops had to work to get into position. (Special Collections and Archives Division, Nimitz Library, U.S. Naval Academy)

deep mud. Nor could Farragut feed his crews over the long haul. With no practical supply route or infantry reinforcements on the horizon, a lieutenant on the USS *Cayuga* wrote, "We may be in a tight fix now, if the forts do not fall, and it is not safe for any one to leave our ships and go anywhere in a boat."[20] Farragut's position would remain precarious as long as the forts held firm and kept him separated from the rest of his expedition.

If anything, Commander Porter of the mortar squadron had even more cause for alarm than did Farragut. As his ships lay downriver from the forts, the CSS *Louisiana*, a powerful ironclad ram, still remained tied up alongside the forts. Potentially more fearsome than the CSS *Virginia* (or *Merrimac*), which had recently sunk two large Union frigates in the Chesapeake, the *Louisiana* needed only working engines in order to become operational. After Farragut's fleet passed the forts, the *Louisiana* remained moored next to Fort St. Philip as engineers worked to finish the ship's engines. They were very nearly done with that work. Fearing the worst and regarding his mortars as easy prey for the *Louisiana* if it ever got moving, Porter pulled his ships back from Fort Jackson and retreated toward the mouth of the Mississippi. "These forts can hold out still for some time," a concerned Porter wrote on April 25, "and I would suggest that the Monitor and Mystic (if they can be spared) be sent here without a moments [*sic*] delay to settle the question." For his part, General Butler doubted the wisdom of Farragut's dash past the forts and complained the day after it that Farragut had "left a *ram* and two rebel boats under cover of

The parade ground of Fort Jackson, where the mutineers assembled.
(The Historic New Orleans Collection)

the Forts. They are proving troublesome." In other words, if the forts continued to hold out and the engineers finished the *Louisiana*'s engines, the Union campaign to gain control of New Orleans could still end in disaster.[21] At a minimum, it could take many more weeks.

The tenuous military balance along the river makes what happened next mysterious and very important. On the night of April 27–28, the third night after Farragut had blasted through the Confederate defenses, the garrison of Fort Jackson mutinied. Brazen and successful, the mutineers staged the Civil War's largest mutiny and essentially handed the keys of the city to the Union forces. William J. Seymour's detailed eyewitness account of the revolt confirms the large size of the rebellion and the determination with which it was conducted. A volunteer aide to the forts' commander, Seymour had served in Fort Jackson for about a month. Seymour's father now served as colonel of a Louisiana regiment in Virginia, and he had supported secession as the editor of the *New Orleans Commercial Bulletin*. Seymour's remarks would thus not be impartial, even more so because General Duncan—his commander—would soon be his brother-in-law.[22] Nevertheless, his description of the mutiny mostly corresponds to the facts (but not the mood) in the other accounts we have from Fort Jackson.

Fort Jackson and the Defense of New Orleans

According to Seymour, the mutineers first appeared at about eleven o'clock on the evening of the 27th. They seem to have been very organized. Without any orders from their officers but instead "at a given signal," they "fell into line on the parade plein, under command of their Sergeants, with loaded muskets." Ordered by their startled officers to go back into their quarters, the soldiers refused, "declaring at the same time that they would fight no longer." Seymour states that about four hundred soldiers mutinied and that they persistently refused to obey orders. Matters grew steadily more tense inside the ill-lit brick walls. Only one company, an artillery unit known as the St. Mary's Cannoneers, sided with the officers. The well-organized mutineers, however, had anticipated opposition from the Cannoneers. With the Cannoneers stationed just outside the fort's brick walls in an earthen-work battery, the mutineers had raised the fort's drawbridge and "a strong guard [was] placed at the sally-port, and all communication from without effectively cut off." Furthermore, Seymour relates, a group of mutineers "went up on the ramparts and spiked the guns that bore up the river to prevent us . . . from firing upon them as they left the Fort." Despite continued pleas from their officers and a Catholic priest, Father Nachon, the mutineers held firm. Outnumbered and left with few options, the officers agreed to allow about 250 mutineers to leave the fort and surrender themselves to the Union infantry that had landed in the back of the forts that day. Other mutineers returned to their quarters, but "not until the promise had been extracted from us [the officers] that the mutineers who still held out should be permitted to leave." When dawn broke the next day, General Duncan and his officers agreed that even the remaining men would not fight for the Confederacy, and they contacted Porter and agreed to surrender the forts that afternoon.[23]

Seymour's account emphasizes the organized nature of the mutiny and seems mostly accurate. Union accounts agree, for example, that about 250 Confederate soldiers abandoned the fort that evening to surrender to the Union infantry encircling them.[24] But Seymour's account seems very static, with officers making speeches and the mutineers listening passively before quitting the fort. The testimony of Lieutenant Colonel Edward Higgins, the immediate commander of Fort Jackson, suggests a more fluid situation in which mutineers controlled the flow of events and Confederate officers scrambled to react. His words give the mutineers a more active role, and his shorter sentences convey his surprise, confusion, and haste. He wrote in a letter, "Suddenly at midnight I was aroused by the report that the garrison had revolted, had seized the guard and were spiking the guns. Word was sent us through the sergeants of the companies that the men would fight no longer. The company officers were immediately dispatched to their commands but were driven back. Officers were fired upon when they appeared in sight upon the parapet. Signals were exchanged by the mutineers with Fort St. Philip. The mutiny was complete and a general massacre of the officers, and a disgraceful surrender of the Fort appeared inevitable."[25] Higgins may have been right that the lives of the officers were in far more peril than Seymour's account suggests. A Union correspondent who spoke with the mutineers afterward wrote that the three hundred rebellious soldiers "trained a loaded gun upon the interior of the fort and threatened to slay their officers if they were not allowed to depart in peace." Arriving at the Quarantine the morning after the mutiny, a Union sailor recorded that he had "found 500 rebels who had spiked some of the guns at the Forts, killed one of their officers + ran for our vessels where they gave themselves up to our men."[26] What Higgins's report suggests is that the mutineers acted with more speed and determination than one senses in Seymour's account.

Taken as a whole, the mutiny seems to have surprised the officers, even though it must have been planned under their noses for some time. Mutineers took decisive measures to secure the fort's drawbridge, ramparts, and artillery. General Duncan's official report again suggests the extent to which the mutineers dominated the events of the early morning. In Duncan's account, even more so than in Higgins's and Seymour's, the officers barely play any role at all. According to Duncan, the garrison remained peaceful until midnight, when it "revolted in mass; seized upon the guard and posterns; reversed the field pieces commanding the gates, and commenced to spike the guns, while many of the men were leaving the fort in the mean time under arms. All this occurred as suddenly as it was unexpected. The men were mostly drawn up under arms and positively refused to fight any longer, besides endeavoring by force to bring over the Saint Mary's Cannoneers and such other few men as remained true to their cause and country." Duncan's report continues in this vein for several paragraphs, and nowhere do the officers occupy the active, cajoling role in which Seymour cast them. Rather, Duncan concludes, the revolt was "so general" that "the officers were helpless and powerless to act." Only after

Fort Jackson and the Defense of New Orleans

the most mutinous men had left did the officers again make decisions. In conference with three visiting officers from Fort St. Philip, who "were not at all confident of the garrison there after the unlooked-for revolt at Fort Jackson," Duncan and the other officers elected to surrender.[27]

By forcing the fort's commanders to surrender, the rebellious garrison guaranteed Union control over New Orleans. Almost immediately, U.S. supply and troop ships rejoined Farragut's squadron off the wharves of New Orleans. By the late afternoon of May 1, only three days after the forts pulled down their Confederate flags, Butler's troops landed in New Orleans, and control of the city passed to the United States. Farragut's passage of the forts in the early morning of April 25 was important, but the mutiny at Fort Jackson meant that his efforts would not be wasted. At a minimum, the mutineers' actions made the Union victory much quicker; at the most, they saved the U.S. Navy from the destructive power of the css *Louisiana* and won the Crescent City for the Union.

The mutiny was fraught with implications for how the people involved imagined that their society and government should work. By refusing to obey the orders of their government's chosen officers, mutineers are, in essence, revolting against their government. This is not a casual business. Mutinies are hard to organize and horribly dangerous. Detection can easily be fatal, and we should remember that danger when we think of the men in these Confederate units trying to plan and recruit men for their enterprise. Death awaits the failed mutineer, but a successful mutiny accomplishes drastic results. The Fort Jackson mutiny leveled one of the most rigid hierarchies in the world—a military command structure. The United States, which had begun its life as a revolution for a more egalitarian world, still had a regular army known for its harsh discipline and distinct boundaries between soldiers and officers. The Confederate States of America inherited that tradition, and much of American and especially European society remained strictly hierarchical—all of which makes the Fort Jackson mutiny exceptional. To enlist in a mutiny involved stepping out of the ordered world of ranks and hierarchy and into mortal peril, all for the sake of making the world, and one's place in it, more just and more equal.

So we must ask: Why did these men take the enormous step of mutinying? Unfortunately, no written record survives that tells the story from the mutineers' perspective, and so we can only infer their motives from what we know about their actions. We can also learn from the actions of other people who share the social characteristics of the mutineers: What did they do when the Union attack was reaching its climax? In these ways, we can try to reclaim the mutineers' past, a history too long ignored by historians. In the course of doing so, we will get a fuller rendering of what the Civil War meant to the people of New Orleans. We will also come to understand what it meant for these people to be Confederate or U.S. citizens.

CONTEMPORARY EXPLANATIONS OF THE MUTINY

Union and Confederate commanders often speculated about why the garrison had revolted. Their writings serve as a useful point of departure for our effort to determine the garrison's motivations. The three main Union commanders each offered his own explanation, and Confederate leaders volunteered a fourth. Of these four rationales for the mutiny, only the last seems to send us off in the right direction. Nevertheless, since recent historians of the campaign have tended to accept the other three as valid to one degree or another, we need to see what the Union military leadership said about the extraordinary events inside Fort Jackson.

The three ranking Union commanders in the region, Farragut, Porter, and Butler, each claimed credit for the Confederate surrender of the forts. Civil War commanders tended to claim exclusive credit for victories large and small, a practice that created rivalries and ill feelings with their brother officers. In retrospect, their postbattle disputes for glory seem petty and even embarrassing, but for career military officers such as Porter and Farragut the Civil War would determine their rank and reputation throughout the rest of their professional life. For Benjamin Butler, who had been a lawyer and politician during the prewar years, military glory could mean election to higher office. Even the presidency had gone to previously little-known militia officers, including William Henry Harrison and Andrew Jackson. Professional soldiers could look at the presidency of Zachary Taylor as an example of what was at stake. Efforts to claim credit for victory, therefore, tend to dominate the official reports and private correspondence of Butler, Porter, and Farragut. As a result, their explanations for the mutiny reflect their own needs, not necessarily the motivations of the Confederate privates and noncommissioned officers who had mutinied. In each case, their official military reports distort historical realities.

David Dixon Porter worked the hardest to grasp the laurel wreath of

Fort Jackson and the Defense of New Orleans

victory. By doing so, he became immersed in a bitter conflict with Benjamin Butler. One Butler biographer refers to the resulting war of words as "the celebrated Butler-Porter feud that was to last almost thirty years."[28] But Porter's reports warrant attention. He claimed that his week-long mortar barrage of Fort Jackson had spurred the mutiny. This could be true; his mortars fired almost exclusively on Fort Jackson, and the mutiny occurred there, even if some men in Fort St. Philip may have sympathized with it.

Porter's claim rests on the idea that his mortar fire made life in Fort Jackson so horrible that the garrison mutinied in order to escape its stinking confines. In a letter to Montgomery Meigs, Porter said that a Confederate deserter had told him "that the Fort, Jackson, was too much shattered to stand any fight, and the men too much demoralized to stand to their guns." The enemy had surrendered to him rather than Farragut, he boasted, "because they said 'we had carried it.'" The damage to the fort was immense; he claimed to an Iowa senator, "I never saw so perfect a scene of desolation and ruin, nor do I believe there was ever such perfect mortar practice." His official report made his case most fully. More than eighteen hundred mortar shells had fallen inside the work, he wrote, and every nonbrick building in it had burned to the ground. He assured the secretary of the navy that "Fort Jackson is a perfect wreck."[29]

Commander Porter was not alone in believing that Fort Jackson had been terribly damaged by the mortars. Porter could take comfort from the detailed official report of F. H. Gerdes, commander of the U.S. Coast Survey steamer *Sachem*. Gerdes inspected Fort Jackson closely before writing to his superior officer, A. D. Bache. Of the fort, he wrote: "I cannot understand to this minute how the garrison could have possibly lived so long in the enclosures. The destruction goes beyond all description, the ground is torn by the shells as if a thousand antediluvian hogs had rooted it up—the holes are from three to eight feet deep, and are very close together, sometimes within a couple of feet. All that is wood in the fort is completely consumed by fire, the brick work is knocked down, the arches stove, guns are dismounted, gun carriages broken and the whole presents a dreadful scene of destruction."[30] Such mortar fire, he implies, must have forced the Confederates to surrender.

Nor did one have to be a high-ranking officer to agree with Porter's theory. In the days and weeks that followed the Union victory, Fort Jackson became a popular destination for curious Union soldiers and sailors.

David Dixon Porter. (Library of Congress, Prints and Photographs Division,
Civil War Photographs)

Most (though not all, as we will see) were impressed by the destruction they saw when they toured the bastion. Many wrote only brief notes, saying that the fort was "very badly riddled," "in a dilapidated condition," or "well shattered."[31] Others, though, wrote extensive comments about the damage they saw around them. Captain Richard Elliott, who served in one of Butler's Massachusetts regiments, thought "the fort was blown all to pieces inside." But the worst thing about the fort, he added, was the "filth" that had pervaded it after water had broken through the levees and flooded the moats around it. Reflecting the racism of many of the expedition's army officers, Elliott complained that "everything is in a most dirty condition. I can not see how white men could live there[.] [I]t is 6 or 8 inches deep in Stagnate wate[r] in some places."[32] A man in the 12th Connecticut, allowed leave to tour the fort, described the destruction of the fort's wooden buildings. But he saved his strongest words for the living conditions inside the fort's brick gun casemates, where the Confederate troops had lived during the bombardment. "The appearance inside of the casemates beggars description," he wrote; "stagnant water stood in large pools in and around them; filth was everywhere to be seen."[33] The writings of these eyewitnesses give powerful support to Porter's idea that the mutiny could have been sparked by the wretched living conditions of the Confederate soldiers, especially after his mortars had broken the levee and caused flooding in the fort.

Further, we should remember that men stationed at Fort Jackson had reason enough to hate the place even without living through a bombardment. Horace Morse, a Union soldier who had the ill fortune to be assigned to Fort Jackson in the summer of 1862, complained bitterly about the place to his family. Mosquitoes predictably topped his list of grievances, earning mentions in two letters. (The first griped that "such swarms of mosquitos I never saw before," while the second quipped that they "are not as large as robins but they are large and very thick in number.") But insects were only part of the problem. Morse also found himself hemmed in by "impassable marshes that swarm with frogs aligators birds and other vermin." For exercise or variety, he could only make the very short walk to the river and row upstream against the current, though even then there "are no plantations or villages or even stores anywhere near us."[34] Whether Confederate or Union, soldiers must have found duty in Fort Jackson to be unpleasant, isolated, and extremely boring. Perhaps mutiny was a quick way out of a bad position that had been made even worse by Commander Porter's shelling.

But not everyone agreed that Porter's mortars had rendered Fort Jackson a "perfect wreck." It was generally acknowledged that the Confederates had enough food on hand for another two months.[35] Nor did everyone think that the fort was in such bad shape. John Hart went ashore at Fort Jackson about a day after the mutiny and saw only five dismounted cannon, small enough damage to a fort with seventy-five guns. True, there was water two feet deep in places, and the fort smelled "so bad that it all most made [him] sick," but he knew that only 13 of the fort's garrison of more than 600 men had been killed.[36] Other Union soldiers left the fort with even graver doubts about the effectiveness of Porter's fire. Looking at the forts, a crewman from the USS *Mississippi* found that "barring a few dismounted guns and a great many holes in the ground, they were comparatively uninjured and might have held out indefinitely, it seemed to me." A naval lieutenant visited the two forts and regarded them as "entirely uninjured" and still "impregnable . . . if properly defended." Even a crewman from a mortar boat, Richard Edes, found the results of his work underwhelming. The mortars, he wrote, "had knocked down considerable brick work, made many holes in the ground, dismounted one or two guns, & in places penetrated the casemates. The fort was, however, by no means untenable."[37]

The remainder of Richard Edes's letter raises legitimate questions about Porter's attempts to garner the credit for causing the mutiny. Continuing, Edes wrote that "if there had been that amount of desperation & firm resolve of which the Secesh are so fond of bragging, . . . there is no doubt they might have held out for some time longer. If they had wanted to 'die in the last ditch,' they certainly had an excellent opportunity. At Fort Jackson which is entirely surrounded by a ditch full of nasty green water—not to mention considerable in the interior—apparently they were not anxious to wind up in that fashion, nor to bled [sic] the last drop of their blood, for 300 deserters made off in one night."[38] Obviously, Edes enjoyed mocking hollow Confederate rhetoric, and thus his letter was mostly a joke for his relatives to enjoy. But he also made a serious point. At other places and times in the war, Confederate soldiers endured situations far worse than what the Fort Jackson soldiers were experiencing. The Confederates guarding Fort Sumter in Charleston Harbor, Lee's troops living in the water-filled trenches of Petersburg, and Hood's cold and hungry troops waiting for battle outside Nashville in 1865, for example, defended positions at far greater peril and for longer periods of time.[39] Especially with full rations still being served and rather light casualties, why did these Confederates give up the fight? Furthermore, why would they mutiny *after* Porter's mortars had withdrawn down the river out of fear of the *Louisiana*?

For his part, Benjamin Butler sought credit for the victory with a passion equal to that of Porter, and his writings offer his own explanation for why the Confederate soldiers mutinied. Butler reasoned that since the garrison mutinied just hours after his infantry appeared in the swamps immediately upriver from the two forts, it must have been his troops that dispirited the garrison. In this regard, chronology is on his side. Writing about the landing of the 26th Massachusetts Volunteers and portions of two other regiments behind Fort St. Philip, Butler asserted that "it was due to their efforts . . . and to those alone, that Forts Jackson and St. Philip surrendered when they did." Sarah Butler, the general's wife and companion on the expedition, agreed. "It was because the Army were so close in their rear that they mutinied and pulled down their flag," she wrote. Indeed, she added that the landing of Butler's infantry was "the sole cause of the *immediate* surrender of the Forts."[40]

Part of Butler's case rested on what he saw as the superb condition of Fort Jackson. Butler sent in three military experts to confirm his evaluation of the fort, perhaps already anticipating that Porter would say that his mortars had broken the enemy's will to fight. The experts, all with ties to Butler or his staff, confirmed the general's suspicions about the strength of Fort Jackson. Though clearly partisan in their conclusions, their reports contained detailed analyses and were based on personal observation. Lieutenant of engineers John C. Palfrey thought the fort was "as efficient as before the attack." Chief engineer Godfrey Weitzel also found the fort to be in good repair, as did the detailed report of Captain Charles Manning of the 5th Massachusetts Artillery Battery. After itemizing all the materials of war he had found in Fort Jackson, Manning listed the minimal damage he had found: "Two of the Guns En Barbette were dismounted, and three more had carriages badly broken. All others in Good Order, Excepting that one had the knob of the cascable broken off." Considering that he had found seventy-three cannon of various calibers in the fort, this list of disabled guns seemed brief indeed. Word of the engineers' reports spread quickly, and a sailor on the USS *Winona* reacted sharply to Porter's claim that he had reduced Fort Jackson to "a perfect ruin." "This is incorrect," Smith wrote to his brother after reading Porter's words in a newspaper account, "as a committee of engineers appointed to examine it say that it is as good as it was before the bombardment. . . . Porter might have bombarded a year without reducing it."[41] If Porter's mortars had left Fort Jackson defensible, then it must have been the timely arrival of Butler's infantry that disheartened the Confederate soldiers, or so Butler reasoned.

Captain David Farragut's official report made much the same argument for why the garrison mutinied. Both Farragut and Butler believed that their combined efforts to isolate the garrison from New Orleans had been the deciding factor in weakening the Confederate troops' morale. This rationale allowed credit to be extended to both of them, since Farragut had cut off riverine communication while Butler had sealed off the land routes to the city. Farragut's report to Assistant Navy Secretary Gustavus Fox explained that the mutiny occurred because "we were in their rear," a statement that credited both the army and his ships. Captain Theodorus Bailey, who served as Farragut's dispatch bearer and one of his most trusted subordinates, phrased this argument succinctly in his report to Secretary Gideon Welles. "This landing of the army above, together with the passage of the fleet," he wrote, "appears to have put the finishing touch to the demoralization of their garrisons (300 having mutinied in Fort Jackson)."[42]

Although aspects of the Farragut-Butler thesis for the mutiny make sense, other parts do not. Perhaps the garrison, sensing itself newly isolated, began to plan its mutiny immediately after Farragut's fleet passed the forts, but if so, we have no evidence to support that idea. Did Butler's soldiers create still more despair? The garrisons should not have had any fears that they would be immediately overwhelmed and butchered by Butler's forces. Butler had landed only one reinforced regiment—about fourteen companies of infantry—above the forts, and so the garrisons still outnumbered Butler's force. In addition, they had the advantage of imposing brick walls, full moats, and no small amount of heavy artillery, some of which covered the land approaches to the forts. Butler's men had no artillery; nor had they brought ladders with which to scale the walls. Even if the Confederates could not know all the shortcomings of Butler's force, they could not have been too frightened by what they saw. After all, only about two hundred of Butler's infantry had actually crossed from the Fort

Fort Jackson and the Defense of New Orleans

David Glasgow Farragut. (Library of Congress, Prints and Photographs Division,
Civil War Photographs)

The formidable brick walls, artillery, and moat of Fort Jackson rendered it secure from anything Butler's outnumbered infantry could do on the day of the mutiny or anytime soon thereafter. This photograph was taken in the 1860s after the fort was repaired by Union forces. (The Western Reserve Historical Society, Cleveland, Ohio)

St. Philip side of the river over to the rear of Fort Jackson. Such a force could hardly be called intimidating. Granted, those two hundred U.S. troops guaranteed the arrival of additional forces and did cut the garrison off from all communication with New Orleans, but we are still left to wonder why the Confederates mutinied when their situation was so far from desperate. In that sense, Butler and Farragut's attempts to explain the mutiny in terms of the surrounding of the forts make as little sense as Porter's rationale. Both hypotheses rest on the garrisons becoming demoralized by the desperate situation they were in on the night of the 27th, when, in fact, they were in no immediate peril.

While Union commanders attempted to explain their enemy's collapse, Confederate generals issued their own statements about why the mutiny had occurred. In many ways, their ideas have greater credibility than those of their opponents. Often eyewitnesses, they understood the condition of Fort Jackson and had some knowledge of their soldiers. Their accounts suggest a wholly different explanation for the mutiny, though they do not pursue the full implications of their ideas. According to the Confederate

Fort Jackson and the Defense of New Orleans

The drawbridge and moat of Fort Jackson. This face of the fort opposed Butler's infantry, which would have approached from upriver. (The Western Reserve Historical Society, Cleveland, Ohio)

commanders on the scene, the soldiers mutinied because they felt no attachment to the southern republic.

Confederate officers almost unanimously agreed that Fort Jackson was in good shape when the mutineers struck. Naval officers thought that Fort Jackson had come through the bombardment practically unscathed. Lieutenant Alexander Warley, commander of the small ironclad ram css *Manasses*, testified under oath that he had dined with General Duncan and Colonel Higgins in the aftermath of Farragut's passage of the forts. The fort commanders, he said, informed him "that Fort Jackson was stronger than it had been when the fight commenced; they having taken advantage of the cessation of the firing [by Porter's mortars] to protect their Magazine." Furthermore, Duncan and Higgins had assured him that they had six weeks' worth of food on hand and "felt perfectly able to hold the fort." Looking around, Warley had found the fort "perfectly unhurt." C. W. Read of the css *McRae* also had visited Fort Jackson, in this case the day before Farragut ran the gauntlet. He thought that Fort Jackson was "injured . . . somewhat," while Fort St. Philip was "entirely uninjured." His account does not even hint at any alarm over their condition. For Read and Warley, Fort Jackson looked ready to give battle for some time to come.[43]

The fort commanders also vouched for the strength of their position.

Fort Jackson and the Defense of New Orleans

The mutiny also caused the surrender of Fort St. Philip across the river. This postbattle photograph shows the large size of the fort. (The Western Reserve Historical Society, Cleveland, Ohio)

After the mortar bombardment began, an anonymous officer assured his hometown editor that "no damage had resulted to the fort except burning wooden buildings." Additional testimony about the strength of the forts came even after Farragut's passage, when "a gentleman of veracity" left Fort Jackson for New Orleans with word that "the damage received by the fort during the terrible bombardment of the mortar boats, and the fight with the enemy's fleet, have been repaired; and that [Duncan] is prepared, as heretofore, to defend his position to the last." Even after the mutiny, officers talked about the excellent condition of Fort Jackson. Lieutenant Colonel Higgins wrote only days after the mutiny that "our fort was still strong; our damage had been to some extent repaired." In an editorial on May 1, three days after the mutiny, the *New Orleans Daily Picayune* reported that it had heard that Duncan "was confident in his ability to maintain both posts, having a sufficiency of ammunition and provisions, a strong and well served armament, good officers, and a force which, considering the duration and severity of the siege, had met with a wonderfully insignificant diminution." Indeed, Duncan believed this, they wrote, until "the very last moment."[44]

With the forts in solid condition, how could Confederate leaders explain

Fort Jackson and the Defense of New Orleans

The "front view" of Fort St. Philip. (The Western Reserve Historical Society, Cleveland, Ohio)

their men's mutiny? Although some, including navy captain John Mitchell, thought that the mutineers acted to prevent Duncan from volunteering them for a suicidal defense of the fort, most Confederate officers suggested a more plausible explanation.[45] The mutineers, they thought, rebelled because they felt no passion for the survival of the Confederacy. In General Duncan's words, the soldiers "were mostly foreign enlistments, without any great interests at stake in the ultimate success of the revolution." Captain William Robertson, who commanded the water battery just outside Fort Jackson, agreed with Duncan. Writing after the war, he said little of the mutiny, pausing only to reassure his readers that "no officers and I believe no native Southerners were involved in this disgraceful affair." A naval officer thought that the mutineers "were mostly of foreign birth and low origin," while Major General Mansfield Lovell, the Confederate district commander, railed against the whole people of southeastern Louisiana. The rich, he said, cared only for their property, and "the poor, miserable, mixed breed, commonly called Dagos or Acadians," had earned "not the slightest dependence."[46]

Lovell's official report called the revolt "one of those strange anomalies for which I do not pretend to account." Yet, while he claimed that "the causes will probably never be known in full," the government and the public wanted to know who was responsible.[47] In the end, he and the other

Confederate leaders blamed the working-class and immigrant soldiers who garrisoned Fort Jackson. Unlike the explanations offered by Union commanders, those of the Confederate officers place responsibility for the mutiny exactly where it belongs, on the soldiers who staged the revolt. By granting the mutineers a reason to rebel, the Confederate officers move us closer to an understanding of what happened inside that isolated, soggy, and smelly fort. They also alert us to the fact that the social and economic status of soldiers is directly linked to what happened on the battlefield. To understand why soldiers performed as they did, we must know about their lives before they were soldiers, and we must understand the communities from which they came. The New Orleans campaign, and the mutiny at Fort Jackson in particular, did not happen in a vacuum.

But the Confederate commanders fall short in their efforts to determine why the garrison mutinied. While they blamed the mutineers' working-class status and immigrant backgrounds, they failed to explain why such men would regard the Confederacy with more indifference or hostility than would richer men or native-born American citizens. Rather than elaborate on why such men failed to fight for their new country, the generals wrote condescendingly about poor immigrants, almost as if no better could be expected of them than treason.

The men of the Fort Jackson garrison must be the focus of any attempt to understand what happened that decisive night, and in the chapters to come, we will explore the complex social mosaic of New Orleans and see how it affected the Confederate war effort. How did poor people experience the first year of the war? How did Confederate politicians regard immigrants? How did other working-class people react when the Union campaign to retake the city got under way? In order to fully comprehend the mutiny in Fort Jackson, or the history of the Confederacy itself, we must explore the social and economic underpinnings of the southern republic. In the face of the reality that nothing written by the mutineers has survived, we must use their actions as a way to come to an understanding of how they saw the Civil War. Mutiny, as a historian of the French army in World War I explains, is a political act. When soldiers choose to refuse orders, they become "free political actors."[48] In other words, the Fort Jackson mutineers voted with their guns and their bodies on April 27 and 28, and it is our job to discover what they were voting for and against that night. By doing so, we can finally understand how a large but previously unexamined group of people in New Orleans felt about the Confederacy and the United States. Silent though they may be in the archives, their actions will tell us a great deal about why the United States became the nation of choice for so many of the world's free people in the nineteenth century.

2

confederate new orleans,
february 1861 to may 1862

Most of the Fort Jackson mutineers enlisted in New Orleans, and any search for their motives must start with a long look at the Crescent City. Civil War historians have increasingly focused on the connections between soldiers at the front and their families and communities at home—links continually reinforced by letters, gifts, newspapers, and men and women traveling back and forth between the army and home. At Fort Jackson, soldiers, whether on leave, discharged on account of sickness, or detailed home to recruit, carried messages and physical reminders from the men at the front. Visitors also came to the fort from New Orleans, including new recruits, civilian and military guests, and, one suspects, a healthy number of fishermen, boat crews, and peddlers. So, even though many of the men who mutinied probably did not see New Orleans again after being posted downriver, they still would have heard about how the war affected their friends and families. In order to understand why the men in Fort Jackson mutinied, we need to look at how their lives, and those of their intimates, had been changed by the war. The soldiers in the garrison had been Confederates for a full year by the time they rebelled, and this period had given them a good opportunity to size up what the new nation would offer them. Many of the soldiers in Fort Jackson had chosen to immigrate to the United States. Had the Confederacy treated them so well that they would consider the southern republic an even better choice? Or was living in the Confederacy perhaps worse than life in the United States had been, making them eager to be part of the Union once again?

The possibility that the mutineers might have made a conscious choice to support the United States instead of the Confederacy has a direct bearing on which of the explanations for the mutiny might hold the most weight. If the Union commanders are correct, then the mutineers acted because they had become disheartened about their ability to resist the Union onslaught any longer. Either Porter's mortars or Farragut's and Butler's movements to cut them off convinced them that further defense was pointless. The Union commanders' explanations imply no larger political motives for the mutineers. But the Confederate commanders suggested something different. They implied that the mutineers were not wholeheartedly Confederate—that, as immigrants, they did not care whether the Confederacy won the Civil War. By looking at how New Orleans fared during its year in the Confederacy, we might well advance another theory for why the mutineers struck. New Orleans, especially the white working class from which the Fort Jackson soldiers were overwhelmingly drawn, had suffered grievously during its Confederate year. The economy had withered, employment had dropped, political repression had climbed, and for what? The men serving in Fort Jackson certainly knew the full extent of the economic collapse, even if they lived sixty-five miles away. Perhaps they mutinied not out of indifference to the Confederacy but out of an active dislike. They may have heartily wished to return to their old allegiances. Examining New Orleans in its Confederate year will not only show that white workers had reasons to deplore the consequences of secession but will also reveal that opposition to the Confederacy existed among whites even as the government did everything it could to suppress that dissent.

Confederate New Orleans

William Howard Russell came to New Orleans just as the Civil War was starting, and his writings are a sound introduction to the city. Russell was a veteran English correspondent, having reported on conflicts in Ireland, the Crimea, and India. He found great enthusiasm for the new nation but also saw signs of weakness that would come to full fruition before April 1862.

William Russell crossed the Atlantic in early 1861 to report on the dissolution of the American Republic for the *London Times*. Aristocratic in his bearing, he was not inclined to give his full approval to the United States or to its democratic form of government. The dispatches he filed concerning Lincoln and his cabinet are reasonable portraits untinted by any particular bias. After seeing Lincoln's inaugural, Russell rode through much of the South, watching the Confederate States of America come to life. By May 20, he was ready to see New Orleans, where he would stay for two weeks. Once there, he admired the city's cosmopolitan atmosphere, its wide boulevards and the mix of languages he heard in cafés. The Crescent City's culture reminded him favorably of Europe, and he thought that the city's size was "imposing." He ate superb food at John Slidell's house. He liked the caged mockingbird that sat next to him when he wrote his dispatches. When he praised the bird's "restlessness, courage, activity, and talent," he could have been describing traits he admired in many of the people he had met in the city.[1] And yet, Russell's seasoned eye detected signs of trouble for the new country.

While in New Orleans, Russell tried to determine how many Louisiana men had joined the Confederate army. The authorities could not give him an accurate, or even consistent, figure. So he guessed. There were, he estimated, about 50,000 men of military age in Louisiana, and he thought the state would need most of them in arms to repulse the coming attacks. Perhaps, he surmised, 15,000 had volunteered. Russell judged this a shortfall, no doubt using as his standard of comparison the high rates of mobilization seen in Europe during the Napoleonic wars. Louisiana's enlistment rates, he wrote, "militate against the truth of their own assertions, 'that they are united to a man, and prepared to fight to a man.'"[2] With its ability to recruit soldiers the key to its future, the Confederacy, he thought, might be failing the test in Louisiana.

Russell could hardly avoid the issue of Confederate recruitment; it invaded the very household of his host, William Mure, the English consul in New Orleans. Russell's visit to New Orleans followed the firing on Fort Sumter, a time that historians have represented as the golden age for military enlistments in the North and South, with towns and cities raising companies and regiments with ease. Russell's estimate that roughly one-third of Louisiana's military-age men enlisted seems to confirm such enthusiasm, but Russell questioned whether all the recruits were volunteers. Residing in Mure's house, he saw that "British subjects living in New Orleans have been seized, knocked down, carried off from their labor at the wharf and the workshop, and forced by violence to serve in the 'Volunteer' ranks! These cases are not isolated," he raged. "They are not in twos and threes, but in tens and twenties; they have not occurred stealthily or in byways, they have taken place in open day, and in the streets of New Orleans." Mure eventually freed more than sixty men, and the governor was forced to publicly denounce the forced conscriptions. Nor did the Confederates only kidnap British subjects; Russell suspected that "the 'moral susion' of the lasso, of head-shaving, ducking, kicking, and such processes," was used "not unfrequently to stimulate volunteers."[3]

Poverty forced a second kind of involuntary enlistment. As early as Russell's visit in May 1861, the city's economy was reeling from the twin shocks of secession and war. Trade had virtually stopped. The city usually exported about 500,000 bales of cotton in a year; 11,000 bales left the port in 1861. The slump caused the municipal government to discuss shutting down schools and laying off police because of tax shortfalls. Private employers, Russell wrote, "refuse to pay their workmen on the ground of inability." More and more people were laid off as commerce slowed. Left without wages, urban workmen were desperately pinched. Some immigrants appeared at Mure's house, where Russell saw them begging for tickets home to Ireland, England, Scotland, or the North.[4] Mure could not help them. As a last resort, many of these unemployed men took jobs as soldiers. "The Irish population," Russell wrote, "finding themselves unable to migrate northwards, and being without work, have rushed to arms with enthusiasm to support southern institutions." Other men showed less enthusiasm, and about them Russell added gloomily, "Nothing remains for them but to enlist."[5] While rich men rushed to serve in elite units such as the famous Washington Artillery, Russell looked at the poor and saw an "absence of great devotion to the cause."[6] Recruiting proved to be a lasting problem in New Orleans throughout its Confederate year.

But Russell was troubled by more than just the coercive elements of Confederate recruiting. He had seen the Sepoy rebellion in India at first hand, and New Orleans's intense heat and surrounding forests and swamps—which he called an "Indian jungle"—seem to have reminded him of those very unpleasant times. He seems to have found parallels between the tenuous hold the elites of New Orleans exercised over the city's poor and the fragile British administration in India. Certainly, Confederate leaders worried about the allegiances of the people around them, much as the English had in India. Slaves might revolt at any time, and the start of a civil war could give them greater opportunities. Nightly fires, thought to be set by slaves, fed these fears. Nervous Confederate authorities worried that antislavery agents would infiltrate their city and spark slave revolts.[7]

Russell was puzzled by the city's fixation with alleged abolitionist conspirators. The arrest of four men for abolitionism in a single day left him outraged. Although they had admittedly criticized slavery, some, like Bernard Cruz, had only said something privately to their wife. Nevertheless, all seemed destined for the workhouse or jail. "Such is 'freedom of speech' in Louisiana!" wrote a sarcastic Russell. He also discovered that stating one's "belief that the Northerners will be successful" was a crime that resulted in six months in jail.[8] Despite Russell's scorn, the heavy-handed justice continued long after he left. Under these conditions, Russell could not determine whether there was a substantial white Unionist community in the Crescent City. No such group was visible, but he credited their absence to "the intimidation of the mob." Confederates, he found, spied on strangers, watched letter boxes, and deported people suspected of disloyalty.[9] Sitting atop a social pyramid made unstable by the restless white and black workers below them, the city's elite looked to the new Confederacy to give them a conservative government. Democracy, the watchword of the city's first American hero, Andrew Jackson, had fallen into disrepute among the men in charge of New Orleans. On May 30, Russell wrote that a rich man had told him that government would not work "until universal suffrage is put down." Others agreed. "The opinion of the wealthy and intelligent men in the community, so far as I can judge,"

Russell wrote, "regards universal suffrage as organized confiscation, legal-ised violence and corruption, a mortal disease in the body politic."[10]

By the time William Russell left New Orleans, he had explored several fault lines that threatened the new nation. Slaves did not support its social and political arrangements. That much could be predicted, then as now, by an impartial observer. But Russell had uncovered other weaknesses as well. Recruitment was sluggish, and the government seemed nervous and willing to jail anyone it suspected of disloyalty. The city's Confederate leadership seemed distrustful of democracy and free speech. Russell may not have been personally disturbed by those ideas, yet he could not help but notice the gulf between Confederate practice and the ideals espoused by the old United States. In all, the Confederacy seemed to be lurching backward, away from the mainstream liberalism of the nineteenth century and back toward a more aristocratic world. And so it was too in econom-ics. At least one Confederate senator, Louis Wigfall, told Russell that he wanted "no manufactures: we desire no trading, no mechanical or man-ufacturing classes."[11] He wanted neither cities nor wage workers in his new nation.

In New Orleans, Russell saw that the "mechanical or manufacturing classes" responded with some ambivalence to the Confederacy. Many ob-viously embraced the new country, but Russell saw that some men were looking for ways to escape the coming war and its economic disruptions. He also saw working men "idling about the streets" even as recruiters went looking for more men to make into soldiers.[12] Many of these men would continue to eye the Confederacy with caution, wondering whether there was any place in a slaveholders' republic—with all its agrarian dreams—for city dwellers who owned neither slaves nor land. Would they have jobs? Would the rich roll back democracy? In other words, would the Con-federacy give them the promises of the old America: economic oppor-tunity, political equality, and social and religious freedom? What the Con-federacy did to win over the working poor would help to determine how wage laborers would react when the "Yankees" came to town.

TROUBLE IN THE SHIPYARDS

Had Russell wanted to get a feel for New Orleans's working class, he could have walked to the city's wharves and shipyards. Here stevedores and ship's carpenters, wage workers and slaves, natives and immigrants all worked long hours in the economic heart of the Confederacy's largest city. How much these men and women supported the new southern republic would prove critical to its success. Nowhere was that more true than in the city's ten shipyards, home to an impressive array of foundries, dry docks, and skilled laborers. Here, if anywhere, the Confederacy could build a navy capable of challenging Federal fleets.[13] In addition, many workers from these places would find their way into the Confederate army—and into Fort Jackson.

As Russell might have predicted, not everything went well in New Orleans for the Confederacy's Navy Department. Workers quickly remade riverboats into wooden gunboats, but the real test came with the production of ironclad rams. Virginia's Gosport Navy Yard built the ironclad ram css *Virginia* by early March 1862. Confederate authorities in New Orleans planned to launch two such ironclads, the *Louisiana* and the *Mississippi*, and they would need them by the time Farragut struck in April 1862. The ability of the shipyards to produce these two vessels would help to determine the city's fate.

Confederate navy contractors soon ran into difficulties, however, because of the bitter division between shipyard owners and their employees. Even with the war well under way, shipyard workers engaged in strikes and industrial sabotage. While not all of this behavior makes them Unionists in the fullest sense of the word, the shipyard workers demonstrated a casual attitude toward Confederate naval imperatives. Shipyard laborers steadfastly refused to work whenever the navy failed to pay their wages promptly. This situation left the builders periodically scrambling to get the government to cover their drafts while workers sat idle.[14] The commander of the Confederate navy in the region, Commodore George Hollins, later complained that he had "had every mechanic . . . knock off there at once for two or three days—right in the middle of work." Hollins would then scramble about the city, borrowing money from merchants until the government sent more funds. Hollins's financial heroics aside, the Confederacy was losing time.[15] Although the Confederate Treasury was responsible for the delays, it was the city's workers who elected to stop work on ironclad ships whenever their self-interest was at stake.

More time was lost when the ship carpenters working on the *Mississippi* went on strike on November 6, 1861. They sought to boost their wages, which had already been undercut by wartime inflation.[16] The chief build-ers, Asa and Nelson Tift, refused to meet the workers' demand that wages increase from three dollars a day to four. Nelson Tift testified later that New Orleans–based mechanics walked out first, then returned to the shipyard "and forced [twenty] Richmond mechanics to quit work." The authorities arrested and imprisoned the strike leaders, but the workers stayed out.[17] With time slipping by, the Tifts appealed to the workers' patriotism. Asa told them about the urgent need for ironclad ships. He "asked them if there was any complaint or disagreement with us or the Government. They said no, but the wages were insufficient." It is interest-ing to note that the workers expressed no dissatisfaction with the Confed-erate government; indeed, Nelson Tift went so far as to testify that workers "said they would go with the Army or serve the Government in any other way rather than work for less than they demanded."[18] However patriotic that may sound, the strikers could not have said anything else given the government's record of arresting both strikers and dissenters. They also knew that they would not be asked to serve in the army, since their skills were so badly needed in the shipyards. And, despite their professed patrio-tism, they still hurt the Confederacy every day they stayed away from their jobs.

Asa and Nelson Tift could take only limited comfort from their workers' patriotic statements. With the strike continuing, they consulted with other New Orleans shipbuilders. To them the Tifts mentioned that they would have to give in and raise wages. Their fellow builders protested vehe-mently, however, and told the brothers about a ship carpenters' strike two years earlier. Then, the employers had held out. The builders boasted to the Tifts that their hard-nosed approach had "finally brought back the strikers" at their old wages after a struggle of six weeks.[19] Now, they urged the Tifts to follow the same course. But the Tifts, unwilling to delay con-struction for a month and a half, settled with their workers after six days, agreeing to pay $4 a day. Months later, pay increased to $4.50 a day.[20]

Courtesy of this strike, the Tifts learned tough lessons about business in New Orleans. Despite the press to complete the work at hand, the Tifts had encountered two groups determined to pursue their own interests. Workers and management had already seen one strike, no doubt involving many of the same people, only two years before. By antebellum standards, a six-week strike was extremely prolonged, a testament to the strikers' dedication and to their status as skilled workers who could not be easily replaced by scab laborers. Workers would long remember a six-week strike (just as management obviously did), and the hostilities created then continued to poison their relationship with the Confederacy, for which they now indirectly worked. On management's side, its eagerness to break the strike before building ironclads attests to its real priorities. Such actions have led the historian of Confederate shipbuilding in New Orleans to call the overall effort "a disaster."[21]

And still, the *Mississippi* was not yet in the water. While worker actions should so far be considered as self-interested rather than disloyal, there were Unionists working in the city's shipyards. In late June 1861, city authorities arrested Lorenzo Minot, a carpenter, when he tried to leave New Orleans for his native Maine. When he was apprehended in Memphis, Minot was carrying a letter that "a ship carpenter in Algiers" named Chapman had written to his wife, who lived in Maine. Chapman's letter gave full voice to his Unionist politics. Chapman had written his wife that "he was all right on the Northern question" and that he "hoped to see the stars [and] stripes soon waving over New Orleans." Both Minot and Chapman were arrested and handed over to military authorities for punishment, but city politicians must have worried about disloyalty among their skilled workers.[22]

The *Mississippi*'s launch must have added to their concerns, since it was clearly sabotaged. Not discussed in the city's press, the matter came to light during an official inquiry into the Tift brothers' work. During the launch of the *Mississippi*'s hull, steamers tried to pull the ironclad off its slip. At the critical moment, however, the ropes to the *Mississippi* snapped and the hull remained in place. An investigation discovered that the ship had been cleverly fastened to the launch with a large locust pin or pins. As Commodore Hollins testified, the hidden "wooden bolts were put down through her into the bed below. This was done by some person to prevent her from being launched." Hollins even had a suspect, a foreman "who was discharged." Although Hollins was merely repeating a rumor, he in essence blamed the industry's strained labor relations for delaying the navy's efforts. Whether the similar failure during the launching of the ironclad *Louisiana* was also caused by sabotage remains unclear.[23]

Unionists also sabotaged the construction of the *Mississippi* in at least one other way. The Tifts contracted to have the ship's iron plating rolled at the firm of Schofield and Markham in Atlanta, one of the two factories in the South capable of producing the ship's protective coat. Unfortunately for the Tifts, Atlantans Lewis Schofield and William Markham were secret Unionists who worked to undermine the Confederacy. Initially, they did this by turning down contracts to work on the *Mississippi*. But when the Confederacy threatened to seize their business, Markham and Schofield reluctantly accepted the next contract. The two industrialists began, however, what historian Thomas Dyer calls the "risky strategy" of "conspiring to keep production low and to operate the mill at minimum capacity." Just how long Schofield and Markham managed to delay the completion of the *Mississippi* is unknown, but clearly the Tifts did not receive full cooperation from one of their most important contractors.[24] The Confederate navy must have looked upon the New Orleans shipyards with frustration. Needing ironclads, it found only delay.

There is a large gap, of course, between being a self-interested worker and being a politically motivated Unionist. One could be both, but a worker could still hope for Confederate success as long as it put enough food on the table. We might well want to employ strict criteria in determining what made a person a Unionist: we could expect Unionists to have been true to the United States, to have taken public stands or significant secret actions even when doing so could have brought them, or did bring them, real harm. Such Unionists existed; we have seen them on the levee and sabotaging Confederate ships. More will appear in the pages that follow. These Unionists enlisted in the U.S. military, quickly took the oath of allegiance, stood for Federal offices, voted in Union-sponsored elections, and otherwise lent their public support for the United States. But it might be more beneficial to view political allegiances as a spectrum, with a person's degree of political commitment determining where he or she falls along the continuum. Unionists who went to jail or braved gunfire for their beliefs would be at the Unionist end of the spectrum in New Orleans, with Confederate nationalists at the other end. Workers who struck could be just about anywhere, except at the far end of Confederate nationalists, those who were willing to sacrifice for their cause. Examining other parts of New Orleans society will reveal that many residents occupied the gray spaces between the two politically committed ends of the spectrum. At times, these wavering men and women proved very useful to the Union cause.

We also need to consider that people's political allegiances, and their willingness to show them, changed with time and circumstances. The Confederate governor of Louisiana, Thomas Moore, recognized in June that his country's deteriorating fortunes would bring Unionists out of hiding and bring some formerly undecided people to the Union cause. He complained to President Jefferson Davis that "dormant disloyalty has awakened with the disaster that brings our enemy so near, and the murmers [*sic*] of the suffering mingle with the complaints of the mercenary, the taunts of the disorganizers, and the whispered tones of treason."[25] Unionists, in this letter, were both the people who had whispered treason all along and those whose "dormant disloyalty" was only now springing to life. Both kinds of Unionists were dangerous to the Confederacy and as such earn a deserved place on the Unionist side of the spectrum. Other people about whom Governor Moore complained, those who griped when stung by the hardships of war or sought to make as much money out of the crisis as they could, were less worrisome to the Confederate cause. Workers who struck may not have been Unionists, but if the saboteurs enjoyed widespread support, then perhaps the mutineers who enlisted out of this community acted out of a consistent preference for the United States over the Confederacy.

THE IMPORTANCE OF WHITE UNIONISTS

Before we continue our search for white Unionists in New Orleans, it is useful to consider just what is at stake. Considered narrowly, the discovery of a large white Unionist community in New Orleans will help us to determine whether the mutineers in Fort Jackson were active Unionists. To connect Unionist southerners with a significant U.S. military victory, the winning of New Orleans, would add importance to the study of white Unionism and encourage military historians to pay further attention to the social and political worlds from which common soldiers emerged.

But for people in the 1860s, white Unionists mattered for other, larger reasons. At issue was nothing less than the legitimacy of the Confederate nation and the righteousness of the Union cause. As northerners saw it, the Civil War could be justified on only a handful of grounds. Most northerners felt that the election of Abraham Lincoln had not provided the southern states with significant grounds for rebellion. True, they believed that people had a right to revolt if their government was repressive (as their Revolutionary forefathers had done), but Lincoln's constitutional election did not meet that criterion. Others felt that any revolt against the United States, a nation they believed to be the world's best chance to establish Protestantism, democracy, and civilization, was immoral. A small number of others would see the Civil War as a legitimate crusade against slavery. But a fourth idea loomed large in the minds of northern Americans. Many people justified their efforts by claiming that the Confederacy did not represent the true wishes of the southern people.

If this was the case, and if indeed white Unionists existed in large numbers throughout the Confederacy, then the war was an effort to liberate Americans who had fallen under the shadow of a coercive government. Many Americans, including Lincoln, remained convinced that the secessionists had been able to seize control only through lucky timing and demagoguery. With time and encouragement, Lincoln thought, white southerners would realize that the U.S. government meant them no harm, that the Confederate leadership did not reflect their interests, and that they should return to their old loyalties. While some historians have criticized Lincoln's hopes for a Unionist resurgence in the South as unrealistic, the United States needed to believe that there was a large Unionist presence in order to avoid the accusation that it was invading a people united in their desire for secession. At issue in any discussion of how many white Unionists there were, then, is the question of just which of the two governments sought to repress the true desires of white southerners.

Northerners in 1862 still hoped that a large number of Unionists lived in New Orleans. Journalists ran reports from Unionist refugees fleeing the city, happily crediting even their most inflated figures. A Vermont newspaper, for example, discovered a Burlington native who had traveled throughout the South and said that "a majority of the people [of New Orleans] were for the Union. Some said two-thirds were Union men, some three-fourths, but all said a majority." The news got better. One of the men the Vermonter had interviewed said that 5,000 men were organized and ready to "assist the United States troops as soon as an opportunity was presented." Two New York City papers passed along the words of New Orleans Unionists who had fled north: 12,000 Unionists were "organized into clubs." Indeed, talk of "Union lodges" and other secret clubs offered northerners hope throughout the spring of 1862.[26] Such Unionists would not only serve as valuable allies in the field but would also legitimize an increasingly bloody war.

Confederate New Orleans

Northern optimism about the Unionist leanings of New Orleans whites led to speculation about which segments of the city's population viewed the old country most favorably. Most refugees claimed that merchants formed the backbone of Unionist networks. They said that trade and profits would secure the loyalty of southerners to the old Union. The *Portland (Maine) Advertiser* took joy in reports that representatives from New Orleans commercial houses had made their way to New York, just as the *New York Times* predicted that "the moneyed and commercial classes" would be loyal. Perhaps the longest refugee report affirmed the Unionist tendencies of the city's richest merchants. The refugee, a Chicagoan who had spent three years in the South, maintained that New Orleans harbored many white Unionists, "especially in the heavy business circles." These men, he said, were "attached to the North by business interests or consanguined relations, [and] are also sincere in their professions of allegiance."[27] Many of the refugees probably came from this business class, and they felt comfortable making the trip north because they had business or family contacts to sustain them once they arrived. These refugees never mentioned the possibility that the white wage workers would side with the United States.

Editors had broader hopes than the refugees, however. They also had bigger worries. As the Civil War ground into its second year, and with the battle of Shiloh showing just how bloody the war could be, editors considered the nature of civil war. How could the nation rebuild? Was it desirable to keep the country together by force? How could the government function without the consent of the governed? These were tough questions for Americans raised on the idea that a republic rested on the sovereignty of the people. The editor of the *Hartford Daily Courant* considered these issues after a string of Union victories brought hope that the war would soon be over. "What shall the Government do with the South?" it wondered. Would the southerners "ever consent to live with us in the holy bonds of the Union?" As a supporter of the war, the editor had no choice but to answer, "Yes, they must and will," but certainly the presence of white Unionists would be an enormous comfort to him.[28]

Many of the same concerns bedeviled the editor of the *Boston Courier*. When he heard that Farragut had captured New Orleans, he downplayed the news. "Mere possession," he wrote, matters little "except so far as the fact meets with the present or future wishes of the inhabitants." Here was an editor who wanted no part of government "by force." Instead, he hoped to find Unionists there. The editor took heart from the "indisposition on the part of the citizens, to make very desperate sacrifices for the Confederate cause; and from this fact we derive some gleams of hope, that there is an influential class in the city, to whom we may look for co-operation." Still, he urged the nation to convince New Orleans whites to "become allies, and finally friends."[29] The Civil War would be to little purpose if the South became nothing more than an occupied territory. If all white southerners opposed the restoration of U.S. power, then how could the United States justify its actions?

Eager to find Unionists, the editors imagined southern society as they hoped to find it. Many editors followed in the footsteps of the refugees and hoped that commerce would keep Louisianians loyal. Though unsure of how many Unionists Farragut would find, the *Eastern Argus* (Portland, Maine) contended that "the interests of New Orleans are all on the side of the Union and it has been believed that the feelings of the people, or a very large portion of them, were strongly on that side." If true, that would speed "the work of reestablishing the authority of the Union." If not, such work would prove "protracted." The *Portland (Maine) Advertiser* agreed. It proclaimed that "a large majority of the people of Louisiana are Unionists; *and always have been*. The State was taken out of the Union by the conspirators, on a minority vote." Louisiana, it thought, stood to gain more than any other southern state by its commercial connections with the rest of the country, "and no State would lose more by a dissolution than it."[30] Always, these editors portrayed New Orleans as a commercial city controlled by its elite merchants. But these editors neglected the city's urban working class. If merchants might be Unionists because of their commercial interests, would day laborers and mechanics such as ship carpenters also befriend the United States out of self-interest? Their actions throughout 1861 indicated that they might.

A handful of northern editors imagined a South in which poor whites would prove to be the most loyal Unionists. Horace Greeley's influential *New York Tribune* saw the working class as the only real hope for finding southern white Unionists. Slaveholders ruled the Confederate states, Greeley wrote, and they ruled them like "petty and domineering oligarchies." Poor Americans, he believed, would naturally despise such governments. Greeley argued that non-slaveholding whites already knew that the rule of the planter class did not benefit them, and the recently passed Confederate draft law would alienate the poor even more. "A battlefield is an uncomfortable place for a man who feels he has no business to be there," he wrote, "and who knows that he is there only because three or four negro-owners swore to hang him unless he marched instanter and without grumbling." With slaveholders able to avoid service, poor whites would be the only ones drafted. They were now to be "stripped to the skin" and inspected by conscription agents—an inspection that would forcefully remind the draftees of the slave auction block. Greeley drove home the analogy, envisioning "the recruiting-sergeant going about with a long whip, and driving up poor whites in droves of five or six to the shambles."[31] Ambivalent about fighting for a slave labor system that did not help them, non-slaveholders would soon welcome reunion.

When he wrote about New Orleans specifically, Greeley argued that the poor there had even fewer reasons to be loyal Confederates. "The great mass of [New Orleans] whites" were moving to Unionism, he wrote soon after the city came under Union control. In Greeley's eyes, the United States represented a dynamic capitalism that offered the world's poor their best chance for happiness. Certainly, reforms were needed to create a more just economic order within capitalism, but northern society promised wage workers much more than a slaveholding republic ever could. With slavery driving down the cost of labor, paid workers struggled in the southern economy. Greeley trusted that urban wage workers understood how slavery crippled their efforts to earn a decent wage. Those who "live by their own industry" would be "easily reconciled to the Union, if indeed they were ever hostile to it," Greeley thought. Picking up the thread of class conflict, the *New York Herald* surveyed New Orleans society and found everyone to be a potential Unionist except for the rich men who controlled Confederate politics. "It is only your native born Southerner, the owner of a sugar plantation, or cotton estate and a gang of slaves, who . . . swears by Jeff. Davis as the only true prophet."[32]

Northern editors needed Unionists, in other words, and they conjured up a series of visions about southern society in which such loyalists would appear. Self-interested merchants might look forward to reunion, and wage workers might hope for a revolution against slavery. These sketches of southern life would prove to be largely accurate in New Orleans. Merchants and white wage workers, in addition to African Americans, came to

Confederate New Orleans

support the Union in large numbers during the war. Despite the Confederates' attempts to claim that they alone represented the will of southern whites, New Orleans offered considerable aid and comfort to the United States.[33]

But to what extent did white Unionism exist during the city's Confederate year? Finding white Unionists in New Orleans during the first year of the war would broaden our understanding of the nature and size of white resistance to Confederate independence. Historians of white Unionists have focused their attention on whether disloyalty to the Confederacy contributed to its military collapse.[34] For the most part, historians have found Unionists in a limited number of places or only late in the war as defeatism and the reality of war became broadly apparent. Unionists, historians have said, lived on non-slaveholding family farms in the Appalachian Mountains and in the piney woods counties of the Gulf states.[35] More recently, some attention has been paid to Unionists in southern cities and also to the ethnic composition of Unionist populations, but to find them in large numbers in New Orleans would mean that Unionism had a broader constituency—an urban one, and one that included wage workers in addition to rich merchants and poor farmers—than we had previously thought.[36] In addition, to discover white Unionists in New Orleans in 1861 and 1862 would change our perception of when the movement began. In general, Unionism has been seen as growing only as southerners learned that war and the Confederacy made their lives miserable with conscription, high taxes, inflation, and death. The Confederate government arguably mismanaged its economy, writing legislation that favored planters at the expense of the poor.[37] The resulting Unionist behaviors, including draft resistance, desertion, military aid to the Union, and tax evasion, no doubt hampered Confederate efforts to win the war. But many of these issues had only just surfaced in April 1862, and most historians do not look for large numbers of white Unionists (outside the Appalachian Mountains) before 1863. Indeed, some historians have found that Confederate nationalism in one form or another remained strong throughout much of the South's white population even as the military situation became increasingly grim.[38] But the Unionists of New Orleans and many other places give us compelling evidence that many white southerners lost faith in the Confederacy (if they ever had it) and that their absence from the cause (and often from the army) shortened the Civil War considerably. Looking deeply into the causes of the Fort Jackson mutiny raises the possibility that Unionists existed earlier and in even more places than we have previously thought. That reality would prove a lasting comfort to Lincoln and other northerners.

DISSENT AND MARTIAL LAW IN CONFEDERATE NEW ORLEANS

So, did New Orleans teem with Unionism during its Confederate year? Is there enough evidence of Unionist action or sentiment to argue that the Fort Jackson soldiers recruited in New Orleans might have been part of a broader Unionist community in the Crescent City? While evidence suggests that Unionism existed in the city in 1861, the repressive nature of the Confederate administration in New Orleans meant that Unionists needed to keep their heads down and their mouths shut. Their secrecy makes uncovering them now a challenge, but New Orleans in its Confederate year seems to have borne a likeness to the society Horace Greeley imagined. Many of the city's workers disliked their bosses and doubted the wisdom of secession. As a result, the Confederacy was forced to wage a long campaign to suppress dissent. Throughout 1861, Confederate leaders viewed the city's people warily, always on the lookout for traitors. By March 1862, General Lovell declared martial law in the city, giving him even broader powers to detain dissenters. His declaration of martial law proves how much force the secessionists needed to compel allegiance to their new government.

The sabotage of the CSS *Mississippi* was not the only clandestine blow aimed at the city's Confederate war effort. Fifteen minutes before midnight on December 28, 1861, a vast explosion on the west bank on the river shattered the calm of Confederate New Orleans. The blast came from a large gunpowder mill in the old U.S. Marine Hospital, and it broke windows even on the other side of the river. Reports varied about how much gunpowder exploded, but the press agreed about the cause. The *New Orleans True Delta* spoke for all when it accused "traitors in our midst" of the "diabolical work." Six months earlier, a similar plot to blow up the city's powder magazine had been narrowly foiled.[39]

That loud bump in the night made the city jumpy. So when men secretly tried to set fire to one of the ironclads a few months later, the *New Orleans Bee* was alarmed. Even with the fire extinguished, the editor recom-

Confederate New Orleans

Confederate major general Mansfield Lovell, who commanded the defenses of New Orleans. (Library of Congress, Prints and Photographs Division, Civil War Photographs)

mended stationing guards to protect war work. The *Bee* warned of "traitors, who are in such large numbers in the Crescent City." Hiring guards, it thought, would mean that "we would not hear of powder-mill explosions" again.[40]

Worried about "traitors" lurking "in such large numbers," city authorities suppressed what they saw as unpatriotic speech. The task kept them busy. Throughout the Confederate year, some people voiced doubts about secession, the Confederate government, and slavery. The government responded by denying the right to a jury trial to anyone charged with sedition or abolitionism. Instead, the accused received hearings before Mayor Monroe.[41] People found guilty by the mayor received jail sentences. An analysis of the *New Orleans Commercial Bulletin*'s City Intelligence column from April 1861 to April 1862 reveals that the government arrested at least nineteen men for abolitionism or seditious language. This is by no means a complete count, however, since there were other arrests that were not mentioned in the *Commercial Bulletin*.[42] Still, these nineteen cases reveal the fates that awaited people convicted of Unionism in Confederate New Orleans.

The City Intelligence column only briefly described most of the anti-Confederate behavior it mentioned. We learn little about the barber Edward Hansen other than that he was bailed out after being charged with "preaching incendiary villainy." Thomas Drummond's crime—"being an abolitionist"—also goes unexplained. A man named Reynolds received more attention, perhaps because of the more flamboyant nature of his crime. Reynolds had called Jefferson Davis a "scoundrel and liar" and added that the United States should confiscate the property of anyone who supported the Confederacy. Punishments for these offenses were not slight. As the *Commercial Bulletin* noted approvingly, Drummond the abolitionist would be "in a bad way if what they say about him can be proved before the Mayor."[43]

The city usually sentenced people guilty of anti-Confederate or abolitionist talk to six months in the city's workhouse. This sentence awaited David O'Keefe, who was found guilty of using "treasonable language." O'Keefe pleaded guilty to abolitionism, though he may not have actually forced his children to "give three cheers for Lincoln," as the indictment charged. What happened to his children during his imprisonment is not known. But we do know that O'Keefe had like-minded company in the

Confederate New Orleans

workhouse. The *Commercial Bulletin* noted three weeks later that another convicted abolitionist, Stephen Lickenham, had been sentenced to an identical term. The paper gloated: "There are now some five or six Abolitionists doing the city some service by cracking rocks or picking oakum at the workhouse."[44]

Punishments were worse if the crime had been committed in front of free or enslaved African Americans. When John White and James Hill were both arrested on the same day for "imprudent talking," White faced a harsher sentence because of the "aggravating circumstance" that his words had been heard by black people. When Louis Huber spoke "incendiary language" that could have provoked blacks to unrest, the court refused to grant him bail. Even after Samuel Murdoch, an elderly man who had spent years visiting jails to give religious comfort and bibles to inmates, was found innocent of abolitionist talk, Mayor Monroe still "repremanded [sic] him for his talk with negroes."[45] Given the harsh sentences that awaited dissenters, Unionists must have felt torn between their political convictions and their need to keep silent in the face of persecution.

In addition to covering the official trials of Unionists, the City Intelligence column mentioned extralegal actions taken against other "abolitionists." Confederates in Houma, Louisiana, whipped a man named Fogay one hundred times for being an "abolitionist of the worst stripe" (pun intended?) before shipping him out of town. A Unionist in Avoyelles Parish in central Louisiana was murdered and two others wounded in a scuffle with "a Confederate mob" before all Unionist property in the region was confiscated. In New Orleans, a mob tarred and feathered Charles Ellis for using "seditious language."[46] With such extralegal actions augmenting the work of the police and courts, Unionists faced perils at every turn.

Unionists called this repression a "reign of terror," a term that referred to when French revolutionaries in the 1790s arrested and executed their political opponents. Such capital punishment rarely occurred in Confederate New Orleans, and it was seemingly reserved for soldiers who had committed military offenses.[47] But the Confederate "reign of terror" did resemble its French predecessor in that it was aimed at stifling political dissent. One man wrote to his father immediately after secession that "it was hardly safe for any one to avow Union sentiments." A. P. Dostie, a dentist, complained that "many were daily arrested and imprisoned for expressing the Union sentiments of our fathers." A local doctor, he added, had been arrested for saying nothing more than that he thought Lincoln would retake Charleston and New Orleans by force. Given the level of repression, some Unionists fled the city, but others could find no way out. N. Maria Taylor was fired from her teaching job in Gretna, close to New Orleans, because of her Unionist politics. A bullet was then fired through her window by a man who was later elected justice of the peace. Maria Taylor was not silenced, but her son—also a Unionist—enlisted in the Confederate army to protect his mother from further violence.[48] By conducting a reign of terror, Confederates hoped to silence Unionists and gain the apparent unanimity that the Confederacy needed in order to be seen as legitimate. For Unionists, the Confederate year was an ordeal that could not end soon enough.

The *Commercial Bulletin*'s coverage of the city's campaign against sedition provides glimpses into the motivations of Unionists. The Unionists apparently acted from a range of causes, including economic distress and a hatred of slavery. Many of the Unionists were also immigrants, and ethnic tensions may have played a part in their arrests. As the commanders of Fort Jackson suspected, many immigrants did not sympathize with the Confederacy. Charley Hensen, locked up for abolitionism, was a "Dutchman," a term meant to insult German Americans. Another immigrant in court was John Frenzel, a Prussian. Frenzel warned the court that "there was a club of the friends of Lincoln in this city, numbering over five thousand," and that it would take up arms as soon as Federal forces arrived. Despite being found guilty of abolitionism, Frenzel regained his liberty (at the price of a one-thousand-dollar bond for good behavior) only because Mayor Monroe could not take action against a Prussian citizen.[49] Immigrants such as Hensen and Frenzel probably brought their liberalism and antislavery beliefs with them from Europe, but others found their motivation in America.

Two of the reports mention economic rationales for Unionism. David O'Keefe, jailed in May 1861, came to his abolitionism through self-interest. "White labor," he said in court, "was put on a par with slave labor" throughout the South. By this he meant that when slave labor is unpaid, it is hard for wage laborers to compete unless they lower their own salary demands to near the level of slaves. In saying this, O'Keefe expressed what Greeley would write many months later. William J. Dewey voiced similar concerns, and at much greater length. Dewey, a businessman, made the mistake of writing a long letter describing New Orleans to a cousin in New York.

Intercepted by the Confederate military, the letter was forwarded to Mayor Monroe, who had Dewey arrested. The letter's bleak assessment of the Confederate experiment earned Dewey jail time, but for some reason the *Commercial Bulletin* decided to print it in full. Dewey described "the awful state of affairs" in his city, starting with the moribund economy. His own business had been "destroyed," Dewey complained, causing his "disastrous change" from prosperity to "exhausted" resources. New Orleans seemed to him "fatally injured." The Confederates had not just ruined the economy, however. Dewey noted that they had also crippled civil liberties. Calling the Confederacy "a slavery despotism," he worried that only slaveholders would be able to live happily under it. "Freediscussion [*sic*] is destroyed," he added, "and if the South ever gains its independence . . . all free literature must be abolished."[50] Dewey's pessimism regarding the city's economy and civil liberties seems fully justified.

While individuals spoke against the hard times caused by Louisiana's secession, the city's poor worked as a group. Their collective actions must have unsettled the Confederate elite. On August 1, 1861, three hundred women demanding food jammed into City Hall and the mayor's office. Several of the women (whom the press would not call "ladies") "used abusive language" toward the mayor.[51] Most of the women had male relatives serving in the Confederate military, which paid poorly and infrequently. Their protest called for the restoration of a moral economy in which the city government ensured that the poor would not starve. About two weeks after the protest, the city and wealthy citizens established a "free market," which distributed food to poor relatives of Confederate soldiers twice a week. The free market no doubt helped many families (it fed more than two thousand people in its first week and more each month), but it did not serve all the needy families in the city. Not everyone had relatives in the military, and many people had lost their jobs. Those who found work often discovered that their wages did not kept pace with inflation. To meet such needs, the city set maximum prices for basic foods.[52] By such actions, the local authorities hoped to keep the poor, especially the families of Confederate soldiers, from becoming demoralized by hunger.

The debate over a proposed state "stay law" proved to be more contentious. Another part of the moral economy tradition, stay laws blocked creditors from collecting certain debts for the duration of the economic crisis. Depending on how they were written, stay laws could protect the poor from losing everything they owned to their lenders. Stay laws often stopped foreclosures, and they could also halt evictions. They were, however, unpopular with creditors, and the proposed stay law in Louisiana encountered stiff resistance from the city's Confederate press. The *New Orleans Daily Crescent* opposed the measure, saying, "Thank God, we of Louisiana are not yet cursed with a stay-law, and we hope we never shall be." Editors in rural parts of the state also opposed the measure, with the *Franklin Planters' Banner* calling it "one of the most pernicious laws that could possibly be crowded through the Legislature." Opposed by the state's wealthiest citizens, who most often were creditors, the stay law bill failed in the legislature. Nevertheless, the poor in New Orleans needed a stay law, and their need was so great that the Confederate military commander Mansfield Lovell finally took unilateral action. On March 20, 1862, Lovell declared that all legal actions in Orleans and Jefferson parishes "for the eviction of the families of soldiers now in the service of the Government . . . for rent past due, is hereby suspended, and no such collections shall be forced until further orders."[53] Faced with soldiers worried about their families, Lovell acted to protect their interests. That the state legislature failed to take a similar stand says something about the priorities of the planter class that dominated both houses in Baton Rouge.

Lovell's stay law and the free market protected the families of Confederate soldiers, but poor women and men who had no such ties to the military still faced uncertain employment and rising inflation. Eager to make a living, they often engaged in activities seen as disloyal to the Confederacy. Oystermen and fishermen found a ready market in the Federal fleet, and for a time trade boomed. Such commercial traffic with the blockaders, attributed by Lovell's predecessor to Unionists, sparked a series of clampdowns. In June 1861, the Confederacy dispatched the schooner *Antonio* "to arrest all persons dealing with the enemy." More such orders followed in November 1861, but with so little success that General Lovell had to restate the order on January 31, 1862: "In consequence of the continued communication with the federal fleet off Ship Island," he wrote, "it is notified to oystermen and all others engaged in trade to that point, that no passes will, on any account or to any person, guilty or innocent, hereafter be granted, unless such correspondence with the enemy is promptly suppressed." In the twelve months prior to the Union victory, the City Intel-

Daniel Nestell's sketch of an old fisherman in his boat on the Mississippi River on April 15, 1862. Fishermen such as this one moved from ship to ship selling goods at exorbitant prices. (Special Collections and Archives Division, Nimitz Library, U.S. Naval Academy)

ligence column of the *Commercial Bulletin* mentioned seventeen fishermen arrested for trading food or information with the Federal fleet. One Unionist refugee knew of three oystermen who had been jailed for more than eight months and of seven fishermen who had been secreted out of the jail and hanged for their crimes. Lovell had hoped that his orders would stop "any further traitorous conduct," but he was bound to be disappointed.[54]

Lovell's efforts to interdict trade with the Union fleet failed, even though in April 1862 he was still arresting people found "fraternizing with the Lincolnites." Records from the Union fleet show that as late as April 1862 sailors regularly bought oysters from local men. The correspondent for the *Boston Journal* relished the "bivalves of enormous dimensions" he secured near Pilot Town. Poverty motivated much of this trade with the Union. Freeman Foster Jr. wrote to his father about the "feast" of oysters he had enjoyed, and his letter makes clear how much the poor in New Orleans had suffered in the past year. After talking with the oystermen, he wrote that they were "most starved until we came but now are doing well. A deserter from N. Orleans says there is but little [to] eat there." Foster then predicted how the Union could win the allegiance of the city's poor: "We will soon be there to feed the loyal ones." Foster's letter highlights the ways in which secession had hurt people, but it also proves his belief that he would find "loyal ones" in the Crescent City and see his government help them. In that, he was an able forecaster.[55]

Confederate New Orleans

In the months right before the mutiny, refugees and captured sailors described the working people of New Orleans as lukewarm Confederates, their enthusiasm dampened by a withering economy. Eight refugees fled New Orleans to Ship Island in "a small boat" in March 1862. Their arrival caused a stir among the Union troops. "They said they were almost starved," wrote Daniel Durgin to his mother. Flour, he noted, sold at fifty dollars a barrel. Union captain Richard H. Elliott also talked with the refugees, who told him that New Orleans had "no provisions, no ammunition & no anything, and not much feeling for sesession [sic]." Such hunger, the refugees predicted, would translate into apathetic Confederate resistance. Freeman Foster wrote about a man from New Orleans who had said that "he thinks they may fight some but not much."[56] Captured sailors taken off the schooners css *Eugenia* and *President* in April confirmed the refugees' depiction of indifferent Confederate soldiers. They told their captors that the garrison at Fort Jackson would "fight a little," but not as hard as it might because everyone expected "the rich and big men" to "all clear out and leave the rest" when the Yankees arrived. Everyone was out of work, they added, except the ship carpenters, whom they correctly reported as earning four dollars a day. Even the carpenters, however, were paid in Confederate notes that "many stores" now refused to accept. This assessment of New Orleans on the brink of its capture highlights the differences in how the Confederate year had treated the rich and the poor. It also accurately predicts how the different social classes would react to Union victory. In a foreshadowing of the mutiny at Fort Jackson, the captured sailors predicted that the Confederate soldiers there would fight, but only so much. The poor, they noted, distrusted the Confederate leadership and would soon work their way free.[57]

With conditions worsening throughout his command, Major General Mansfield Lovell declared martial law in four parishes, including the New Orleans metropolitan region and Plaquemines Parish, home of Fort Jackson, on March 15, 1862. As he explained to the secretary of war, martial law was needed in order to "root out our enemies." Lovell's martial law decree proved so sweeping that Louisiana's governor later complained to President Davis about "the urgent and persistent complaints" he had received. Lovell's major goal was to force all "grown white male residents" except unnaturalized foreigners to take the oath of allegiance. In addition, anyone "unfriendly to our cause" was required to leave the district immediately.[58] Lovell hoped to rid his command of traitors, but his order inadvertently revealed a lack of enthusiasm for the Confederate cause. People did not flock to the provost marshal's office to swear their allegiance to the new country. On April 6, three weeks after martial law went into effect, the *New Orleans Bee* expressed "surprise" that only 12,984 native-born men had taken the oath. Although that number grew to 19,324 by April 14, four days after the deadline for taking the oath, the turnout disappointed Confederate leaders.[59]

Sabotage, trade with the enemy, and verbal dissent may not be adequate proof that there was widespread Unionism in New Orleans in the year before the mutiny. But they are proof that not everyone was happy with the Confederacy. Considered as evidence, these actions are even more impressive given the fact that Unionists had every incentive to keep their mouths shut. Faced with six-month sentences in the workhouse—if they were lucky enough to avoid the extralegal violence of the mob—Unionists probably stayed silent or talked only with trusted friends or family members. And there is one more thread of evidence to consider. The ongoing search for volunteers for the Confederate army affords ample evidence that the new nation did not hold the allegiance of as many southern whites as it would need.

VOLUNTEERS AND CONSCRIPTION: CONFEDERATE RECRUITING IN NEW ORLEANS

We would expect ardent Confederates to disagree with William H. Russell's bleak assessment of Confederate recruiting early in the war, but the city's press nervously agreed with him. Editors worried about the slow pace of enlistments. At other times, they doubted the motives of the men who had joined the ranks. Recruits, they thought, joined because they lacked work and were offered cash bounties for enlisting as early as the first months of 1862. As historian John Winters writes, "In New Orleans patriotism was rarely the motive inducing . . . men to enlist." This is not to say that thousands of Louisianians did not flock to the Confederate colors with enthusiasm. Many did. Still, the rebellion's leadership and men in the ranks wondered why more had not joined them. Edward Murphy, serving in the ranks in Virginia, captured this blend of patriotism and doubt when he complained that while he was "willing to sacrifice all to get Independant [*sic*] of the whining Yankees, there are at the South and more particularly in the lower Parishes of our state Men who have not given anything like what they ought to give considering what they have at stake."[60] He was not alone in his suspicions.

New Orleans newspapers became increasingly concerned about the pace of recruiting in the two months before the city fell. The *New Orleans Daily Crescent* condemned the city's foreign-born residents for avoiding state conscription by claiming exemptions because they were not citizens. In March, a letter to the editor regretted "the backwardness of volunteers" and belittled the excuses offered for staying at home. Also in early 1862, the *New Orleans Bee* bemoaned "an apathy and indifference which are truly surprising." It listed six parishes that had failed to provide any companies for the war. Eight larger parishes, it said, had raised only one company. All these "laggard" parishes were in the southern part of the state, with most touching the Gulf of Mexico or the Mississippi River south of Baton Rouge. These southern parishes remained rather indifferent to calls for Confederate volunteers. Their "culpable lethargy" made the editor angry, and he welcomed a resort to military conscription.[61]

Military drafts started early in Louisiana. The state resorted to compulsory military service long before the Confederate Congress passed a conscription law on April 16, 1862. On September 28, 1861, Governor Moore ordered all white men between the ages of 18 and 45 into state militia units. Once enrolled, the men would drill for military service in the defense of Louisiana. Shirkers, the state militia's adjutant and inspector general warned, would have their names and residences recorded on a "blacklist," together with any women or ineligible men who were their "aiders, abettors, and advisors."[62] The Louisiana legislature also passed a law on January 23, 1862, authorizing the state to call up militia units to serve in the state for six months. In February, the city's militia was called into active duty in the field. This meant that men in the militia could no longer return to their homes at night, and complaints followed hard on the heels of the new orders. The aggressively Confederate *Bee* noted, however, "We can tell all those who might wish to evade the law and their duty to their country, that no earthly means can avail them. The law will be enforced."[63] Such warnings proved necessary, but only so effective.

Anecdotal evidence suggests that informal conscription continued as well. Like the press gangs that compelled Englishmen and others to serve in the Royal Navy during the Napoleonic wars, Confederate "recruiters" used coercive methods to get New Orleans men into the ranks. Much of the evidence of street impressments comes from refugees to the North or in letters to Benjamin Butler after he assumed command of the city. While these people had a vested interest in presenting their Confederate service as coerced, the frequency of such statements (together with Russell's and Mure's testimony about abductions in May) suggests that they may have been accurate. A woman told a *New York Times* reporter that her Unionist brother had been "seized at night and hurried off to Virginia," where his officers abused him for his political beliefs. Men of northern birth, like Unionists, may have been targeted for compulsory service. A man born in Brooklyn and a 15-year-old boy from Syracuse, New York, independently reported that they had escaped from Confederate service after being, in the words of the boy, "impressed in New Orleans." Refugees spoke of a "vigilance committee" that "impressed men without hesitation." Butler suspected that the sheriff of New Orleans evicted any Unionist whom he could not "force . . . into Confederate service."[64] Though not as sweeping as the militia law or the looming national draft, such forced enlistments enlarged the army even as it revealed the tepid nature of Confederate volunteering in New Orleans.

Confederates hoped the draft laws would force malingerers into the ranks. When the New Orleans militia was called into the field in February 1862, Confederate editors rejoiced. Joyous at the thought that slackers would finally be forced into soldiering, they wrote with a gleeful spite. The *Bee* delighted in the fact that "all who have shirked duty so far will have to 'toe a chalked line.'" The *Daily Crescent* condemned the militia men as "lukewarm patriots" who spent their days "courting their ease and comfort" while others fought and died for their country. Now, the *Crescent* smiled, their time had come. "It was amusing to observe their terror and to hear the miserable excuses they gave, with a hope of getting off," the editor wrote. By taking such joy in the pain of others—of men called away from families— the editors indicated their commitment to the Confederacy but also showed how far removed they were from the cares of ordinary people.[65]

Men could be forced into the ranks, but that did not mean that they obeyed orders readily. The Louisiana militia in New Orleans became known for its poor attendance at drill, slack discipline, and occasional outright disobedience. Especially before it was ordered to military camps, the militia proved to be a haphazard affair. It had a reputation as a way for Unionists to seem patriotic while avoiding active Confederate service. The use of the militia as a front by Unionists may explain the poor reputation the units had in Confederate circles. Certainly, militia drills had impressed few spectators after the first few months of the war. The infrequency of drills, coupled with absenteeism, damaged the militia's credibility. Poor attendance at a review in November 1861, for example, forced the commander of the state's militia, Major General John L. Lewis, to order officers to report the names of absentees to his office. Despite Lewis's efforts, a steady rain kept enough soldiers away from a January 1862 grand review to catch the attention of the press. Conscientious officers, such as Captain John Knight of the Crescent Blues, were driven to frustration by their men's apathy. Knight went so far as to print up his orders about absenteeism as a public broadside in February 1862. The order observed, "We have a large roll, and ought to turn out at every meeting 65–75 men. Those that attend know that our number at drills falls far short of the above figures. It is discouraging to those that drill and pay dues to know that others of the company do neither." Away from New Orleans, a muster in Fort Jackson's home parish on March 4, 1862, saw only 200 of the local militia's 600 soldiers turn out. "Patriotism is very Low in this parish," an observer concluded. Even the local justice of the peace in that parish, Dick Corbett, told Union naval officers a month later that he "would like to see Jeff. Davis and his colleagues swinging at our yardarm."[66] Officers were supposed to enforce attendance with fines or dismissal from the unit, but even with punishments looming, officers had a hard time motivating their soldiers.

Louisiana's militia laws contained a provision that surely angered at least some people in New Orleans and throughout the state. Worried that slaves might rebel if left unsupervised, the state exempted one white man from the draft for every plantation. This exemption freed some of the state's wealthiest men from the draft, and poorer citizens grumbled about the iniquities of the governor's order. Later national draft laws also allowed rich men to escape service either by hiring substitutes to serve for them or through a similar planter exemption. Non-slaveholders in Louisiana and elsewhere complained that the war to protect slavery was being fought only by men who did not profit from the institution. It was, they said, "a rich man's war but a poor man's fight."[67] It is tempting to make connections between the passage of the first Confederate draft law in

April, which allowed for the hiring of substitutes, and the mutiny less than two weeks later, but such connections would be only conjecture. However the garrison troops reacted to the new legislation, they knew when they mutinied that the Confederacy would compel their continued service for the duration of the war and that, in contrast, the United States did not (at that time) have a draft.

Whatever their reactions to the draft laws, New Orleans soldiers proved to be a fractious bunch. New Orleans troops earned a reputation for mutinying before the end of 1861. The crew of the small ironclad CSS *Manasses* had rebelled when the navy ordered a new commander to take charge of the vessel. According to a diary by one of its gunners, the announcement of the new officer "almost created a mutiny on board." The new commander, Lieutenant Alexander Warley, prevented more serious trouble only by allowing men to leave the ship rather than serve under him. As it was, however, the *Manasses* lost "all our best feremen [*sic*]" and others "who left in disgust." Other New Orleans troops mutinied in Memphis on August 2, 1861, and on the same day "two companies of the Polish brigade of Louisiana volunteers" raised havoc in Grand Junction. The men "disbanded" their units, apparently illegally, since two other companies of Confederate troops were dispatched to control them. In other words, the mutiny at Fort Jackson was not an isolated incident. Mutinies occurred with enough frequency to suggest that many soldiers resented their officers. Some had been forced to enlist by privation, others by extralegal force, and still others by state law. As even the *New Orleans Daily Crescent* observed about the militia, the men had "no friendship for their officers, and the officers no sympathy for the men."[68]

With the Union attack looming, some of General Lovell's troops appeared ready to break with the Confederacy even before the Fort Jackson mutiny occurred. An officer wrote home that at his post, a small fort near New Orleans, "the discipline is awful, in fact there is none." Confederate general Braxton Bragg's wife warned him from New Orleans that the army appeared to be spinning out of control. "Lovell is more & more distrusted," she wrote in mid-March 1862; "persons are open and plain in the expression of their opinions of him—it will in time of danger, be followed by *open mutiny*."[69] Lovell himself knew enough about his command not to trust many of his troops. "I issued no ammunition to the militia at the camp near the interior line because . . . they had, in some regiments, manifested such an insubordinate disposition, that I felt unwilling to put ammunition in their hands," he wrote. Some of the most mutinous of his troops were among those he had earlier "ordered to the support of Fort Jackson." These troops, Lovell later told a court of inquiry, had "mutinied and refused to go, and had to be forced on board the transports by other regiments."[70]

It is possible, then, to see the mutiny at Fort Jackson as the natural end to a year of Confederate rule. The rebellion had not made life easier for ordinary families in New Orleans. The Confederate experiment, successful elsewhere, had failed in several ways in New Orleans. Many of the city's businessmen and workers had placed self-interest above national defense. Recruitment was slower than the governor or General Lovell would have liked. Efforts to make up for the shortfall of volunteers with conscription had filled militia ranks, at least on paper, but those soldiers often proved to be absent or undependable when it came time to drill. Attempts to get them into the field met with resistance. Finally, the men coerced into the ranks often proved mutinous even before the Yankees arrived, and we have to wonder if Generals Lovell and Duncan spent their days and nights worried about the very troops they supposedly led.

cannoneers, regulars, and jagers

INSIDE FORT JACKSON BEFORE THE MUTINY

Henry E. Lawrence and Alexander Ashton had very little in common. They were born in different parts of the world and did different work. One was rich, the other poor. The Civil War and the fighting at Fort Jackson, in all likelihood, did not mean the same things to the two men. But together, Lawrence and Ashton hint at what went wrong for the Confederacy inside the fort's brick walls.

Henry Lawrence never served in Fort Jackson, though a company from his parish, St. Mary's, joined the garrison in the spring of 1862. Lawrence was an established businessman in the sugar-rich parish, and he donated money to the Confederate cause. He was badly disappointed by the mutiny at Fort Jackson, which he heard about from a private correspondent in the garrison. Likely a member of the Know-Nothing Party, Lawrence knew whom to blame for the military collapse, and he spared his enemies no rhetorical blows when he wrote in his diary. By turns maudlin and furious,

Lawrence believed that the Confederacy had been betrayed at Fort Jackson by "Democracy + Foreign voters." Immigrant voters, he continued, were "the Curse of this once magnificent + Beautiful Union." Andrew Jackson and his Democratic Party had ruined a fine country by embracing manhood suffrage in the 1820s. Like many conservatives, he blamed the Democratic Party for allowing immigrants to vote. By late April 1862, Lawrence also held Democrats responsible for the Confederacy's military defeats. "The Rule + Ruin democrats *die, die, die* and down to hell they go," he wrote when New Orleans fell. A day later, he added: "So fell the Great and proud City of the South[,] traitorous[ly] betrayed by the Foreign population, the . . . petted favorites of the *Rule* + Ruin democracy[.] So we will fall fall Ruined damned."[1]

Lawrence's melancholy words, mixed with such anger, point to an important part of the Confederate defeat at Fort Jackson. Like Lawrence, many Confederates looked down on immigrants, even though they might have won valuable allies by treating them more equitably. Nor would Lawrence ever shake his sense that the new nation remained too egalitarian. St. Mary's Parish remained under Confederate control for many more months, and Lawrence was eventually accused (by his social inferiors) of not accepting Confederate paper currency at face value. In a blow to his dignity that he found hard to forgive, some zealous Confederates dragged him off to Opelousas in the dead of night to answer this charge.[2] Although he was soon released, Lawrence must have felt that the Confederacy had failed to reverse the United States' ruinous slide into democracy. He had expected little from the immigrant wage workers who made up much of the garrison of Fort Jackson, but the new nation's inability to control them depressed him. The unwillingness of Lawrence—a representative of the Confederacy's many wealthy backers—to cozy up to immigrant soldiers spelled trouble for the new country.

Alexander Ashton was one of the men who upset the likes of Henry Lawrence. Almost certainly, Ashton was one of the mutineers in Fort Jackson, where he served as a private in Company D of the 1st Louisiana Heavy Artillery. Ashton arrived in the United States in September 1847, when he was 9 years old. The boy, accompanied by his mother, Ann, and his younger brother, George, had come to Boston from Glasgow, Scotland. Ashton's father, Samuel, may well have preceded them. By 1850, the family had moved to Philadelphia, where Samuel found work as a sailor. Such work did not pay well, however, and by November 1850 the 14-year-old Alexander seems to have been farmed out to a household in Greenwood Township, New Jersey, as an apprentice or general laborer. By 1860, the family's fortunes had not improved; the census taker that year still listed Samuel as a "mariner," and he decided that the Ashtons' entire worth was about one hundred dollars. Alexander was now back with his parents and also working as a sailor.[3] At some point in 1861, Alexander Ashton's job took him to New Orleans, where the Union blockade bottled him up and made it impossible for him to escape the city.

Stranded and probably unemployed, Alexander Ashton volunteered for the Confederate army. He proved a recalcitrant soldier. In the fall of 1861, Ashton and another soldier, Willis Reynolds, were charged with attempted desertion and conspiring to convince other men to join them. They had planned their escape in advance. Ashton and Reynolds had hidden their muskets, bayonets, ammunition, and food where they could grab them on their way out of the fort. They also planned to leave before they were issued their back pay, reasoning that officers would be more on guard against desertion after pay day. Their plan implies that officers knew that members of the garrison were disheartened but that the promise of deferred pay kept men in the ranks. A court-martial found Ashton and Reynolds guilty; they were sentenced to be executed by firing squad. General Duncan urged Lovell to approve the sentences "for the good of the service." Luckily for the two men, however, Lovell rejected the sentences because of a legal technicality.[4]

Ashton and Reynolds might have had many reasons for wanting to escape from Fort Jackson. But it might be more fruitful to ask why they would have wanted to stay. Why would a Scottish immigrant who had lived in the free states for much of his adult life want to fight for the Confederacy? If Henry Lawrence's diary is any indication of the welcome given to immigrants in the Confederacy, then Ashton must have felt alienated from the country whose uniform he wore. Indeed, disloyalty to the Confederacy may have plagued officers in Fort Jackson as men who had already chosen once to immigrate were faced again with the choice of which country, the United States or the Confederate States, offered them the brightest future. True, prosperity had eluded Samuel Ashton and his son Alexander as they plied the seas on Philadelphia's ships over the previous fifteen years, but the South arguably offered an even bleaker pros-

Cannoneers, Regulars, and Jagers

pect for wage laborers, white or black. At least some of the immigrants, and maybe some native-born Americans, chose to live in the United States when they mutinied that April night. Some may have voiced their preferences even earlier.

Joseph Harris was among the first Union officers inside Fort Jackson, and he spent time talking with the members of the garrison. Charged with determining the condition of the fort after the mortar bombardment, Harris interviewed the men who had survived the Union fire. The former Confederates he talked with complained about the "very young and entirely inexperienced officers" who commanded them. They also said that "the discipline in the fort was very strict." This harmonizes with what the Confederate records say. But Harris also reported that the fort's officers had suspected that some of their soldiers were guilty of disloyalty to the Confederacy. These men "were closely watched," he wrote, and if found guilty of "improper talk," they were hung by a rope and left to "float in the 'stinking ditch.'"[5] "Improper talk" meant disloyal talk, and the context of Harris's letter indicates that the officers suspected that Irishmen, Germans, and northerners wavered in their Confederate patriotism. Some members of the garrison pledged little or no allegiance to the new government, despite the threat of being sentenced to death or left suspended in the stagnant water of the fort's moat for hours at a time. Henry Lawrence, it turns out, may have had every reason to be worried that men would decide that the United States represented a brighter future for them and their families. For Alexander Ashton, escaping from Fort Jackson—even into the miles of wild swamp that surrounded it—was worth risking his life. How much more tempting must it have been when he saw Butler's troops just a few hundred yards away?

THE CONFEDERATE GARRISON of Fort Jackson consisted of eight companies, five of artillery and three of infantry, though the infantrymen were also trained to work the fort's heavy guns. Most of the 630 men in the garrison had volunteered for service early in 1861. Such early enlistment dates would seem to indicate enthusiasm for the Confederate cause. Why would such early volunteers mutiny?

Anyone looking for a political motivation for the mutiny—for example, evidence that the mutineers rebelled in order to help the United States or hurt the Confederacy—must also recognize that other factors may have contributed to the disaffection of the garrison. Life in Fort Jackson during the first year of the war, for example, was not pleasant, and several aspects of it may have weakened morale. Soldiers in Fort Jackson soon became familiar with mosquitoes, heat, hard work, and isolation. Such conditions could prove especially wearing on the many men who served in Fort Jackson for months—or even a full year.[6] Morale might also have been weakened by the scattered nature of Confederate units in the region. The garrison of Fort Jackson included four companies of the 1st Louisiana Heavy Artillery (companies B, D, E, and H), the independent St. Mary's Cannoneers company, two companies of the 22nd Louisiana Volunteers (H and I; infantry), and Company I of the 23rd Louisiana Volunteers (also infantry). All these regiments had troops scattered across Louisiana. Civil War soldiers often built strong allegiances to their regiments, but the troops in Fort Jackson could not develop these loyalties because their units were so spread out. Their allegiances to their home, neighborhood, or ethnicity would remain that much more intact.[7]

Poor officers no doubt also hurt morale. In the 1st Louisiana Heavy Artillery alone, General Johnson Duncan urged the governor to dismiss two lieutenants because of their unfortunate "habits."[8] An even worse situation arose from the conduct of Captains James Anderson and Frederick Brand. In September 1861, Captain Anderson ordered some gunnery drill, and Captain Brand accused him of wasting ammunition. An argument followed in which Anderson told Brand that he was "a God damn shit arse and . . . a damn liar." Brand responded by punching Anderson. All this unbecoming conduct took place in front of their men. A court-martial found both officers guilty but only stripped them of their seniority as captains.[9] When Brand took a leave of absence to try to find another command, General Duncan pointedly refused in January 1862 to write him letters attesting to his "capability and good conduct."[10] Such discord could not have made rank-and-file soldiers happy or confident as they went into 1862. Although poor officers, scattered commands, and harsh living conditions helped keep the garrison of Fort Jackson from developing into an effective unit, these factors probably were not enough to start the mutiny. The varying backgrounds of the men—their histories before the war started—had a substantial impact on whether they joined the mutiny. In many ways, the key to the Fort Jackson mutiny was forged long before the Confederacy came into existence.

Cannoneers, Regulars, and Jagers

Since the men in Fort Jackson came from very different backgrounds, an examination of three of the units stationed there will provide us with some possible reasons for why these men acted as they did during the mutiny. By looking at the St. Mary's Cannoneers, the 1st Louisiana Heavy Artillery, and an infantry company known as the Jagers, we can see the diverse social worlds from which Confederate soldiers came. The Cannoneers distinguished themselves by being the only unit in Fort Jackson that did not mutiny. The mutineers suspected that they would prove loyal, and they took the precaution of locking them out of the fort. The second unit, the companies of the 1st Louisiana Heavy Artillery, was part of the Regular Army of the state of Louisiana. Most men in the Heavy Artillery companies had enlisted even before the war started at Fort Sumter. The third unit, the Jagers, volunteered before Confederate conscription became a serious threat. But the men in the Regulars and the Jagers were mostly first-generation immigrants, and their prior experiences varied greatly from those of the rural Cannoneers. The men's reactions to the situation at Fort Jackson stemmed from their diverse personal backgrounds.

THE ST. MARY'S CANNONEERS

The St. Mary's Cannoneers came from a Gulf Coast parish so deeply enmeshed in the global sugar economy that a local editor called it "the sugar parish."[11] The sweetener had made some men in St. Mary's Parish very rich. Not everyone was so lucky, however. Sugar cultivation required heavy, often fatal, work under the hot Louisiana sun. Here and on the sugar islands of the Caribbean, men and women died to bring in the crop before time robbed it of its sweetness.[12] Free laborers would not do this work—at least not fast enough for maximum profits—so Louisiana planters, like their predecessors around the Caribbean, resorted to forced labor. Before long, racial slavery formed the central component of life in St. Mary's Parish.

The booming economy of St. Mary's brought in an increasingly diverse free population. The 1860 census found 3,589 whites in St. Mary's living alongside 174 free mulattoes and blacks. Of the whites, 475 people (about 13 percent) had been born in Canada or Europe. People in the parish, no doubt including some of these immigrants, worked in 1861 to build the first Catholic church in the parish. Sugar profits also brought in dozens of

Cannoneers, Regulars, and Jagers

Drawing of a St. Mary's Parish sugar plantation in 1863 by Daniel Nestell. Note the industrial-looking smokestacks in the left center, conveying the size and complexity of the plantation economy. (Special Collections and Archives Division, Nimitz Library, U.S. Naval Academy)

northerners. Still, when Confederate recruiters talked to men in St. Mary's, their audience was drawn mostly from traditional southern families.[13]

Free people, however, constituted only a small part of the parish's population; the roughly 3,600 white people in St. Mary's claimed ownership of 12,978 people, about 77.5 percent of the population. Seriously outnumbered, whites tried to reassure themselves that this captive group could be held to their work. Some whites did this by telling themselves that slaves had it easy and therefore had no reason to revolt. Enslaved people, a local editor wrote, were "perfectly quiet, happy, and contented, with plenty to eat, drink and wear, and nothing to disturb their thoughts by day, or dreams by night. They are, indeed, truly happy creatures."[14] But this was pap, and people with years of experience wringing work out of involuntary laborers knew it. Men in the fields and workshops of St. Mary's knew that slaves did not regard their status as a blessing. White people also knew that, ironically, the war designed to safeguard their human property put the slave system at momentary hazard because of the imminent threat of invasion, violence, and anarchy. Aware of the risks their war for independence posed, they set about securing an even firmer control over their slaves.

Twelve days before Louisiana seceded from the Union, St. Mary's governing body, the Police Jury, passed seven new regulations designed to keep slaves quiet. The new laws made it easier for masters to retrieve fugitive slaves (including giving owners the right to search other people's property without their consent), prevented slaves from earning money (which could be used to buy weapons), and required owners of thirty or more people to secure overseers to "maintain a good police among them." In early 1862, when Federal attack loomed, the Police Jury banned outside peddlers from the parish (they might be abolitionists) and encouraged masters to keep their slaves home on Sundays.[15] With Union troops threatening the parish, its government reinforced racial and legal boundaries.

The slaves in St. Mary's Parish had other ideas. In May 1861, slaves near the town of Jeanneretts conspired to revolt against the government. Southern whites rarely wrote publicly about slave revolts (for fear of giving other slaves the idea), and the May slave conspiracy in St. Mary's is no exception. The historical record consists of a single letter to the editor published more than a month after the events it described. But clearly something had happened to alarm the outnumbered white inhabitants. In tones meant to reassure, the anonymous writer described how their "well-drilled patrol" eavesdropped at every doorway and searched slave quarters and surrounding woods. Guilty people would hang from the parish's stately magnolias, he wrote. Investigators also pointedly interrogated a handful of white men who lived "in a marital manner with the woman slaves." This "vulgar practice" excited considerable attention from the author, who deemed sex across the racial and free/slave lines "very inconvenient to the peace and safety" of society. "A few natives" of the state might have interracial sex, and they must be stopped, but he mostly railed against foreigners, who he thought committed most of these sins. Assuring readers that Jeanneretts was "wide awake" to the danger, the author went on to blame a German named Miller, who was a hired cooper, of being "an abolitionist of deep dye." Perhaps Miller slept with a black woman; maybe he was seen talking to slaves who later were thought guilty of conspiracy. We don't know what Miller did to arouse suspicions. But blaming Miller— an outsider to St. Mary's and the South—allowed the writer to preserve the myth that people of African descent, if left to themselves, would passively accept slavery. Still, no one could rest easily, even after Miller was forcibly banished from the parish. Having relayed the dismaying news of the conspiracy, the writer called for employers to question new workers such as Miller "adroitly."[16] Perhaps then slavery might be safe.

Or perhaps not. Authorities detected another slave conspiracy in St.

Mary's Parish later in 1861. Evidence for this possible revolt is sparse—only a brief newspaper report that thirteen slaves had been shot in St. Mary's Parish after a "dangerous insurrection." Even dating this conspiracy is difficult. It was "within the past few months" of a report filed in late January 1862. But such an event would explain General Lovell's decision in December 1861 to keep three infantry companies and a battery of artillery in St. Mary's Parish, even though the Confederacy sorely needed those troops on other fronts. Writing to the secretary of war, Lovell said that the troops were "intended for moral effect in that densely slave-populated section."[17]

The artillery battery mentioned in Lovell's report was almost certainly the St. Mary's Cannoneers, which had formed in June 1861. The Cannoneers soon became the darlings of the parish's free population. They received their flag from Miss Louisa McKerall of the Franklin Female Institute on June 20 and the last of their rifles and cannon in July.[18] They were not, however, formed for active duty in the field. The parish had already sent a company to the front lines, and the Cannoneers were meant to serve as local militia, seeing duty mainly in the parish and perhaps in the state during an emergency. Many of the members enjoyed a social status that usually protected them from danger or rigorous exercise. No less a man than Jules G. Olivier, a 61-year-old planter and lawyer who had served as a state senator and a delegate to the state's secession convention, held a lieutenant's commission.[19] Meant to operate primarily against poorly armed slaves, the Cannoneers drilled only three times a week, and briefly at that. Nor were the drills really mandatory. Parades and drills started at 4:30 in the afternoon, and country mechanics were allowed to miss two of the three weekly drills. Men who missed drill could "make their excuses" at the next meeting.[20] The Cannoneers seemed unlikely to cut a respectable figure on the battlefield.

Sometime in early April, however, a desperate Louisiana government ordered the Cannoneers to Fort Jackson. Leaving behind their field artillery, the Cannoneers would have less than a month to train on the fixed heavy artillery pieces of the fort's exterior water battery.[21] They may not have been great shots—when Farragut steamed by, Confederate cannons inflicted far fewer casualties than might have been expected—but they performed above everyone's expectations. General Duncan went out of his way to praise the St. Mary's men, even to the point of taking out a news-

Cannoneers, Regulars, and Jagers

This sketch by Daniel Nestell resembles the casemates of the Water Battery, the earthenwork extension of Fort Jackson where the St. Mary's Cannoneers served during the bombardment. Because the Water Battery was outside the fort's brick walls, the mutineers could effectively lock the Cannoneers out of the fort during the mutiny. (Special Collections and Archives Division, Nimitz Library, U.S. Naval Academy)

paper ad praising them after the battle. General Lovell also weighed in, writing a glowing letter to the unit's captain, Florian Cornay, who forwarded the praise to his hometown paper. Despite their lack of training, the Cannoneers "stood firm and true." The general continued: "When the greater portion of them around you were false to the country, you evinced a heroism greater than that which carried you through the terrific bombardment."[22] Who were these largely untrained men, and why did they fight so well?

The St. Mary's Cannoneers came to the unit from different segments of the parish's white population. Of the 90 names from the Cannoneers' December muster roll (the surviving list closest to the date of the mutiny), 34 (37.8 percent) can be found in the 1860 Federal census. That is not a particularly large percentage, but we can begin to see why the fort's officers called the Cannoneers the "sons of planters." Of the 34 people located in the census, 18 owned slaves themselves, were the sons of slaveholders (and thereby stood to inherit), or were listed as "planters." Some were from very rich families, including 20-year-old Oscar Berwick, whose father, David, owned 128 people in 1860. Others owned only a handful of people, including Bill Tophan, whose father, a carpenter, owned 4 people

Cannoneers, Regulars, and Jagers

(though one of them, a 40-year-old woman, had escaped his reach and was listed as a "fugitive").[23] Whether they owned only a few people or many, more than half of the Cannoneers located in the census had intimate ties to the slave economy.

Further, men with deep ties to slavery held the company's leadership positions. The captain and the three lieutenants who served in 1861 owned slaves themselves, and some had earned the designation "planter" from the census taker. Fewer of the noncommissioned officers could be found in the census, but all the ones who could be found owned people, including First Sergeant John Tarlton, who possessed 27 slaves. The father of the unit's guidon, Ludovic Delahoussaye, held 11 people as property.[24] For these men, the success or failure of "the slaveholder's republic" could mean the difference between financial security and possible impoverishment.

Looking at the 16 Cannoneers who did not own slaves helps to show the range of wealth and poverty experienced by rural whites in the Civil War South. Many of the men who marched off to Fort Jackson had little or no wealth at all. Nor were they settled members of the St. Mary's Parish community or even the state of Louisiana. The place of birth of 15 of the non-slaveholding men is listed in the census. The non-slaveholding Cannoneers, all privates, came from almost everywhere—though birth in Louisiana was noticeably rare. Almost half (7 of 15) had emigrated from Europe. Three had come from Germany, but England, Ireland, France, and Italy were also represented. Four Cannoneers had been born in northern states, 3 of them in Pennsylvania. Only 4 of the non-slaveholders had been born in the South, and only 1 in Louisiana.[25] These men seem to have no direct ties to slavery; indeed, it is hard to imagine them ever moving up in the world given their status in 1860. Quite simply, the non-slaveholders seem very poor in comparison with their comrades in arms.

Even middle-aged, relatively well-established men who did not own slaves seem several steps below their slaveholding neighbors. Valentine Weber might have become middle class in another society. At 31 years old, the German immigrant was married and had been stable enough to have his two children born in Louisiana. He also owned a modest house valued at $1,200. But the census taker listed no occupation beside his name, and the Webers' possessions totaled a mere $500 in value. Alcee Whaley should have been able to carve out a living as a blacksmith by age 40, but instead he roomed, single, with another Scottish blacksmith and owned no property worth the census man's attention. (Whaley would die after having his shattered arm amputated at Fort Jackson.) Pennsylvania-born carpenter Augustus B. Larmer owned nothing at age 26; Irishman John Finnigan and his wife, Brigit, had belongings worth only $200, even though he was 34 and she was 29 years old. Even though the Finnigans were in their prime earning years, his work as a "laborer" and her efforts to care for their three boarders barely got them through the week.[26] Given their mixed national origins and their poverty, why did these non-slaveholding men fight so hard for the Confederacy?

Historians have offered many explanations for the loyalty that many, even most, of the South's poor whites showed for the Confederacy. Certainly many fought to defend their homes from invasion, some believed in states' rights as a constitutional theory, and others no doubt wanted African Americans to be kept in subjection even if slavery did not benefit them directly. The fact that the parish boasted a chapter of the Knights of the White Camelia, a secret organization resembling the more famous Ku Klux Klan, as early as May 1867 suggests that white supremacy was alive and well in Civil War–era St. Mary's.[27] But economics played a part as well. Most of the non-slaveholding men needed the economic patronage of the slaveholders and their sons who marched alongside them. Some of the poor men earned their living directly from slaveholders. Private James McDonald captained the schooner *Jeff Davis*, owned by the Footes, a planter family that sent a lieutenant and a corporal to the Cannoneers.[28] Other connections are less obvious, but the poor men must have worked for neighboring planters. The homes and workshops of the richer parish residents served as the primary markets for coopers' barrels, brickmasons' handiwork, and tailors' clothing. The man who wrote about the Jeanneretts slave conspiracy used this economic dependence to try to influence the coopers who had hired the abolitionist named Miller; the writer warned the coopers to question their workers closely or else planters would start to make their own barrels (by ordering their slaves to do so).[29]

We can also find evidence of how much poor whites relied on the patronage of the planter elite in the local editorials that bemoaned the business slowdown caused by the war. With the parish Police Jury issuing its own paper bonds (further diluting the value of Confederate paper currency), local businesspeople found it hard to keep shops open. In May 1861, the newspaper blamed "the tightness of the times" for the sale of a "young negro boy 'Walter,'" who was being auctioned to pay his owner's taxes. As times worsened, poor people became increasingly unable to purchase the goods and services of artisans or unskilled laborers, and the parish's wealthiest citizens became even more important customers. By the start of 1862, St. Mary's opened its own free market, a tacit admission that poor families could not afford to eat on the (often unpaid) wages earned by the nation's soldiers. But, since the wealthy organized and attended the charitable events that sustained the free market, and given that their support might be removed at any moment, poor white soldiers knew that any failure to please the planter class could send their families back home hungry.[30] Poor white men served for a variety of reasons, but economic dependence on the business and largesse of their planter neighbors must have provided some motivation. Frederick Heyl may have been the genuine Confederate patriot envisioned by a local scribe after his death at Fort Jackson, but that seems unlikely given the fact that he had been born in Pennsylvania, had no wealth, occupation, or local family, and had boarded with two other northern-born men in 1860.[31] The presence of so many wealthy planters and their sons in the Cannoneers, especially as officers, ensured that non-slaveholders would have to fight hard if they wanted to stay in the good graces of the men who ruled their world. The Cannoneers might not have been rigorously trained, but they displayed the steadfast loyalty to the Confederate cause that distinguished units drawn from slaveholding regions. In that way, the men of St. Mary's stood out from the men in the fort's other seven companies, all of whom enlisted in the broad, often anonymous, expanse of New Orleans.

THE REGULARS

Four out of the eight companies in Fort Jackson came from the 1st Louisiana Heavy Artillery, known as the Regulars. The Regulars were different from the state's volunteer regiments, which mustered in after the war started in April 1861. Unlike the volunteers, who enlisted for one year of service, the Regulars signed up for a three-year term. Also unlike the volunteers, Regulars had their hair closely cropped and did not enjoy the luxury of electing their own officers.[32] Most of these men signed their recruiting contracts in early March 1861, some even before Lincoln was inaugurated, and they had no guarantee of glory or excitement. It is un-

Cannoneers, Regulars, and Jagers

likely that people with promising jobs and bright futures would be willing to sign away three years of their lives without knowing that a war was under way. Indeed, southerners and northerners alike needed months of fighting before deciding that enlistment periods of longer than three months or a year would be necessary.

Enlisting in the Regulars meant more than signing away three years of one's life to a hard job. Before 1861, becoming a Regular Army soldier carried with it a strong social stigma. Historian Edward M. Coffman writes that American citizens regarded soldiers with "contempt and fear," an attitude with deep roots in the nation's ideas about itself. Americans disliked the Regular Army because its command structure smacked of hierarchy instead of the equality that white men were supposed to enjoy. Also, Americans condemned the idea of a peacetime army, finding it a drain on the Treasury and a possible means by which the government could oppress the people. Thomas Jefferson disliked the army so much that he had cut it to just over three thousand soldiers, including coastal garrisons and men stationed on the western frontier. Since American men were supposed to be independent, equal citizens, an institution like the army that placed men in dependent positions could not hold the love of the people at large.[33]

Given these social realities, volunteers for the Regulars tended to be motivated by chronic poverty, which gave them little choice but to take on a job that others regarded with suspicion. As the nineteenth century wore on, an increasing percentage of soldiers were immigrants who lacked the skills or personal connections that would gain them a solid foothold in the economy. Edward Coffman has noted that enlistments in the Regular Army rose dramatically during economic depressions and that eastern cities with large immigrant communities proved to be the most fertile grounds for recruiters. By the 1850s, two out of every three soldiers in the army had been born outside the United States, with the Irish constituting the majority of the foreign-born soldiers.[34] These trends in the antebellum U.S. Army seem to have continued into the formation of Louisiana's Regulars.

Enlistment records give us tantalizing hints about the men who volunteered for the 1st Louisiana Heavy Artillery. Three out of four of the regiment's companies in Fort Jackson enlisted before the war started, with the fourth recruited slowly in the summer and fall of 1861. The age of the recruits fell into a normal, even desirable, pattern, with more than

75 percent of soldiers enlisting in their twenties. None was over the age of 40.[35] The historical record offers stingier clues as to the backgrounds of the men, but there are indications that the men fit the same profile as volunteers for the antebellum U.S. Army. Unfortunately, Confederate officers and U.S. census takers recorded names with a spectacular disregard for standardized spelling, so it is impossible to track the recruits back into their civilian lives through the census. We are left, therefore, with only a handful of cases when unusual circumstances required additional paperwork about a specific soldier. Most frequently, this means the discharge papers that officers and surgeons completed when they wanted to get rid of a soldier who could not perform his duties. In more than a dozen cases, these records tell us details about the men who joined the Louisiana Regulars.

While these cases cannot offer a scientific profile of the 1st Louisiana Heavy Artillery, they point in exactly the direction that one would expect given the profile of the antebellum U.S. Regulars. In the 17 cases in which we know the ethnicity of a volunteer, 12 of the men (71 percent) were born in Ireland. Two started life in Germany (12 percent), with 1 each from England, Jamaica, Pennsylvania, and Virginia. They were not an overly skilled group of workers. Of the 17 men whose prior occupation is known, 8 (47 percent) held the least-skilled job in the Civil War vocabulary: "laborers." Others had more specific careers, but 5 (29 percent) had skills that put them near the bottom of the labor pyramid: shoemakers, painters, and sailors. Two men, a printer and a musician, may have enjoyed more status, but they may also have been underemployed. Only one man, Henry Sitman, could claim a middle-class job. Sitman's training as a clerk could have eventually allowed him to become an independent storekeeper or merchant. Sitman also stands out because he was the only native-born southerner in the group. He had been born in Richmond, Virginia, in about 1834.[36] So was Sitman, perhaps, an ardent Confederate?

As it turns out, Henry Sitman was at least as unemployable as his fellow Regulars. His example adds proof to the rule that the Regular Army served as a catch basin for men who could not find a better job as civilians. Sitman proved to be unfit even as a soldier, and not just because of the physical disabilities that caused officers to throw other men out of the regiment. The medical staff at Fort Jackson discharged Sitman because he was "addicted to self-abuse; so much so that he has rendered himself unfit for the duties of a soldier, and is sometimes very crazy." Given to "fits of insanity,"

Sitman presumably had trouble holding down a civilian clerkship and had found it necessary to join the Regulars in spite of his southern birth and professional training.[37]

The men who joined the 1st Louisiana Heavy Artillery, then, formed the bottom layer of their society's labor pool. Historian Peter Way has chronicled these men's lives from the time they left impoverished farms in Ireland and elsewhere, and he has found many of them building the canals (and later railroads) that flourished in antebellum America. Working in canal construction, he finds, isolated these men from the rest of the society. They lived in temporary shanties, moving on whenever they finished a section of canal. The work was dangerous, with blasting conducted with little regard for worker safety. Contractors gave daily rations of alcohol, up to sixteen ounces of hard liquor, to every man, making workers docile and sometimes literally addicted to their jobs. Distanced from any communities they might have lived close to by their ethnicity, transient status, and their Catholicism, the canallers suffered not only from hard labor, poor shelter, poor wages, and periodic unemployment but also from outside social pressure that turned canallers and their anger inward, often producing violent and destructive behavior within their own communities. Without permanent addresses or citizenship papers, they were usually denied the vote, their society's most basic measure of masculine equality.[38]

Life on the bottom of the paid labor market took a toll on these people. Men and women broken down by the harsh living conditions, work, and disease filled city almshouses and other charitable institutions. The discharge papers of some of the Regulars from Fort Jackson bear testimony to the lives these men had experienced. Four men discharged from Company H were physically used up by prior employers before reaching the brick walls of Fort Jackson. William Doyle, 40 years old in 1861, was discharged for "being too old and too much worn out to attend to any duty." Another 40-year-old, Thomas Grogins of Kilkinny, Ireland, proved "too old and weak to use a musket." Thomas Goggins of Cork, Ireland, was physically broken at only 33 years old. He was, the surgeons said, plagued by an "old, infirm constitution." Finally, Irishman John Downey, all of 30 years old, was discharged because he tired too easily and was always fatigued.[39]

But workers, even the most unskilled immigrants, were not without means of defending themselves. Canal workers and others often clashed with their bosses on antebellum job sites. Historian Peter Way finds a marked increase in labor-management conflicts in the hard times that followed the Panic of 1837. As they had been as canallers, the immigrants, to whom the 1st Louisiana Heavy Artillery would have meant little more than steady work for three years, proved to be intractable workers as soldiers. By the end of February 1862, a full 10 percent of the 288 privates and noncommissioned officers serving in the Regular companies in Fort Jackson had been formally punished by their officers. This figure no doubt underestimates the true total, since it only includes men who were confined when the payroll muster was completed at the end of every second month or if their sentence diminished their pay. The punishments they received could be quite harsh—an echo of the violence canal management could inflict on its workers. Edward Sullivan, an illiterate 23-year-old private, was sentenced in May 1861 for an unspecified crime. He forfeited half of his pay for two months, was confined in solitary for ten days, and then was made to carry a twenty-four-pound cannonball back and forth between two spots for eight hours a day. This went on for five days. Sullivan's sentence typified many of the punishments handed down in the fort, which also included reducing the rank of many noncommissioned officers.[40]

While Civil War histories often portray warm relationships between officers and enlisted men, Fort Jackson's officers had little in common with their men. If we look at service in the Regulars as a job (rather than as a patriotic imperative), then the enormous gap in salaries between officers and men takes on added significance. The Confederate government paid privates the decidedly working-class wage of $10 a month, whereas officers earned a middle-class income. Lieutenants earned $90 a month (nine times a private's salary), and captains received $130.[41] Nor was the gap between officers and men only a financial one. The documents left behind by officers indicate the contempt in which they held the men under their command. Often separated from their men by education, ethnicity, and religion, officers sometimes insulted the soldiers they commanded. Officers expressed their contempt most clearly in the discharge papers that sent men back to civilian life. Samuel Young of Company D was discharged for "*unsoundness of mind*," a reasonable medical statement except that the officers reinforced their judgment by underlining it. Nor could they resist taking another swing at Samuel Young, an unskilled laborer from Cork, Ireland. "So great a fool is he," they went on, "that he knows not how or when to execute an order."[42]

Under the circumstances, we would expect men who had been canallers and railroad workers to resist the dictates of their employers. As some of America's most exploited workers, canallers had developed means of coping with the pressures that were placed on them. Some of these techniques may help us to understand the mutiny that occurred at Fort Jackson. Desertion was an obvious choice and proved to be a persistent problem, just as it had been in the antebellum U.S. Army. Surrounded by swamps and alligators, however, the men in Fort Jackson had few chances for desertion. Officers approved few furloughs for men to go home to New Orleans, perhaps because many of the men who had taken them never came back. Others stayed longer than their pass allowed. Over the year that most of the Regulars stayed at Fort Jackson, only about nine men deserted successfully, though others were caught trying. Among the men who deserted was private William H. Duncan of Company H. Duncan had enlisted on July 1, 1861, only to desert about ten days later while the unit was still in New Orleans. After eight days of freedom, he returned to his unit. One month later, he fled again; he was reported missing the day after his unit left the city for Fort Jackson. He remained at large until drafted back into the company in September 1862, serving until he was captured at Vicksburg in the summer of 1863. He deserted again on October 31, 1863, when he disappears from the historical record. Even one sergeant, James Jackson of Company E, deserted while on furlough. The issue of desertion probably loomed larger for officers and men after a new group of soldiers arrived in January 1862 to reinforce Company H. These seven men included five who had deserted from other commands earlier in the war, only to return under an amnesty program that sheltered them from prosecution. Originally enlisted in cities in Tennessee, Alabama, and Mississippi, these men may very well have stood apart as a distinct, and not overly patriotic, group when the battle started.[43]

But desertion was usually an individual choice, even if Alexander Ashton and Willis Reynolds had conspired together to flee the service. How could the men in the garrison have staged such an organized act as a mutiny? Returning to the work of historian Peter Way, we see that antebellum canallers frequently used organized resistance against their employers. As the economic downturn known as the Panic of 1837 continued through the early 1840s, companies often paid wages late or not at all, forcing workers to fight for their pay. Laborers started staging work stoppages and using force to prevent scabs from working at the site. In addition, disguised workers would threaten or brutally beat management's representatives. In the most intense labor-management conflicts, unpaid workers would destroy canal corporation equipment or sections of already completed canal. Complicated lock mechanisms proved tempting targets for workers who had been denied their wages. In one case, workers seized 140 casks of gunpowder and threatened to blow up canal locks unless they were paid. Like the mutiny at Fort Jackson, these actions were illegal and had to be organized in secret. Irish workers, schooled in resistance to the English, excelled at forming what Way calls "secret societies" that "used terror to achieve their ends." The mutineers at Fort Jackson also organized secretly, taking the officers who employed them by surprise. As at Fort Jackson, where officers were threatened and finally shot at, canal worker protests embraced the idea that laborers could organize extralegal forces against management to achieve their goals.[44]

Half of the Fort Jackson garrison consisted of Louisiana Regulars, and three-quarters of them chose to become professional soldiers before the war started. Schooled in confrontational management-labor relations after decades of exploitive employment on both sides of the Atlantic, the men in the Regulars proved to be unreliable soldiers. The best guess is that about 35 percent of the Regulars fled the fort on the night of the mutiny, leaving behind a remnant that proved unwilling to fight the next morning.[45] Perhaps the fact that only 35 percent of the Regulars left that night, a rate lower than that of the volunteer infantry companies in the fort, attests to the power of their officers' strict discipline to compel obedience.

Fear may have kept an unusually large number of the Regulars from mutinying, but it did not win over the men in the ranks. It is hard to track the later service of these men in the Confederate army, but very few privates from the Regulars chose to be exchanged back into Confederate service. Only about 2 percent of the privates in the Regular Army companies later served in the 1st Louisiana Heavy Artillery, a figure that compares with 24 percent of corporals, 39 percent of sergeants, and about two out of three officers.[46] The commanders at Fort Jackson, and the nation as a whole, clearly failed to convince the rank-and-file soldiers in their Regular Army units that the Confederacy was a worthy cause.

Cannoneers, Regulars, and Jagers

Immigrants made their presence felt in the other companies in Fort Jackson. Three of the eight companies at the fort came from the 22nd or 23rd Louisiana Volunteers, units raised mostly between June and September 1861, though some men joined as late as February 1862. In many ways, they should have been good Confederate soldiers. Their enlistment dates, for example, indicate that these men knew they were signing up for a war, and many would have heard of the serious casualties at the Battle of Bull Run. While we cannot know what kind of financial pressure the failing New Orleans economy may have put on them, they were volunteers.[47] Other Confederate troops who enlisted at the same time from rural regions (such as the St. Mary's Cannoneers) became good Confederate units. But the three companies from these two regiments would disappoint General Duncan. On the night of the mutiny, the rebellious soldiers found many allies in these three companies. About 46 percent of the men in these companies left the fort that night.[48]

The unit with the most mutineers appears to have been Company I of the 22nd Louisiana Volunteers. Early in its service, the company had called itself the "Sappers and Miners," a name given to engineering units, not common foot soldiers. That distinction was short lived, however, and the unit quickly became an ordinary infantry company. Still, like most Civil War companies, the men of Company I gave themselves a nickname; in this case, they picked "The German Jagers." Under the leadership of their captain, Friedrick ("Frederick") Peter, the Jagers bore a distinctly German flavor. Although we only know the place of birth of two of the unit's seventy-five men, (one Silesian and one Frenchman), surnames such as Ertling, Graf, Reichmann, and Scherer permeate the muster roll and reinforce the central European aura of the unit's nickname.[49]

The Jagers' service record before the mutiny gives few hints that they would be leaders in the rebellion. Only one man deserted; officers confined only one other man, Christian Jacobs (or "Jacob," or "Jackob"), who returned of his own volition after being absent without leave. When Captain M. T. Squires assessed the unit a few weeks before the mutiny, he found much to admire. The soldiers' "military appearance" was "good," and their clothing "very good." He rated their arms, accoutrements, and level of instruction as "fair."[50] Their discipline, an obvious weak point in

The training the Jagers received would have included working heavy artillery.
This illustration by William Waud portrays Fort Jackson after it fell into Union hands.
(The Historic New Orleans Collection)

other units, was also "fair." Despite their solid record, the Jagers would join the mutineers in large numbers; the best estimate is that forty-four of seventy-five (59 percent) men in the company left the fort that night. Further, only three of the men in the unit, two privates and one corporal, give evidence of further Confederate service after Fort Jackson.[51] In spite of their tight ship, the German Jagers mutinied and abandoned the Confederacy for good.

The men in the Jager company came from an immigrant community whose experiences in both Europe and the United States afforded them a critical perspective on the Confederacy. Their background warrants investigation, since it suggests many reasons for their willingness to embrace the United States when its army appeared outside the fort's walls. Although we cannot know precisely the origins of the men in the Jager company, certain assumptions about the experiences of German immigrants can be safely made. If the Jagers followed the traditional pattern of Confederate enlistees, most of them would have been born in the late 1830s or early 1840s. Since the high point of German immigration to the

Cannoneers, Regulars, and Jagers

antebellum United States was in the years immediately after 1848, this means that most of the Jagers had been born in Europe and came to North America as children.

The German men who would serve in the Jagers probably came across the ocean as the sons of revolutionaries. Even if they were not the direct sons of women and men who had taken part in the 1848 German revolution, the ethnic community they lived in had been shaped by the refugees who came to America in the aftermath of the failed uprising. In 1848, German revolutionaries joined with other people across Europe to demand a more representative government and a more egalitarian society. In France, the German states, Hungary, Austria, and Italy, revolutions threatened the conservative, monarchical governments that had reigned since the Congress of Vienna in 1815. Ever since 1815, monarchs had worked hard to erase the revolutionary equality espoused during the French Revolution (especially its propensity for regicide). For the better part of three decades, they succeeded in stamping out revolutions that sought more democratic governments. In 1848, however, much of Europe demanded radical change. Revolutions started in France and spread throughout central Europe, with middle- and working-class men and women banding together to overthrow monarchs and write more equitable laws. Democratic in their ideologies, the revolutionaries debated, and often enacted, laws that abolished slavery in overseas colonies and increased women's rights. Fueled by the revolutionary principle that men (and perhaps women) deserved equal rights, the 1848 revolutions nearly succeeded in remaking European society and government.

Momentarily successful, the revolts drew men and women out of their homes long enough for them to proclaim their support for equality and democracy. But the revolutions failed. As European monarchs and their armies rallied against the poorly armed revolutionaries, the people who had declared their revolutionary beliefs were in mortal peril. Many, especially middle-class Germans who could afford the passage, chose to emigrate rather than face persecution at home. The United States proved to be an alluring destination for these revolutionaries, in part because it had already implemented many of the changes they had sought for Germany. Democracy, freedom of expression and religion, and a rough social equality among men all seemed part of the American promise. By the tens of thousands, German revolutionaries, known as liberals, flocked to the

United States, eager to live in the country that they saw as a model for the society they had tried to create at home.

Once on American shores, the Germans often allied themselves with the antebellum Democratic Party. The Democrats presented themselves as the friend of immigrants and working-class people. Urban Democratic machines often got immigrants jobs, sometimes with city governments, and usually worked hard to naturalize immigrants. Most immigrant men rewarded the Democrats with their votes, and some ethnicities became fixtures in Democratic politics. But the German liberals proved an awkward fit with the antebellum Democratic Party on the issue of slavery. As Abraham Lincoln and other Republicans pointed out, the continued expansion of slavery clashed with the egalitarian beliefs of German liberalism. By 1860, a majority of German Americans in the North voted for Lincoln, and he won support from Germans as far south as the slave city of St. Louis. The shifting German allegiances may even have given Lincoln his margin of victory in key states.

Given these political developments, the question of German loyalties hovered over the South as it embarked on its independence movement. Would German liberals support the Confederate States of America? Would the Confederates work to win the allegiance of the German revolutionaries by making concessions, even rhetorical ones, to egalitarianism? Enough German immigrants and their children lived in the South to make a difference in the Confederacy's ability to field a large army. In New Orleans, Germans made up 11.7 percent of the white population (19,752 of 168,675). Second only to the city's 24,398 Irish immigrants (14.5 percent), the Germans would help to determine how many men the Confederacy's largest city would put into uniform for the secessionist cause.[52]

Weighing the two nations against their own ideals, many German liberals came to express their preference for the United States over the Confederacy. This was true both in New Orleans and in the broader Confederacy. Many Germans had ended their transatlantic flight in Texas, a rapidly growing state in 1848 and the years that followed. Texas Germans proved to be a thorn in the side of Confederate authorities. Ambivalent at best about the new southern nation, they began the war by trying to stay neutral. In 1862, when Confederate draft laws made it impossible to avoid taking sides, some German families fled to Mexico rather than fight for the South and slavery. Others organized to hide draft-age men from conscrip-

Cannoneers, Regulars, and Jagers

tion. By the summer of 1862, violence became common, especially after Confederates had tracked and massacred a party of German Americans trying to reach Mexico. More than twenty Germans were killed. Other sporadic killings occurred throughout the summer, prompting further resistance to Confederate rule. Confronted with a growing resistance movement, the Confederacy eventually made some concessions. Hit hard by the earlier Confederate repression, the German communities mostly cooperated with the new regime for the rest of the war. Historian James Marten cites the Germans' "well-known opposition or indifference to slavery" as the root cause of their strained relationship with the Confederacy. While Texas Germans had other reasons besides antislavery sentiments to resist the Confederacy, the egalitarian ideals of the Forty-eighters would also mean trouble for the Confederacy in New Orleans.[53]

The New Orleans German community distinguished itself from its native-born neighbors on the slavery issue. Historian Lauren Ann Kattner finds that when German immigrant households joined the ranks of slaveholders, they forged relationships with African Americans that differed from traditional master-slave dealings. Noting that Germans in New Orleans held egalitarian ideals, Kattner finds evidence that they regarded their slaves as traditional "servants," not as slaves. She writes that German immigrants usually refused to see racial inferiority as legitimizing permanent enslavement and degrading treatment; also, slaves living in German households enjoyed greater liberty and less supervision during their nonworking hours. In the most radical households, she finds, German immigrants expressed "a spirit of sisterhood with their enslaved women, a sisterhood that crossed both social and racial boundaries."[54]

With slavery a major topic on the streets of antebellum New Orleans, the German community's ambiguous position caused southern nationalists to doubt the Germans' loyalty. Suspicions grew stronger when some Germans failed to rally to the Confederacy during the early months of the war.[55] In 1862, readers of the *New Orleans Daily Crescent* learned that "nearly one-half of our male population . . . have sworn that they are aliens, and claim exemption from military service in consequence thereof." This may have been true, since about 38 percent of the city's white population was foreign-born, and this number probably included a disproportionate number of young men. The *Bee* reported that even those foreigners serving in militias did so only to avoid service outside the city.[56] Germans seemed the most troublesome of all foreigners. The city's Confederate newspapers referred to Union soldiers as "Hessians," a term that must have rankled Germans. When a German man, Adam Hirsch, "aided and abetted" a slave named Aaron, who had gotten drunk and insulted white women, an editorial suggested that Aaron be beaten. Hirsch, however, should "be silenced by the administration of a hempen cravat." Hanging Hirsch seems like a bit of an overreaction; remember that the cooper's assistant in St. Mary's who had fallen under suspicion after a slave uprising was only exiled from the parish. The editor's harsh sentence for Hirsch may well have been prompted by his fear that Germans represented an abolitionist threat just beneath the surface of white society. As a Confederate lieutenant colonel serving in New Orleans complained, "A large portion of the German population was disloyal."[57]

Union officers and northern journalists soon reached the same conclusion; Germans were viewed as the most loyal white people in New Orleans. The *New York Herald* regarded both the Germans and the Irish in the Crescent City as "Union men" in early May, and it gave credence to reports that Germans had formed local militias to avoid going to the front. Evidence for German disaffection with the Confederacy came to Union commanders and reporters in a variety of forms. A friendly correspondent wrote to Union general George F. Shepley that "the Germans are all Union." Early in the campaign, the only two families not to evacuate Pilot Town on the approach of the Union fleet were German, with one woman proclaiming her willingness to "die on her own threshold" before following Confederate orders.[58]

But for the purposes of understanding the actions of the German Jagers in Fort Jackson, perhaps the most interesting letter was mailed by Ernest Wench of New Orleans to Benjamin Butler. Acknowledging himself to be a former Confederate captain, he claimed that he had enlisted only to protect his family after they were marked by the mob as abolitionists. After his brief Confederate service, Wench made it back to New Orleans by May 1862. We might well doubt this story, as well as what he wrote next, except that his letter makes no request for money, employment, or favor. He had, it seemed, no need to excuse his actions to the new commanders of New Orleans. Wench seems interested only in setting the record straight. He admitted to Butler that Germans like himself had entered the Confederate military, but he claimed they were not devoted secessionists. Rather, he said, "We Germans have concluded [that] if the [Confederate] conscrip-

Cannoneers, Regulars, and Jagers

tion Law should be put in force before we should be relieved [by the arrival of U.S. forces], we would form a volantaire [*sic*] brigade + to surender [*sic*] to the U.S.A. so soon as a chance would offer to do so, which I am willing to prove all the facts and allegations contained in this presents to your full satisfaction."[59] While Wench made no mention of the German Jagers, what he describes is the course of action that most of the Jagers followed in Fort Jackson. Patient Confederates until the moment they could surrender to Butler's troops, the Jagers then seized their first chance to go over to the Union side.

THE NEW ORLEANS KNOW-NOTHING PARTY

Could the Confederate authorities have won over the Irishmen, Germans, and other immigrants in Fort Jackson? We will never know the answer to that question because Confederates in Louisiana made almost no attempt to make immigrants feel at home. Throughout their year in power, Confederates seemed intent on reinforcing the hierarchies that placed wage-earning immigrants at the bottom of white society. At a time when the Lincoln administration and the U.S. Congress worked to secure the loyalty of immigrants in the North, the Confederacy did very little. Indeed, many southern politicians, including ones in New Orleans, did the reverse. By April 1862, many of the city's wage earners and immigrants probably welcomed a new municipal government that operated under the U.S. flag.

By the time the Civil War started, the Know-Nothing Party, known formally as the American Party, had ceased to exist in most parts of the country. Known for its electoral appeals to anti-immigrant and anti-Catholic biases, the Know-Nothings had ridden to victory in many cities and states in 1854. The party failed to coalesce into a national force, however, during the 1856 campaign, when its presidential candidate carried only Maryland. While the Know-Nothings subsequently collapsed in most places, New Orleans was still ruled by a Know-Nothing mayor and city council when the war started in 1861. The party's continued success underlines the extent to which the Crescent City was divided along ethnic and religious lines.

The Know-Nothing Party's rise to power was fueled by the nativist beliefs held by so many American-born citizens. Confronted by waves of immigrants escaping famine in Ireland and failed revolutions in Europe as the 1840s drew to a close, nativists worried that newcomers would subvert

Cannoneers, Regulars, and Jagers

American democracy and Protestantism. New Orleans Know-Nothings shared these concerns, and their campaign literature often depicted Catholics and immigrants as the unthinking minions of a tyrannical foreign power or of the pope, whom nativists regarded as a canny and unscrupulous enemy of democracy and liberty. Historian Leon Cyprian Soulé finds the New Orleans Know-Nothings to be "antiforeign, anti-Catholic, and anti-Creole in sentiment" and that their successful election campaigns in the mid-1850s fanned "the flames of religious and national prejudice."[60] Although the Know-Nothings faded statewide after 1856, they lived on in New Orleans, thanks in part to their use of mob violence during elections. With their armed mobs of "thugs" roaming the streets on election days, the Know-Nothings earned Leon Soulé's condemnation for their use of violence "to disenfranchise . . . political opponents by terroristic methods."[61]

The election of 1858 illustrates how militarized the city's politics became in the late 1850s. Tired of the violence waged against them by the Know-Nothings, opposition leaders coalesced around a vigilance committee under the command of West Point graduate Pierre G. T. Beauregard. Most of Beauregard's vigilantes were Democrats, a group likely to include almost all the city's Irish population and probably most Germans as well. Beauregard also found an ally in Johnson Kelly Duncan, the future commander of Forts Jackson and St. Philip. The vigilantes and the opposing Know-Nothings formed armed camps in the city's parks, each with more than a thousand men under arms. The standoff intensified after Beauregard took the remarkable step of seizing several government buildings in the downtown. Duncan apparently took command of the captured state arsenal building near the cathedral and the main vigilante encampment at Jackson Square. While mutual fear of the other side's army prevented an outburst of organized warfare, the Know-Nothings won a narrow victory at the polls and retained control of the city's police and patronage machines.[62]

It is hard to know whether Duncan's prominent part in anti–Know-Nothing politics helped him with the immigrant soldiers under his command at the forts. Perhaps it did. It may even explain why he and his fellow officers escaped the mutiny unharmed. But it may not have helped him very much. The vigilance committee had overt ties with the Democratic Party, and local working-class men had become suspicious of the Democrats by the time the war started. The Democrats, who controlled the state government, never funded enough public works jobs to satisfy laborers, who relied on government programs like levee repairs for steady paychecks. Further, the Know-Nothings accused the Democrat Beauregard of firing many of the government's white workers and replacing them with black workers. To make matters worse, the Democratic Party's intense attachment to slavery may have caused some of the city's poorer white residents to question their own status. As historian Walter Johnson has discovered, New Orleans in the 1850s hosted a long court case centered around the legal status of Alexina Morrison. Morrison appeared to most observers to be entirely white in appearance, yet Louisiana law and custom enslaved her because her mother was a slave and she had a very distant African ancestor. Thus, Johnson speculates that in the late 1850s, poor whites would be left to wonder whether their complexions would continue to be enough to protect them from enslavement.[63]

New Orleans politics, then, offered workers no consistent champion for their interests. The Know-Nothing Party favored public works spending and took no adverse action against strikers, but it retained its animosity toward immigrants, despite some rhetorical gestures to welcome native-born Catholics and perhaps German Protestant immigrants to the party.[64] The Democrats favored small government spending and slavery, and those positions hurt the city's wage workers. Obviously, native-born workers might revel in Know-Nothing politics, but they turned out to be a relatively slim proportion of the Fort Jackson garrison. With nativist politicians and mobs triumphant in city hall from 1855 to the arrival of Farragut's ships, immigrants in New Orleans might well consider U.S. rule as a positive step toward achieving better government and greater rights.

New Orleans's anti-immigrant politics found expression in the broader Confederacy as well. In several state legislatures, representatives debated measures that would increase the number of years that immigrants would have to spend in the country before becoming citizens. Politicians in Virginia, Alabama, and North Carolina considered measures that would lengthen the naturalization process to twenty-one years, one of the longest such periods considered in American history. Though the bills did not pass, reports about them alarmed the South's immigrant communities. Worse, efforts to postpone immigrant citizenship were only part of a broader drive to stifle democracy in the Confederacy. Doubtful of the ability of poor whites to govern, some politicians saw secession as a chance to turn the clock back to an era when elites held more power. As historian Drew Gilpin

Cannoneers, Regulars, and Jagers

Faust has written, "many conservative southern politicians . . . saw 1861 as a moment to reverse the democratic tendencies" that had brought participatory democracy into almost all corners of the South. Some of their anti-democratic ideas became law; in the most famous instance, Confederate presidents were granted a six-year term, with no chance of reelection. This meant that the president no longer had any reason to respond to the will of the voters. Overall, an elitist dislike for popular participation in government filled the air, as when secessionists pointed to the political power of workers in New Orleans, Baltimore, and St. Louis as something that should be curtailed when southern states established their independence. Viewed in this national perspective, the study of New Orleans reinforces the consensus being formed by Drew Gilpin Faust, Frank Towers, George Rable, and others that Confederate political thought regarded democracy with suspicion and saw immigrants as potential threats.[65]

WHEN HENRY LAWRENCE railed against immigrants and their Democratic allies, he displayed just how well he had absorbed the nativist lessons of the Know-Nothings (and probably of the Whig Party before them). Schooled to hate the Democratic Party and its immigrant allies, Lawrence epitomizes the ethnic divisions that split the Confederacy and the Fort Jackson garrison as it looked out on Butler's encircling troops. For the men of the St. Mary's Cannoneers, the South was a place where native-born men could dictate to the handful of immigrants in their midst, guiding them into a brotherhood of white supremacy. But in New Orleans, the rest of the Fort Jackson garrison had learned other lessons about what southern politics and the Confederacy meant. Never entirely welcome except when their brawn or their skills were needed, the immigrants in the garrison had witnessed the city's violent Know-Nothing regime from the bottom of the city's white social ladder. The advent of the Confederacy had changed little, and what changes occurred seemed to erode their rights, not promote them. By April 1862, some were ready to climb the city's levees to greet the U.S. warships with waving flags. Others perhaps remembered the United States' egalitarianism when, three months later, the United States extended immediate citizenship to any immigrant who served in the nation's military and earned an honorable discharge.[66] This gesture, even if it was calculated to promote recruiting, was so simple yet so in keeping with the democratic spirit that guided the best aspects of the

Cannoneers, Regulars, and Jagers

first century of American history. And yet it was beyond the pale of what the Confederacy could consider if it was to hold true to its more aristocratic vision of the perfect society. The contrast between the two countries would not have been lost on the men in Fort Jackson, and it may well have guided their actions when they returned to New Orleans after the mutiny.

the mutiny at fort jackson and the collapse of confederate authority

The men in Fort Jackson reacted in different ways to the arrival of Butler's troops outside the fort's ramparts. Secession and the Confederacy had affected the people in the fort differently depending on their ethnicity, class standing, urban or rural backgrounds, and religious beliefs. For some members of the garrison, the Confederacy had brought only hardship and a likely erosion of their rights as citizens. We know that some members in the garrison mutinied after the arrival of Butler's infantry, but we might still ask why they rebelled. Was their mutiny a political act meant to strike a blow for the United States and against the Confederacy?

In light of the fact that the mutineers left behind no written records explaining their actions, that might seem like a very difficult question to answer with any certainty. But there are many hints to help us arrive at an answer. The mutineers' actions provide many clues. So does the way that other Confederate troops in southeastern Louisiana reacted to the collapse of Confederate authority throughout the region. The rebellious actions of other Confederate soldiers around New Orleans as the Union gained control indicate that many of them felt relieved that the secessionists had been routed. Their behavior, plus tantalizing evidence that some of the soldiers in Fort Jackson did not fight especially well during Farragut's passage of the forts, reinforces the hypothesis that the mutineers acted with a conscious political intent, not just to get out of a miserable place or to avoid a prolonged siege. By looking at what men and women did as New Orleans came under Union control, as well as the behavior of the Fort Jackson garrison in combat, we can cast additional light on the motives of the mutineers.

HENRY A. SNYDER'S UNTOLD CIVIL WAR

Henry A. Snyder's diary from 1862 never mentions Fort Jackson, but it captures much of what the white people of New Orleans went through during that difficult year. By reading his reactions to the city's fall, we can understand more about the world in which the Fort Jackson garrison lived, worked, and fought. His experiences suggest that Unionism existed just below the Confederate patriotism that formed the public face of New Orleans. Just below that surface—even when the surface was the Confederate uniform that Henry Snyder donned—Unionists waited to emerge into the light. Henry Snyder's diary suggests that there were many men, even in the Confederate military, who may have mutinied had they been given the same chance as the men in Fort Jackson.

Describing himself in a newspaper advertisement as a "family grocer," Henry Snyder owned a shop at 108 Camp Street, in what is now the French Quarter. He was married to Phebe, and they and their daughter, Anne, seem to have been close. While he made no sentimental remarks about his family, he worried when Phebe was not well and tried to be with her at those times. Information about his business is sketchy, though we know that in February 1862 he had on hand "Choice Yellow Virginia Butter" as well as butter from other southern states. He employed a clerk, but he directly supervised his business. He and his family appeared to be prosperous, though he clearly had to work. His diary focuses on his Confederate military service, his thoughts about the war, and how events in 1862 changed his perspectives.[1] Through his diary, Snyder introduces us to the

The Mutiny at Fort Jackson

people of New Orleans as they abandoned the Confederacy and returned to their old allegiances.

When Henry Snyder first raised his pen above the blank pages of his diary, he did so as a loyal Confederate. The first thoughts he recorded were political; he hated Lincoln, whom he called the "abolitionist president." On January 2, he accused the United States of "waging cruel unholy war" on the Confederacy.[2] Not surprisingly, then, we find him serving in a militia unit, the Confederate Guards. What is surprising is how indifferent a soldier he was and how often his fellow soldiers proved equally apathetic about their military duties.

Even with U.S. troops occupying Ship Island and threatening New Orleans, the Confederate Guards barely prepared for war. Snyder wrote about military drills in his diary, but he did not feel compelled to attend them, even though they were held only a few times a week for an hour or two. His company was restructured on February 14, by state law, but the month before that reorganization shows the careless nature of militia drill in New Orleans. On January 13, battalion drill was canceled because of rain. Four days later, the commander called off a scheduled drill because "of the rain yesterday," which had made the parade grounds muddy. Snyder participated in drills the next week, but he clearly was not used to physical exertion. He complained after a parade that he "was much fatigued, & went home with a severe headache caused by the long march through the dust and hot sun." On February 7, he missed drill because his clerk had quit work. He had hired a new clerk before the next drill, but he received permission to skip training because he was "quite unwell." The Confederate Guards, at this rate, would not be a formidable unit on the battlefield. No one in the unit, including Snyder, seemed upset about this state of affairs.[3]

The February reorganization of the militia meant that Snyder moved to a different company (G) of the Confederate Guards, but the reshuffling did not inspire greater sacrifice for the Confederate cause. As Ulysses S. Grant's offensive into Kentucky and western Tennessee rolled toward Mississippi, calls went up in New Orleans for volunteers to go north to oppose Grant. As a militia unit, the Confederate Guards could not be ordered out of the state, but they were asked to volunteer for service in Tennessee. Snyder recorded that about a quarter of his company volunteered, but repeated pleas—even as the men were in ranks on parade—yielded few

The Mutiny at Fort Jackson

additional enlistments.[4] As rumors spread about the Guards' lack of enthusiasm in this desperate hour, fellow Confederates took note. A New Orleans resident was stunned that those "who should be the first to offer their life's blood for their country" had "actually refused going out of the city for anything but camping. Can you understand them?" Northern editors welcomed the news that southerners were avoiding active service. In New York, the *Herald* rejoiced that almost everyone in the city's two militia brigades (perhaps three thousand men) had *"refused to comply with the requisition."*[5]

While able to avoid fighting against Grant, Snyder and his unit were called up to defend New Orleans on March 11, 1862. In a burst of patriotism and self-satisfaction, Snyder wrote: "What a scene! This regiment composed principally of men of wealth, many of them millionair[es], accustomed to all the ease, comforts, + luxuries wealth can produce, harnessed up in uniforms, marching in the ranks as common soldiers."[6] It is an inspiring image, men from all ranks of society brought together to sacrifice for their country. But in this case, as so often in New Orleans, Confederate patriotism only went so far. Henry Snyder and the Confederate Guards never abandoned their luxuries; nor did they stray too far from home. Five days after the Guards were called up, Snyder described their fancy new camp. The soldiers had decorated their tents with evergreens, drunk wine and champagne from real glasses, and feasted on "sundry delicacies." After less than two weeks, they moved back into the city, setting up camp in prestigious Lafayette Square. Once there, the men received every other day off to see their families and to check in on their businesses.[7] The *New Orleans Delta* mocked the Guardsmen and their Lafayette Square camp soon after they had retreated from it in the face of Farragut's fleet. "The gay, gallant and luxurious Confederate Guards," it wrote, had "occupied the grounds with their beautiful tents and sumptuous camp equipage, their gas-lighted guardhouses, and their elegantly dressed and most substantially conditioned soldiers." The *Delta* then compared the overweight Guards unfavorably with the weatherbeaten and veteran 4th Wisconsin Volunteers, who had replaced them in Lafayette Square.[8] By the end of the first year of the Civil War, real soldiers no longer took to the field with champagne glasses.

And yet Henry Snyder and the Confederate Guards did serve the Confederacy. Snyder describes his regiment's most successful campaign in his

April 7, 1862, entry. It is the only known record of this military engagement. Woken before daylight, Snyder's company and three others quickly marched nine miles to Camp Chalmette, part of the "interior line" of defenses established by General Lovell. Their mission, as described by Snyder, was "to arrest and bring into subjection several companies of a Dago regiment called 'Cazadores.'" The Cazadores were also a Confederate militia unit, but they had risen up against their officers and refused to obey orders sending them closer to the front. Snyder's unit took the situation very seriously. About a mile before they reached Camp Chalmette, the Confederate Guards paused and loaded their muskets. Meanwhile, a second loyal Confederate regiment, the Orleans Guards, slipped around the flank of the "unruly cazadores" in order to "completely surround them."[9] The Confederate military also dispatched three cannons to support the Orleans and Confederate Guards against the mutinous regiment.

With the Orleans Guards working behind the mutinous regiment, Snyder and the Confederate Guards moved forward. When the Cazadores first spotted the approaching Confederate Guards, they "ran for their arms, loaded their pieces, and declared their intention to fight us, but when they saw our superior numbers + the predicament they were in, part agreed to obey orders + go to the Fort—the rest, not willing to go[,] were forced to Surrender unconditionally—laid down their arms and became our prisoners—thus saving us the task of shooting them." Snyder noted that "it is reported they all agreed to go to the fort at night and were sent."[10] Military records do not indicate where the Cazadores spent the rest of the campaign, but this incident shows why Lovell refused to give ammunition to some of his regiments because of their "insubordinate disposition."[11]

Henry Snyder spent the next few weeks in Lafayette Square, alternately getting days off and being restricted to camp. The appearance of Farragut's warships before the city, however, put an end to this peaceful existence. Lovell ordered Confederate military units to retreat to Camp Moore, about seventy-eight miles north on the New Orleans, Jackson, and Great Northern railroad. The Confederate Guards were ordered to report to the railroad depot in New Orleans, where they found a "general State of excitement + confusion everywhere." Many civilians also crowded the station, hoping to escape the Yankees. Phebe and Anna met Henry at the depot. By now it had started to rain, and Snyder wrote of the "gloomy circumstances" of the family reunion. Irritated by the rain, he also "began to fear

The Mutiny at Fort Jackson

we might be Sent up the Rroad" to Camp Moore, a violation of their enlistment contract. Other members of the Confederate Guards reacted to this possibility by melting into the crowd. Snyder mentioned that "some of the members of our regiment left us at the depot + returned to their homes." Officers soon ordered the Guards into the cars and got them under way, but "quite a number more left at every stopping place all along the road up." Although the Confederate Guards enjoyed enough social privilege to ride inside the railroad cars while others had to ride on flat-beds or on the car roofs through the rainy night, Snyder felt only hostility toward the authorities who had ordered him away from his city and his family.[12]

After reaching Camp Moore, Snyder and his fellow soldiers spent the next day grumbling. They had been ordered out of the city illegally, they said. They wanted to go home, not to the front. Snyder wrote about this in personal terms; the men wished to return because they had left their "families there unprepared for such an emergency." The unit's officers got wind of the disaffection in the ranks and tried "to quiet the men but could not." Eventually General Lovell arrived to calm the men. Snyder was not impressed; Lovell looked "nearly frightened out of his wits" and reminded him of "a whipped dog." Further, Lovell had ordered them out of New Orleans, and by now the regiment was convinced that it had been taken into the muddy fields of Camp Moore by an illegal order. Lovell seems to have agreed with them. Confronted with some of the wealthiest men in the city, he apologized for the error. He claimed not to have ordered it. He asked for volunteers to stay with the army. He left them to think over their situation.[13]

A few more days in the mud did not improve Snyder's attitude toward the Confederacy or General Lovell. By April 29, the Confederate Guards were even more ready to go home. "It is the general belief in our regiment that [Lovell] has humbugged + sold us," Snyder wrote; "our regiment censure[d] him severely for taking us out of the city away from our families leaving them exposed to the merciless treatment of a lawless rabble." Since no U.S. troops had yet occupied New Orleans, that "lawless rabble" could only be the city's working-class residents, which gives some idea of how the city's richest men viewed their poorer neighbors. Faced with continued resistance, Lovell ordered the regiment disbanded and returned to New Orleans (in railroad cars) the next day. Amazingly, he also made sure that

The Mutiny at Fort Jackson

the unit was paid before it went home. Snyder's May 1 entry, written either on his way home or after he got there, reflects his joy at avoiding further Confederate service. He wrote that throughout the morning in Camp Moore, "a general hum of mirthfulness is heard in every quarter + a cheerful look expressed on every face showing how they prefer civil life with their families at home, to a life of warefare [sic] among the confederates."[14] He spent that night in his own bed.

Snyder's joy at returning to New Orleans on May 1 is all the more remarkable because it was on that day—presumably at almost the same time in the late afternoon—that Benjamin Butler's first troops marched through the city's streets. Far from upset about this, Snyder was happy to return home to a Union-held city. Phebe, his wife, was even happier. On May 2, Henry recorded Phebe's reaction to the Federal troops in her city: "Phebe's joy was almost unbounded when she saw the beautiful Stars + Stripes floating proudly at the head of the column."[15]

Phebe's euphoria at the sight of the U.S. flag raises a host of questions, most of which cannot be answered. Had Henry known of her Unionism? Did Phebe herself know how she would react when she saw the old flag? If she did, had Henry shared her Unionism despite his professed earlier abhorrence of the "abolitionist" Lincoln and his "unholy" war? Had he merely written that so that he could produce it as evidence if he was brought before Mayor Monroe's antisedition hearings? Had he served in the Confederate Guards to avoid suspicion about his possible Unionism? Or had he and Phebe been loyal Confederates until they were affected by events—the Confederate defeat, Henry's unhappy stay at Camp Moore, or the sight of the old flag? Certainly Henry seemed to share Phebe's delight in the Union flag—if he had disapproved of her sentiments, he would not have described the flag as "beautiful" or as flying "proudly" before the marching troops. Further, he wrote four days later that the U.S. soldiers "make a noble soldierly appearance."[16]

By the end of 1862, Henry and Phebe were integrated back into the old Union. As early as June, Henry enjoyed a brisk business baking bread and selling it to Union troops. On June 17, the whole family went to the docks to wish a bon voyage to a friend, Mrs. Plumb, who boarded the *Mississippi* for a trip to Boston. General Butler had arranged for the *Mississippi* to take Unionists who "wished to rejoin their friends at the North" at a discounted rate.[17] By the end of the year, the war disappears from Henry's diary, and business affairs predominate. Finally, the family ships out for New York on account of Phebe's health. Within weeks of Union victory, Henry Snyder and his family had put the Confederacy behind them. By the end of the year, they lived in New York.

Henry Snyder's diary documents the lukewarm attitude many Confederate militiamen had toward drill and military service. Snyder's diary affords us a front-row seat at the disintegration of the Confederate military as it retreated from New Orleans. It also provides vital evidence that there were far more mutinies in Confederate ranks than just the one in Fort Jackson. Most obvious, the Cazadores mutinied illegally. Later, at Camp Moore, the Confederate Guards also mutinied, though they did so legally. The deep-seated ambivalence visible throughout Snyder's diary sheds light on the mutiny at Fort Jackson by reminding us that the men rebelled within a larger context of willful resistance to Confederate commands.

THE FORT JACKSON GARRISON IN COMBAT

When the Union mortars opened fire on Fort Jackson on April 19, they inaugurated a momentous day in the life of Amos J. Bonney. Bonney began the day as a private in the 23rd Louisiana Volunteers, but by the next morning he could consider himself a free man. He would also become famous among the many bored men serving in Farragut's fleet.

The first day of the mortar bombardment proved to be one of the toughest for the men in Fort Jackson. The mortars played havoc on the fort's wooden buildings. Although the brick walls proved to be largely invulnerable, mortar shells soon had every wooden structure ablaze, including the barracks in the central courtyard. Late that night, fire threatened the fort's powder magazine, and for a time disaster loomed. Officers and their men scrambled to douse the fire or move the powder. After they succeeded, the magazine's charred wooden door bore testimony to how close a call it had been. The fire, however, also gave private Amos Bonney his big opportunity.

With flames diverting his officers' attention, Bonney deserted from the Confederate army. Once outside the fort, he found a skiff, crossed the moat, and plunged into the waist-deep mud of the surrounding swamp. Heading toward the Union fleet, he reached the riverbank by daylight. His red cap, red shirt, and dark pants with a red stripe marked him as a rebel soldier, but he changed that identity even sooner than he did his filthy

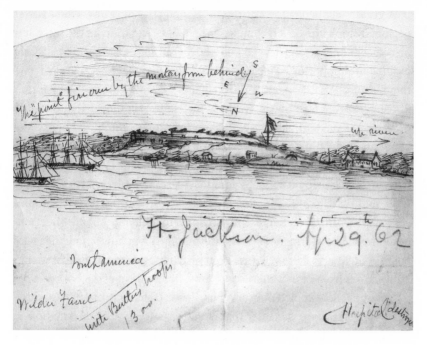

Fort Jackson as it looked to Daniel Nestell on the second day after the mutiny.
(Special Collections and Archives Division, Nimitz Library, U.S. Naval Academy)

uniform. Bonney came from Brookfield, New York, in the upstate county of
Tioga. Sometime before the war, however, work took him on the road.
According to a reporter, he had been part of the famous Dan Rice Circus
Troupe. (Perhaps acrobatic experience had helped him over the walls.)
The start of the war presumably found him in New Orleans, and he had
enlisted on August 15, 1861.[18] Now safely with the Union fleet, he turned
his allegiance to the United States.

Bonney soon found himself the center of attention, a source of information for curious officers, enlisted men, and reporters alike. Picked up off
the riverbank at 5:00 in the morning, he was in Porter's quarters by 7:30
telling him what he knew about the fort's supplies, its garrison, and the
damage it had suffered from the bombardment. He apparently spent the
rest of the day talking to reporters and crewmen, all of whom were eager
to know what was going on and what they were up against. Talking to the
mortar crews who had given him the diversion he had needed to escape,
he uniformly praised their fire as accurate and destructive.[19]

The Mutiny at Fort Jackson

A greater challenge lay in store for Bonney the next day, when Porter personally took him on a reconnaissance up the river to scout the forts. It is unclear whether Porter learned anything from Bonney on this trip. One disappointed reporter claimed that "they were unable to accomplish anything," but one sailor heard a different story. Samuel Massa claimed that Bonney had "showed our men where the chain was shackled and the[n] drew out the pin letting it loose."[20] Almost certainly Bonney did not single-handedly destroy the vast chain that the Confederates had strung across the Mississippi to block ships from passing upstream; it was an enormous mass of iron chain held afloat by stationary schooners arrayed between the forts, and the Union fleet spent the next several days in a series of dangerous (and ultimately successful) attempts to break the chain.[21] But Bonney may well have provided useful information about how to pull the chain apart. A St. Mary's Parish diarist, Henry Lawrence, who received firsthand information from one of the Cannoneers, believed that "the Fort was betrayed by a fellow named Bony a Pennsylvania Dutchman of Allen Guards." His strong language suggests that Bonney had valuable information to pass on to the Union commanders.[22]

Bonney had not been the first local person to offer information to the Union fleet. Even before the bombardment had begun, Union officers had gathered intelligence from loyal inhabitants living along the river. A reporter boasted that Unionists had told them the location of Confederate batteries and "a vast amount of very valuable information," while another correspondent said that the fleet had learned about Confederate deployments from "a deserter from the rebel army." Farragut's men would have learned even more had they realized that the corked bottles floating by their ships contained messages from Unionists in the forts and in New Orleans. Whether Bonney told Porter how to destroy the chain across the river or not, Unionists in Louisiana provided intelligence throughout the campaign.[23]

Amos Bonney had escaped from Fort Jackson, but the rest of the fort's garrison endured several more days of bombardment in the brick casemates. Early in the morning of April 25, the men were called to their cannons to beat back Farragut's attempt to steam past the forts. Much has been written about the fight that ensued. The story usually focuses on the ships on the river: the destruction of the css *Manasses*; the attempts of Farragut's flagship to ward off a fire raft; and the fight between the uss *Varuna* and the css *McRae*. The men in the forts rarely receive much

The Mutiny at Fort Jackson

attention, perhaps because they suffered few casualties and left few written records. It is also impossible to gauge the effectiveness of their shots. But we do know that they failed to stop most of Farragut's ships and that they inflicted so little damage that contemporaries marveled at the fleet's intact appearance when it came to anchor above the forts.

Fort Jackson's officers later complained that pervasive darkness had made it hard for them to aim their big guns. This explanation for their failure effectively blamed the Confederate navy, which was supposed to have filled the river with fire rafts designed to burn the Union's wooden ships and illuminate the river. An army officer protested that "it was the opinion of everyone within the Forts, that had General Duncan's request been complied with by Captain Mitchell and the River sufficiently lighted up to enable us to see to fire with accuracy, not one of the enemy's vessels would have succeeded in passing."[24] But there are reasons to doubt their claim. Even though the navy unleashed only a handful of fire rafts that night, some witnesses thought that visibility was quite good. A reporter for the *New York Times*, who had secured a tiny skiff, rowed himself upriver from the mortar flotilla for a better view. His calloused hands earned him quite a sight as the battle raged, since he was able to see most of what went on thanks to "a fire raft [that] cast a lurid glare near Fort St. Philip." Even more convincing is the testimony of the young artist William Waud. Waud (like his brother Alfred) had the keen eye of an artist, and he tersely described the scene as aglow with light. He saw "signal lights from both sides. Vast bonfire in front of heaviest batteries[.] light as midday." Gun smoke, he added, eventually obscured his vision, but only after Confederate gunners and everyone else could see what was happening.[25]

If the Confederate gunners could see their targets, especially at first, then why did they fire so wildly? At least one observer in the fleet thought that the Confederate guns "were elevated too much, most of the shot passing over" the Union ships. Confederate naval officer C. W. Read blamed the cowardice of the forts' garrisons, who he claimed were driven by Union fire from their posts at the exposed barbette guns. There may have been some validity to this accusation. The garrison's men may have taken cover either for safety or as an excuse to be ineffective in combat. Two Union soldiers later wrote that they had talked with men from Fort Jackson who had attested to the power of the Federal fleet's return fire. A Fort Jackson veteran told a Wisconsin soldier that it had "rained grape and canister" as

The Mutiny at Fort Jackson

the uss *Mississippi* went by, and a Connecticut man was told that fire from the passing ships had made him think "it about time to surrender."[26] But with the army blaming the navy and vice versa, is there another explanation consistent with the garrison's later mutiny?

Perhaps—this is highly conjectural—some of the people manning the guns in Fort Jackson, and perhaps St. Philip, had no desire to hit the Federal ships. This hypothesis would be hard to prove in any event, but the lack of written records by mutineers makes it unlikely ever to be documented. Yet one piece of evidence, beyond the inaccuracy of the forts' fire, suggests that some of the gunners may have intentionally missed the mark. In a report to the U.S. Coast Survey, Joseph Harris, a Union officer who spent time with the garrison after its surrender, included an intriguing story about Captain Samuel Jones, the commander of Company I, the Allen Guards, of the 23rd Louisiana Volunteers. Harris reported that Captain Jones had been entrusted with the command of the battery that fired "hot shot"—the potentially devastating superheated cannon balls that would cause Union ships to burst into flame when they lodged in the dry timbers of a vessel. Captain Jones appears to have performed his duties either very badly or with an intent to sabotage the Confederate defense. Harris wrote that Jones had "depressed the muzzles of his guns very considerably, fearing to fire too high; and, being desirous of working his guns very vigorously, had them run out with a jerk, the consequence of which was that the balls rolled harmlessly into the moat, and the guns blazed away with powder and hay wads at a most destructive rate." Only when a superior officer called his attention to this pattern did Jones change his ways, except that now he concentrated the fire of his battery on "one particular vessel, which he kept at until some one informed him that he was devoting himself to one of their own chain hulks."[27] Jones's performance seems slightly less effective than the Marx Brothers' defense of Fredonia. Could he really have been so inept? Or might he have done this on purpose?

Indeed, Jones's Allen Guards had a poor reputation among the garrison's officers. Each month, Confederate officers filled out muster rolls that concluded with an evaluation of their companies. Raised later than most other companies in Fort Jackson, the Allen Guards were recruited in mid-August 1861, a point when hard times were squeezing many otherwise reluctant men into Confederate ranks. The unit may have been at its best at the very end of 1861, when it earned evaluations of "very good" in disci-

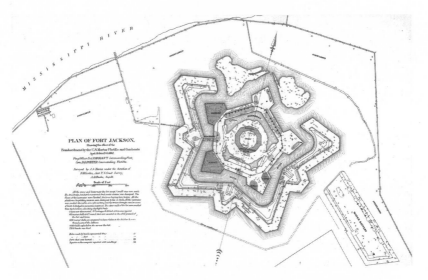

This detailed plan of Fort Jackson, showing the effects of the battle, was drawn up from notes taken by Joseph Harris, a Union officer. Harris also spent time right after the battle talking with former members of the Confederate garrison. (Library of Congress, Division of Maps)

pline and "very fair in Infantry + Artillery" instruction. Its military appearance was rated "good." The Allen Guards deteriorated from there, however, hampered perhaps by the desolate nature of Fort Jackson and maybe also sapped by a lack of enthusiasm for the work or their cause. By the end of February 1862, the company had dropped to "fair" in discipline and to "fair in Infantry and Artillery" instruction. Its clothing remained good (as we know from Amos Bonney's uniform), but its accoutrements had fallen from "good" to "fair" and its arms from "middling" to "very poor + in poor order." The Allen Guards also received an infusion of fifteen additional privates in March 1862, and these men seem unlikely to have improved the company's appearance or reputation. Eight of the fifteen men were illiterate. They had no uniforms, no accoutrements, and only "very defective" weapons. While their discipline was "good," their "military appearance," not surprisingly, was rated "bad."[28]

The Allen Guards also appear to have been involved heavily in the mutiny. The *New York Times* published an army memorandum listing the number of men who were paroled at Fort Jackson, itemized by company. This list would not have included the men who had mutinied and aban-

The Mutiny at Fort Jackson

doned the fort on the previous night (who would have been paroled outside the fort by Butler's men). Using muster rolls from the end of February and adding the fifteen privates who joined in March, we can estimate that the Allen Guards would have gone into the mutiny with perhaps ninety-eight noncommissioned officers and privates. Of these, only eight of the nine noncommissioned officers and thirty-five privates remained behind in the fort to be paroled, meaning that about 60 percent of the company's men had mutinied. Rumors about the unit's disloyal conduct spread to St. Mary's Parish, where Henry Lawrence complained, "All that Company but 10 Deserted."[29] We don't know whether Captain Jones, or others in the garrison, intentionally missed the Federal ships, but the Allen Guards were among the most ill-disciplined and mutinous soldiers in the garrison.

General Duncan knew that he was in a tight spot after Farragut's ships had made it upriver. Still, the mortar boats soon withdrew, and work resumed on the *Louisiana*. Duncan quickly had his men back at work repairing the fort. But he also suspected that all was not right with his troops. On April 27, he issued a statement to the men under his command that mixed praise for their previous efforts with an ill-phrased look to the future. Their courage in battle had been noble, gallant, and heroic, he told them. But, he added, "more remains to be done." He reassured them about the strength of the fort and claimed, "Your officers have every confidence in your courage and patriotism, and feel every assurance that you will cheerfully and with alacrity obey all orders and do your duty as men."[30] Duncan's emphasis on the obedience of orders—"cheerfully and with alacrity"—may have seemed more like a threat than a pat on the back to men who had experienced the harsh discipline of Fort Jackson. Worse, Duncan was lying when he said that he trusted his men.

By this point, Duncan lacked confidence in his soldiers. Evidence of ineptitude and disloyalty stared him in the face. Nor could the navy's sailors be trusted. On the day of Farragut's passage, so many crewmen turned up drunk that some of the ships could not be moved safely. During battle, many crews had "deserted their vessels at the first gun and fled wildly to the woods," as the navy's own C. W. Read acknowledged. One man reported later to the Union fleet that "some of the crews of the rebel boats were in irons [during the battle] for refusing to fight against the Stars and Stripes and were burnt in the boats" when the Confederate commanders destroyed their vessels to prevent their capture. After the

Confederate brigadier general Johnson Kelly Duncan, who commanded Louisiana's coastal defenses from his headquarters at Fort Jackson. (Library of Congress, Prints and Photographs Division, Civil War Photographs)

battle, when the rush was still on to finish the *Louisiana*, its chief carpenter, Zerah Getchell, deserted. A native of Bath, Maine, Getchell waded seven hours through the swamp to escape, leaving behind a work crew of thirty carpenters. Later in May he explained, "I am a Unionist; and for this have been abused and persecuted by the Secessionists of this place. . . . No man here can charge me with aught, except being a Unionist."[31] The unsupervised ship carpenters he left behind him may not have spent the next crucial days hard at work. Word of all these failures in the navy no doubt reached General Duncan.

Duncan later admitted that his men "were still obedient, but not buoyant and cheerful," during the calm period between Farragut's passage and the mutiny. The men's sullen behavior had spurred him to address his men, but he also took concrete measures to prevent men from following Amos Bonney's example.[32] During the bombardment, he had, a Confederate vet-

The Mutiny at Fort Jackson

eran said, "cut away the bridges and locked the gates of the fort so that no one could get out." Union officer Joseph Harris reported that Duncan had also "filled up" a "secret passage out of the fort" to stop desertion. The anxious general had then placed guards "over the entrance to keep every one away from it."[33] In other words, even though the mutiny surprised him, Duncan had doubted his men. In all likelihood, his clumsy address only added fuel to the mutiny then in the making among his soldiers.

Duncan's soldiers mutinied the night after his address. Two events in the hours before the mutiny help to explain why the rebellion occurred on this particular night, and both suggest that the rebellious troops had only been waiting for an opportunity to escape from Confederate authority. Both events suggested to the garrison that the Confederacy was losing its power to coerce people into its service. By the end of daylight on April 27, the men in Fort Jackson knew for the first time that they could mutiny and probably escape with their lives.

Both of the events seen by the garrison came as a result of Benjamin Butler's troops landing in the rear of Fort St. Philip after a grueling march through miles of waist-deep mud. Butler's men ended their march on the east bank of the Mississippi River at the Quarantine Station. The Quarantine Station impressed at least one Massachusetts soldier, who admired its large brick house and five big wooden houses. Here was "a gay place," he thought, or at least a dry one where he could get some sleep. Happily, he also encountered no resistance from the Confederate garrison of the Quarantine, which had already surrendered to Farragut's ships as they steamed past. The surrendered men belonged to the Chalmette Regiment, a Louisiana militia unit under the command of a local planter, Colonel Ignatius Szymanski. The Chalmette Regiment had surrendered to the uss *Cayuga* without firing a shot, a notable example of just how little resistance most Confederate troops would offer in the coming week. Crewman Samuel Massa and the *New York Herald*'s reporter remembered seeing rebel soldiers lining the shore "waving white flags" before men from the *Cayuga* landed and took about five hundred men prisoner. Diarist Oscar Smith wrote that the Confederates were "in a dreadful condition, some without hats or shoes and looking like drowned rats." Nor were they all upset at having surrendered: "Some of the men appeared glad, other[s] sulky."[34] Thus, the Chalmette Regiment became the first Confederate unit to hastily, perhaps happily, abandon its government in the wake of Farragut's success. It would not be the last.

The arrival of some of Butler's infantry at the Quarantine Station had dramatic repercussions for the men in Fort Jackson. Butler soon threw a small infantry force across the river to watch Fort Jackson, while another body of infantry marched down the swampy east bank to surround Fort St. Philip.[35] These troops would play a crucial role in causing the garrison to mutiny that night. Their arrival outside the walls of Fort Jackson was duly noted by the garrison. Historians have written that Butler's men disheartened the men in Fort Jackson by proving to them that they were cut off from their supply base in New Orleans and therefore may have given them an added incentive to mutiny. But the garrison was already cut off; Fort Jackson had received its supplies by water, and the presence of Federal warships upriver had already signaled the end to their supply route. The real difference was that now, if the men in the garrison mutinied, they could surrender to someone who would protect them from a vengeful Confederate government. It is no coincidence that the mutineers did not bother to seize and hold the fort when they mutinied; all they wanted was a way out of the fort, with assurances that the cannons that could fire on their path to the Union infantry had been disabled. It is not at all unreasonable to suppose that had Butler's troops arrived earlier to offer their protection to any mutineers, the rebellion against Confederate officers would have happened sooner.

Butler's troops also provoked another change by occupying the Quarantine Station. The soldiers found women living at the Quarantine Station, including many wives and other relatives of the men in Fort Jackson. The women had not been allowed into Fort Jackson by General Duncan, and the Quarantine Station was the closest habitable place for them to live. Union officers soon decided that they could use the women to get information to the garrison of Fort Jackson. The historical record is unclear about how duplicitous the Union officers were when they encouraged the women to travel to Fort Jackson. A Memphis newspaper reported that the Union officers gave "the Irish women" money "and urged them to advise their connections to give up the contest. The women did as directed." The women may have taken money from U.S. officers, but other sources suggest that they carried only information with them to the fort. William

Seymour, the volunteer aide to General Duncan, reported only that a woman carried the false intelligence to the fort that New Orleans had surrendered. This misinformation, he thought, demoralized his soldiers. Whether the women were bribed, however, is less important than the fact that the women, in all likelihood desperately poor in light of the Confederacy's irregular paychecks, made it into Fort Jackson. On the way to the fort, they would had smelled the rapidly decaying corpses that lined the river from the battle three days before, and they arrived to say that they had been well treated (and maybe paid) by the Union army.[36] Whether they thought New Orleans had surrendered or not, the women spread the same news that the sight of Butler's troops investing the walls had conveyed: the U.S. military could now protect anyone who mutinied. The era of Confederate coercion was over. Anyone in the garrison who had wanted to rebel could now contemplate taking that leap with some measure of confidence.

On the morning after the mutiny, General Duncan, after talking with officers from Fort St. Philip who could give him no assurances about their men's loyalty, decided to surrender his command. By the afternoon of April 28, Porter and Butler began to occupy the forts. With the U.S. flag raised over the forts at 3:30 P.M., twenty Union sailors from the *Winona* and hundreds of soldiers from the 26th and 30th Massachusetts Volunteers, Manning's Massachusetts artillery battery, and a dismounted squadron of cavalry took possession of the forts. They soon began to deal with the Confederate prisoners now in their custody. Some, like the fort's officers and the St. Mary's Cannoneers, were placed on parole and sent to New Orleans on board the USS *Kennebec*.[37] Other Confederates, however, seemed reluctant to give their parole, which would lead to their eventual exchange and then further service in the Confederate army. These men included the mutineers, now housed at the Quarantine, but also many of the men who had surrendered with General Duncan.[38] Not eager to rejoin the Confederate army, these men looked for other options and delayed their return to New Orleans.

These "prisoners" in Fort Jackson could now give voice to their Unionist sympathies. A reporter for the *New York Evening Post* enjoyed relating what he had seen of the garrison's behavior after its surrender. "To-day we administered the oath of allegiance to our prisoners, and let them go. They all took it willingly and apparently gladly." This was good news to Union

The Mutiny at Fort Jackson

readers, who would see that these men were swearing their fealty to the United States of America. "What do you think of two squads of them," the correspondent continued, "about seventy-five men each, volunteering three cheers for the Union, and giving them with a will? What a comment upon the boasted unanimity of the South! It struck us so forcibly that we all went into a laugh." Another eyewitness to the scene noted that the former rebel soldiers took the oath of allegiance voluntarily and that just as they were taking it "our boat came up with a large flag flying[.] One of their Sergeants stepped out of the ranks and said now boys three cheers for the old flag we'll never again desert her." The same held true at the Quarantine, where the more aggressive mutineers told the *Herald*'s army correspondent that "there was not a private in either fort that would not cheerfully take the oath of allegiance, and keep it after it was taken."[39] All these men, including those who had opted to stay in the fort during the mutiny, clearly had little love for the Confederacy. For these Americans, citizens and recent immigrants alike, the Union victory at Fort Jackson represented a welcome change.

In the days after the forts' surrender, Union soldiers enjoyed visiting the Quarantine Station and Fort Jackson. The damage to the forts provoked debate, but for those who arrived quickly enough to see them, the former Confederate soldiers proved even more interesting. Most visitors focused their attention on the prisoners' ethnic or regional background. Joseph Harris noted that "a large proportion of the forces were Northern men, and there were also many foreigners." These included, as we have seen, many Germans and Irishmen. At the Quarantine, Alfred Parmenter commented that he had met only two native southerners; "the rest were foreigners and Northerners & from the West." A third visitor recorded talking with "Irish and Italians, not many true Yankees."[40] Although these testimonies are somewhat inconsistent, probably depending on which group of prisoners the writers had spoken with, they mostly agree that foreigners and perhaps northerners formed a large part of the garrison. In the course of talking with the prisoners, however, these Union soldiers also got a sense of the former Confederates' political convictions.

While in Fort Jackson, Union soldiers heard their former opponents talk about how they had ended up in the Confederate military and what they thought about the war. A newspaperman walked away from his interviews thinking that "many of them were evidently Union men."[41] Most of

Daniel Nestell's portrait of two of the mutineers, drawn about seven hours after the mutiny began. The men, whom Nestell refers to in his caption as "refugees," not prisoners, hold their heads up and appear contented. This is the only known likeness of the mutineers. (Special Collections and Archives Division, Nimitz Library, U.S. Naval Academy)

the former Confederates, Union observers thought, seemed happy at the change of events that had placed them behind Union lines. Private John Goodhue of Manning's artillery battery was among the very first Union troops inside Fort Jackson, arriving long before anyone even thought of cleaning up "the blood and brains of the killed." He spent his first night there guarding—and talking with—the Confederate prisoners. "I talked most of the night with the rebbels [*sic*] and they seem glad to think that they was taken[,] for they had been used hard," he reported to his mother. Perhaps now convinced that all Confederate soldiers felt the same way, he predicted an early end to the war. Brigadier General J. W. Phelps also thought the prisoners he held were "heartily tired and disgusted with the thralldom under which they have so long labored, and well satisfied with their recovered liberties." Even David D. Porter had difficulty restraining his prose as he thought about the men he had liberated from Confederate authority. "The sun never shone on a more contented and happy looking set of faces than those of the prisoners in and about the forts," he wrote. "Many of them had not seen their families for months, and a large portion had been pressed into a service distasteful to them, subject to the rigor of a discipline severe beyond measure." Porter then went on to enumerate the punishments to which the Confederate officers had subjected their soldiers. Men who had endured these "tortures," Porter continued, "must have been unable afterwards to do any duty for months." Union victory brought the soldiers in the garrison not pain but relief, Porter thought. No wonder they had mutinied. Now free of the Confederacy, the men did not bear "the downcast countenances of conquered people[;] they emerged from the fort . . . like a parcel of happy schoolboys in holiday times, and no doubt they felt like them also."[42]

These "happy schoolboys" told stories as they left, ones that emphasized the coercive elements of their military lives. Union soldiers proved an eager audience, themselves happy to find that the enemy they faced might not be so determined after all. Massachusetts soldier H. W. Howe wrote, "The soldiers are impressed into the service and are held by traitorous officers. . . . The soldiers say the officers, when they were in action, stood over them with loaded revolvers and would shoot them if they did not fire." Another Union soldier, Frank Harding, talked with a former Confederate who claimed to have helped tie up Lieutenant Colonel Higgins after the surrender. The unnamed man told the writer, "He was mighty glad that

The Mutiny at Fort Jackson

we had got along. I asked him how he came to Enlist. [H]e said that he was out one Evening with Some fellows and an officer asked them to drink[.] [T]hat was the last he reccollected [*sic*] for three days when he found himself in the forts. and that he said was the way of more than half of the troops in the Southern army."[43] This statement, which sounds like a confirmation of everything William Russell had heard about the enlistment of English subjects in New Orleans, may have been an accurate assessment of the Fort Jackson garrison, or it could have been an exaggeration told to make friends with an enemy soldier. But unlike testimony about the garrison's ethnicity, which varies somewhat, at no point did any Union soldier write about talking with a determined Confederate soldier.

All the happiness, flag cheering, anti-Confederate storytelling, and loyalty oaths sworn indicate that the men in the Fort Jackson garrison (and perhaps those in Fort St. Philip) had lost any enthusiasm they may have felt for the southern republic. This in turn makes it far more likely that the mutiny had, at its roots, a political dimension that transcended a simple desire to escape an uncomfortable physical or military situation. Had that been the case, the Confederate soldiers would merely have taken their parole and waited to fight again elsewhere, as so many Confederate prisoners would do over the course of the war. These men, however, went further; many of them, even most of them, embraced the United States when it arrived in enough force to guarantee their liberty and their lives. Indeed, some of them proved anxious to help the United States to gain control over the rest of the state.

The mutineers, of course, faced an uncertain future. The Confederate elite in New Orleans held them in contempt, or worse. As mutineers, they faced harsh penalties if Confederate authorities ever got their hands on them. Fears of revenge made them reluctant to return to New Orleans. "Some of them have gone to the city and some have remained here, not daring to go to the city," wrote Alfred Parmenter. He added that "most of them expressed a desire to go any where but there."[44] The men who had fought in Fort Jackson remained poor, however. They needed work, and that meant turning to the U.S. government for employment. An eyewitness estimated that about 100 of the estimated 250 prisoners remaining in Fort Jackson on April 30, 1862, applied for work with the Union garrison. The situation was the same at the Quarantine, where some of the mutineers soon found manual labor jobs.[45]

The Mutiny at Fort Jackson

But the former Confederates did more than lift boxes and rebuild Fort Jackson; the newly liberated men sometimes had valuable skills or knowledge to offer the Union expedition. Two men followed Amos Bonney's example, offering information to David Farragut about Confederate deployments upriver from the forts. These men, Farragut wrote, had "been forced into the Confederate service at Fort Jackson as laborers, or mechanics," but somehow found their way on board the USS *Hartford* on the day after Farragut passed the forts. The men told Farragut of the two small Confederate forts at Chalmette, just below New Orleans, and he maneuvered accordingly as he approached those positions. A third captured Confederate guided a Union captain carrying dispatches overland from Farragut to Porter on a difficult twenty-six-hour trek through the swamps around the forts. Like so many of his peers, the man who showed Captain Boggs the way complained that he had been "forced to enlist," a story that a newspaperman concluded made him "like almost all who have been taken prisoner." In defeat, General Duncan complained publicly that many of his men had "probably decided to share the fortunes of the Federals."[46]

Duncan could only begin to suspect at this point, however, how many of his former soldiers would go over to the Union cause. But within a week of the mutiny, signs indicated that many of the former Confederates would find their way into blue uniforms. At both Fort Jackson and the Quarantine, men from Fort Jackson expressed interest in joining the Union army. In his official report, General Duncan noted that all the loyal Confederate soldiers had been evacuated to New Orleans within a few days but that many men—presumably those taking the oath of allegiance—remained within Union lines. Of the men who had revolted against him, he wrote that "many . . . enlisted with the enemy."[47] The fact that many mutineers would join the Union army, however, as well as the speed with which they often did so, again suggests that the mutiny may have been caused by the Unionist political sympathies of the men.

THE COLLAPSE OF THE CONFEDERATE MILITARY IN SOUTHEASTERN LOUISIANA

General Mansfield Lovell, faced with the fact that his infantry could not stop Farragut's ships, ordered his scattered commands along the Louisiana coast to withdraw northward. Their rendezvous point was Camp Moore,

Sugar Field

located on the railroad line between New Orleans and Jackson, Mississippi. From there, his forces could move to protect Vicksburg and the Mississippi River valley. (It was at Camp Moore that Henry Snyder's Confederate Guards refused to serve any longer.) Lovell's orders could have concentrated a considerable number of Confederate troops, but many of them failed to obey his commands. Instead, much of the Confederate military in southeastern Louisiana collapsed; some commands mutinied, while others disintegrated more slowly, crippled by desertion as soldiers turned themselves back into civilians and headed home. The Confederate and Louisiana forces did not perform well, perhaps because many of the men in them had never intended to serve with a whole heart. As an African American observed to a Union soldier, "The rebils were quite brave till our forces got in sight than they threw their guns and uniforms in evry direction + showed how smart they could be geting out of sight."[48]

The brief fight between Farragut's warships and the Confederate fortifications at Chalmette on April 25 showed how little resistance many Confederates would offer to the Federal advance. The commander at Chalmette, Brigadier General M. L. Smith, described the fight in his official report as a lopsided battle in which his forces fought creditably. He reported that his men fought until they had exhausted "every round of ammunition on hand" and then withdrew "deliberately." With only fourteen heavy guns to oppose Farragut's fleet, they never stood a chance. The Chalmette gunners did fire long enough to wound, if only slightly, the *New York Herald*'s navy correspondent.[49] But not everyone agreed with General Smith's report of a brave Confederate resistance.

Union accounts tell another story. Certainly, the Chalmette line fired on the approaching Union ships, at least until Farragut's ships got in close

The Mutiny at Fort Jackson

Union crewman Samuel Massa depicted the Confederate Chalmette line in two sketches in his diary. This is the battery on the western bank. (Samuel B. Massa Diary, Special Collections Research Center, Syracuse University Library)

enough to turn and fire their broadsides. As soon as this happened, however, the Confederates quickly left their fortified positions. An amateur correspondent reported seeing enemy soldiers "running for life in all directions" from the waterfront batteries. Men from a nearby infantry encampment, he continued, were beating "a hasty retreat," led by mounted officers who "went at their utmost speed." An officer on the uss *Oneida* also noted the rapid Confederate withdrawal. Men from his ship occupied the captured earthworks and noted that the Confederates had left behind valuable munitions, including a considerable amount of gunpowder and ammunition, which tends to refute General Smith's claim that he had retreated only after he had fired his last shot. Even a Confederate diarist admitted that "a French Company took to the woods without further notice, some of them through [sic] of[f] their knapsacks and through [sic] away their muskets" before any order to retreat was issued.[50] Obviously, the Confederates at Chalmette offered some resistance, though not as much as perhaps they could have. (Smith's report listed one man killed and another wounded.) But other Confederate units in the region put up even less of a fight. It was probably those commands that inspired the now-wounded *Herald* reporter to write, "The rebel army in this vicinity are panic stricken, and it is reported [that] the most disorderly scenes have occurred within the last twenty-four hours."[51]

The *Herald* called it a panic; Captain Farragut termed it "a general stampede."[52] Confederate general Lovell might well have called it a disgrace. Whatever term is used, the lack of patriotism exhibited by Confederate troops throughout southeastern Louisiana establishes a context of disloyalty that makes the mutiny in Fort Jackson look like the focal point of a wider protest against the Confederacy by its foot soldiers. Certainly

The Mutiny at Fort Jackson

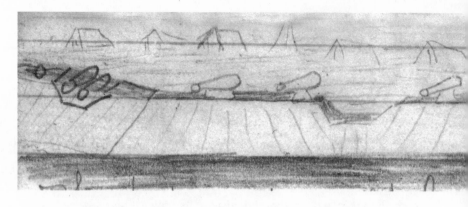

Lovell's reports from this period betray his frustration with his disobedient troops. Lovell ordered the soldiers at five forts, Livingston, Guion, Quitman, Berwick, and Chene, to retreat to Camp Moore. The garrisons of the last two arrived intact, but the men at the other posts "became demoralized, disbanded, and returned to New Orleans."[53] The small garrison at Fort Quitman, he told the secretary of war in June, had failed to obey his orders. Officers as well as ordinary soldiers, he noted, "mutinied and disbanded." He could only regret that punishing the officers was "impracticable" owing to their safe residence in New Orleans.[54] At Fort Livingston, Colonel Theard failed to bring off his command of about 330 men intact. Theard, whose widely scattered regiment also included the Allen Guards in Fort Jackson, would see his troops desert the Confederate flag on the road north from Fort Livingston. A Union navy officer who occupied the position talked to a local man, Angelo Zernata, who said that most of the locals "are union men." Deserters and their wives confirmed that the Confederate soldiers were "chiefly French and Italian" men who brought their part of the Civil War to a close when Union success made it possible for them to do so. At another spot along the coast, Tower Dupres, the Confederates left behind four undamaged heavy artillery pieces and a substantial amount of medical supplies.[55]

The Confederate garrison in Fort Pike, northeast of New Orleans, also proved unruly. While the fort itself was impressive, the soldiers in its garrison were hard to control. Most of Fort Pike's men served in companies of the 1st Louisiana Heavy Artillery, the regiment that made up half of the Fort Jackson garrison, and they proved equally fractious. Arriving at Fort Pike in January 1862, a Confederate officer, Edward J. Butler, quickly

The Mutiny at Fort Jackson

Samuel Massa's drawing of the Chalmette line's fortifications on the eastern bank. (Samuel B. Massa Diary, Special Collections Research Center, Syracuse University Library)

123

formed "rather a poor opinion of my company who are badly drilled and about as stupid a set as I ever saw. I hope, however, to improve them in a few months." He apparently had little luck with his new command, however, perhaps because of his condescending attitude. Two months later, two companies of the Confederate Guards (Snyder's "elite" unit) had to be called out to suppress a riot involving "a lot of drunken unruly regulars who had been Sent up [to New Orleans] from Fort Pike + were being transferred to another point." Snyder thought the matter was quite serious: the Guards seemed fortunate to have "subdued them without killing a single man + only wounded a few with swords and bayonets" before shipping them back to Fort Pike. Not surprisingly, these ill-disciplined elements of the 1st Louisiana Heavy Artillery evaporated in the withdrawal from Fort Pike to Camp Moore. Captain Butler, who had disliked his men from the start, lost control of them during the retreat through New Orleans. He wrote to his mother that he had ordered them to the railroad station "and with about half of my Co. embarked for this place. The rest deserted or were too drunk to be able to walk and there was no earthly way of having them transported." Some of the drinkers later found their way to Camp Moore. Nevertheless, Butler's Company I permanently lost sixteen of its sixty-nine soldiers (23 percent) on its way through New Orleans. Faced with such losses throughout the units under his command, Lovell told the secretary of war that "it was impossible to reoccupy" any of the forts. Desertion would prove to be far more destructive to the Confederate army in Louisiana than the Federal forces.[56]

Desertion plagued Confederate units especially as they made their way through the city. Benjamin Butler, the Union commander, later estimated

The Mutiny at Fort Jackson

that "more than one-half" of Lovell's army deserted, with most of the escaping men returning to New Orleans to put on civilian clothes. Butler's figure cannot be taken as wholly accurate; no one can know how many soldiers seized the opportunity to flee military life. But anecdotal evidence suggests that large portions of the Confederate army melted away. As one Union correspondent explained to his readers, "Disorganized Confederate troops in companies and parts of companies, fled in wild disorder to the depot." Once at the depot, some never found their way onto the trains. So many men from the 20th Louisiana Volunteers deserted that it had to be reorganized at Camp Moore. State militia brigades commanded by Generals E. L. Tracy and B. Buisson disbanded, largely because they agreed with the Confederate Guards that they did not have to serve outside Louisiana. Lovell disagreed, but he could not stop them. Interestingly, one reporter explained the high desertion rate by saying that the deserters had always been Unionists. According to his theory, Unionists had formed companies "and enlisted friends of the Union, to rid themselves of being forced into [front-line] service, and on the arrival of our troops of course disbanded."[57] This explanation gives credence to a political interpretation of the Fort Jackson mutiny and may also explain why Henry Snyder served in a militia unit but lived peacefully under the old flag. In all, the confused scene at the New Orleans railroad depot allowed many people to escape from Confederate service.

The scene at the Oak Lawn plantation outside the city gives an interesting picture of life in the chaotic period during the Confederate evacuation of the city. Oak Lawn was a center for Confederate loyalty in the midst of a moving, unsettled population. Edward Stewart, its owner, gave shelter to "a house full" of people, some of whom had fled the city. As a loyal Confederate, he encouraged people to leave New Orleans rather than live under the old flag. Indeed, when a friend showed no signs of budging from New Orleans, Stewart urged him to take any railroad car or schooner he could find to escape from the Yankees. But loyal Confederates heading north were not the only ones tramping the lawns at Oak Lawn. "Richard + young Thompson were here two days ago," Stewart wrote to a friend about two Confederate deserters who had stopped by. "They left the camp above and were going to try and slip back to the city[; they] had thrown away their guns and uniform[s]." Edward Stewart did not offer the deserters any comfort, but others in the neighborhood did.[58] The nearly anarchic situation surrounding the Confederate evacuation allowed men who had been compelled to enlist to decide how much longer they wanted to serve the southern republic.

Loyal Confederates found the whole situation vexing. How could they explain their defeat? Why had the Union accomplished so much, at so little cost? What could they say about the defections from their army? In the days after Lovell retreated, Confederates rallied around the idea that they had been betrayed by traitors. Some people imagined they had been sold out by one or two corrupted men, while others admitted that there was a broader Unionist constituency. But all confronted the notion that their city's white population had not been united in the face of the enemy.

The city's Confederate press circulated a story from the *New Orleans Commercial Bulletin* the day after Farragut's ships appeared off the wharves. The paper had received a letter from an officer in Colonel Szymanski's regiment that accused some common soldiers of betraying their country. The letter reported that "some of the lookouts on duty at the forts and in the river are supposed to have deserted to the enemy, and given them the necessary information to enable them to effect their object." The paper remarked, "Our informant is confident that had the alarm been given at the forts in time, the ships could not have forced a passage. He also states that a member of the regiment to which he was attached, on being captured by the Federals, volunteered to pilot them to the city." This story of betrayal was picked up by the *New Orleans Daily Picayune* and the *Algiers Newsboy*.[59]

Many Confederates believed the story that treasonous lookouts had caused the military debacle. Perhaps it comforted them. The story allowed Confederates to believe that the disaffection among their troops had been limited and that their military had been otherwise well prepared to defend the city. One Confederate citizen in New Orleans wrote that a lookout's failure to launch warning rockets meant that the forts and the navy had been "taken completely by surprise." The Yankee ships, he continued, had "only four shots fired at them" as they passed the forts. This was not true, but it reassured this man. He also added another detail: "When the man was asked why he did not give the signal he said the rockets would not go off. They were brought to the fort and when tried, went off beautifully.

This proved that the man was a Lincolnite and he was hung at that instant." Such revenge would be a cold comfort, and probably also not true, but he liked it well enough to include it in his letter.[60]

Nevertheless, even this writer had to admit that the city had produced more than one traitor over the past week. As much as he and his compatriots wanted to believe that the white South stood solidly behind the Confederacy, evidence of disaffection was all around them. Immediately after getting his revenge against the Lincolnite lookout, the writer admitted that "there are nothing but traitors surrounding us." Another New Orleans Confederate wrote of the "treachery and falsehood around and among us," noting with anguished surprise that "it is inconceivable how we were deceived—*sold.*" She later blamed the Confederate officers, whom she found to be "*incompetent,* if not unfaithful." It was all very painful for Confederate loyalists, and this writer sought solace in the fact that "some of our men fought nobly."[61] Yet there was no disputing that the city harbored men who had sold out the new nation.

Even the Confederates, therefore, had to admit that the mutiny at Fort Jackson was not an isolated incident. As events at the Quarantine Station, the Chalmette line, and the coastal forts indicate, Confederate soldiers did not uniformly support their government when the chips were down. Many greeted Union successes as an opportunity to go home, since Confederates could no longer harass them. While only some mutinied in order to get there—most preferred the more passive route of desertion—the Fort Jackson garrison was not the only group to pointedly disobey orders. From the Cazadores and the Fort Pike regulars, whose revolts had brought out Henry Snyder's regiment, to the mutiny that marked the end of the garrison at Fort Quitman, Confederate commanders were plagued by their soldiers' willful disobedience. Together, these incidents suggest that the mutiny at Fort Jackson was only part of a larger movement within the Confederate military to resist its elitist and xenophobic government.

The extent of Unionist feelings among New Orleans whites, even among Confederate soldiers, suggests that the weeks after the Union victory would see conflict between different elements of the city's white population. As we will see in the next two chapters, whites in New Orleans split into Unionist and Confederate camps. The two groups would deploy both real and rhetorical weapons in their efforts to gain an upper hand in the Crescent City. But the mutiny at Fort Jackson would continue to hang over the city, giving hope to Unionists and troubling Confederates. The men of the garrison, far from simply slipping into the background, would figure prominently in the fate of the city both as symbols and as political actors in their own right. For now, however, the mutiny and its roots in the city's Unionist movement inspired those people who strove to rebuild the United States. As the *New York Tribune* said, the mutiny and the rapid collapse of the Confederate army around New Orleans gave it "little doubt that the number who are getting sick of this unholy Rebellion are not a few."[62]

The Mutiny at Fort Jackson

the many fates of the fort jackson garrison

Nothing is known about Thomas Graham's life before he enlisted in Company B of the 1st Louisiana Heavy Artillery on February 28, 1861. He was then 22 years old, and he volunteered on the first day the regiment started to recruit. Graham's Confederate military record was uneventful until the mutiny. After that night, Graham becomes a larger figure in the historical record, and his life hints at the motivations of the mutineers as well as the perils they faced after their rebellion.

At some point in the spring or summer after the mutiny, Thomas Graham enlisted in the 8th Vermont Volunteers. The Vermonters had started recruiting soon after they arrived in New Orleans, hoping that Unionists would replace some of the losses they had suffered from disease. In May, the 8th Vermont enlisted six Frenchmen, five men from the German states, one Swiss, and Charles Marrion, a carpenter born in South Carolina. Recruiting picked up again in July, when the regiment was stationed in Algiers, across the river from New Orleans. One of the regiment's officers, Stephen Spalding, reported that new recruits were easily found. Writing that a man in his regiment had drowned, Spalding cynically noted, "I had a man in his place enlisted and drilling just as he was sinking the 3rd time."[1]

The 8th Vermont spent much of the summer in Algiers, but it also established picket lines west of the city along the New Orleans, Opelousas, and Great Western railroad. Patrolling the western approaches to New Orleans was both tedious and dangerous. One soldier jokingly referred to the regiment's post at Bayou des Allemands as "musketoe valley." Confederates also buzzed around the outpost. In July a Confederate recruiter was captured and brought in by local Unionists who probably wanted to avoid being drafted.[2] For Graham and others in his regiment, the summer passed with long periods of boredom.

Disaster struck on September 4, 1862. A surprise attack on the 8th Vermont's outpost at Bayou des Allemands captured 141 Union soldiers, including Thomas Graham. Worse was to follow. The Confederates recognized seven of their prisoners as former Confederate soldiers. The seven men, Bernard Hurst, Deidrich Bahne, John and Michael Leichleiver, Michael Masman, Frank Paul, and Gustave C. Becher, were quickly separated from the other Union prisoners. They were then "taken about five rods [about twenty-seven yards] from the rail-road, a single shallow pit was dug, they were placed on the brink, and without respite were shot down; their bodies tumbled into the ditch, and a few shovelfuls of earth were thrown over them." Thomas Graham—who remained unrecognized—must have been terrified. Nor was he alone. Two other veterans of Fort Jackson were captured that day, William H. Brown and Dennis Kean. Both Brown and Kean had enlisted on June 1. William Brown had been born in Bangor, Maine, and, like Graham, had been 22 years old in 1861. Dennis Kean, an Irish-born laborer, was the eldest of the men at age 29.[3] All three men headed off to a Confederate prison camp near Vicksburg, scared about what would happen to them if their identity was discovered.

Thomas Graham's luck lasted only until October 30, 1862. Recognized as a former member of the 1st Louisiana Heavy Artillery, Graham was tried at a court-martial in Jackson, Mississippi, on December 20, 1862. His accusers said that he "did join in a mutiny and abandon his post of duty in the presence of the enemy." He was also charged with desertion and joining the Federal army. He was found guilty and sentenced "to be shot to death

The Many Fates of the Fort Jackson Garrison

with musketry." Dennis Kean and William Brown were also found guilty that day.[4]

The three men were shot to death on March 6, 1863. Confederates officers had each of the men shot in front of a different Confederate division, the better to impress upon wavering volunteers and conscripts the fate that awaited them if they mutinied or deserted. Confederate private J. A. Wilson described one of the executions, probably Graham's or Brown's, since he described the man as "quite a good looking young man." Wilson wrote that "he was set on his coffin, his hands tied behind, in front of twelve men with loaded Muskets. [W]hen the word was given 'make ready' he slightly inclined forward, but soon to fall back to rise no more. [H]e seemed to bear up with great fortitude." Graham's death marked one of the many different fates experienced by men from Fort Jackson.[5]

In the context of a war that killed so many men, the death of the ten New Orleans men of the 8th Vermont can seem like a small affair. But there were other, similar incidents, such as when General George Pickett executed twenty-two former Confederates who had been captured after volunteering for the Union army in North Carolina.[6] The brief but complicated lives of these and other former Confederate soldiers also suggest new ways of thinking about the Civil War. Thomas Graham and dozens of other men who had served in Fort Jackson enlisted in the Union military, even though that act placed them in great jeopardy. Why did they switch sides? Were they desperate for work, no matter how dangerous? Or were they so angry about their treatment by Confederate officers, or by the hierarchical cast of the new southern republic, that they wanted to fight for the United States? After all, as immigrants, many of them had already chosen the United States once, above all other nations, as the place to live. Particular individuals, such as Thomas Graham, left behind no records of their thoughts. But taken as a group, the garrison of Fort Jackson left behind a trail of evidence about what they did after their mutiny. Their actions suggest that they were motivated by a marked preference for the United States. In the end, we might well remember Thomas Graham and his nine comrades as men who chose the United States because its vision of democracy and equality appealed to them. As for the Confederate officers who ordered their executions, their actions speak of their desperate need to coerce men into the Confederate ranks.

The Many Fates of the Fort Jackson Garrison

New Orleans hosted a confusing swirl of people during the last days of April and the first two weeks of May. Civilians lived between two warring centers of power, the Confederate city government and the Union military. Deserters and stragglers from Confederate and Louisiana units quickly joined the mix. Over the course of the month after the mutiny, the city's loyalty would be won or lost among these civilians and former soldiers. The men from Fort Jackson had to pick their way through these turbulent waters. They would pursue a wide variety of paths as they sought security for themselves and their families. Many volunteered for Union military service, believing that it represented their best chance for happiness.

The Confederate mob gained an upper hand in the battle for control of the city's streets in the days after Farragut's arrival. In many popular depictions, it comes across as almost quaint, the harmless and spontaneous voice of a unanimous white population. In reality, the mob that raged against Farragut's men and later Butler's was not harmless. As we have seen, it massacred people as they stood on the levee to greet Farragut's ships. Nor was the mob spontaneous. It probably closely resembled the Know-Nothing mobs that had dictated the city's election results since 1855. Nor was the city's white population, let alone the city's free and enslaved blacks, entirely supportive of the mob and its secessionist politics. Instead, the mob represented a concerted effort by Confederate leaders to use violence to contest the Union's control over the city. Although it was successful at stifling civilian Unionists, its failure to mount a sustained resistance to the Union military suggests the weakness of the Confederate community and the strength of Unionism in New Orleans.

The first weapon of the New Orleans mob had always been the threat of violence against its enemies. Unionist civilians had been repressed by the city government throughout 1861, but Confederate leaders knew in May 1862 that they were losing control of the courts and prisons. Confederate authorities, therefore, turned to extralegal mob violence to accomplish their goals. Unionist civilians, familiar with the brutality of recent elections, remained cowed for several weeks. But they were no longer alone.

Union soldiers entered the city with more swagger and a greater ability to defend themselves than the Unionist civilians. Nevertheless, elements in the mob sought to kill Union soldiers after their appearance on May 1.

The Many Fates of the Fort Jackson Garrison

Their successes belie the romantic notion that the mob was harmless. On May 3, Private Mark O'Neil of the 9th Connecticut Volunteers was stabbed to death while taking an evening walk in his uniform. By May 6, the *New York Tribune* reporter counted five Union soldiers who had "been found murdered in the streets."[7] Infuriated by the assassinations, Union soldiers fought back. John E. Goodhue, formerly a shoemaker and tanner in Salem, Massachusetts, wrote to his mother on May 3, "Our soldiers are found every day poisoned or murdered by the sesesh." Goodhue, however, took comfort—though perhaps his mother did not—that Union soldiers were now stabbing their bayonets "through" the men who insulted them. George Hughes, another soldier on the streets that week, wrote that a man in his regiment had done just that to "a rowdy [who] drew a revolver on the officer of the guard."[8] During the first week, the city's streets were the site of a sometimes deadly contest between the mob and Union soldiers. Significantly, reports of murdered Union troops disappear by the end of the first week.

The mob also threatened and murdered Unionist civilians. The tireless *New York Herald* correspondent reported that, three days after Unionist citizens were shot on the levee in front of the Union fleet, two more "Union men" were "martyred for no other crime" than their politics in Jefferson City, about five miles north of New Orleans. They had been killed, he believed, by "the citizen patrol," a pro-Confederate force that controlled the streets before Butler's troops landed. George Hughes, whose compatriot had bayoneted a man earlier that week, complained that "several Union men have been killed by the rowdies."[9] Other Unionists were luckier, receiving only threats or imprisonment in return for their political sentiments or their trade with Federal sailors. The *Herald* reporter noted that a "youngster" who had sold him a newspaper had been imprisoned for having done so. The Confederates also arrested Joseph Noel during the interim between the arrival of the U.S. ships and Butler's troops. The *New Orleans Daily Picayune* rejoiced that Noel had been arrested as soon "as he landed from a yawl which had come from one of the enemy's ships, on a charge of communicating with the enemy and acting as a spy. He found that from the levee to the First District Police Station was a hard road to travel. Had it not been for the protection he received from a detachment of our Home Guards, which was called upon to escort him, he would very likely have been hanged by the exasperated people."[10] The *Picayune*'s les-

The Many Fates of the Fort Jackson Garrison

son was clear enough; people who treat with the enemy could expect imprisonment, but only if they were lucky enough to avoid the lynching they so rightly deserved. Especially before Butler's troops arrived, the mob did what it could to enforce a uniform Confederate patriotism on the city's people.

Jailing and killing ordinary people could only do so much, however. Confederates also had to worry about stopping municipal officeholders from going over to the enemy. The case of Judge Somers, a two-term city recorder, illustrates the close eye kept on people with known Unionist sympathies. Accounts place Somers all over town during the busy week after the fleet arrived. He was seen fleeing to the USS *Richmond* by April 29, being jailed by Confederates for condemning Mumford's removal of the U.S. flag from the Mint, and being threatened by the mob for welcoming U.S. officers to the city. On May 2, the mob threatened to hang him as he traveled to and from Butler's headquarters.[11] While it is impossible to reconstruct his day-to-day movements, the mob clearly targeted Somers in an effort to dissuade other officials from defecting to the Union. Later in May, Thomas U. Laster, a Unionist candidate for judge in the city's Fourth District, was killed by two policemen. The police, long linked to the pro-secession Know-Nothings, may well have assassinated Laster for political reasons. Already, Laster had been notorious enough for the Confederates to call him before the extralegal Southern Independence Association, which had duly threatened him.[12] No doubt aware that some people in New Orleans welcomed a Federal resurgence in Louisiana, the Confederates sought to stop municipal leaders from blazing a path to the Union administration.

Hardly harmless, the mob was also probably not spontaneous. Instead, it appears like part of a planned effort by the mayor to retain some control over the city. Part of his campaign included pretending that nothing had changed since Federal warships arrived. Confederate newspapers boasted (erroneously) that the streets of New Orleans and Algiers remained free of Unionist demonstrations. They bragged that the city's women and children still adhered to the Confederacy.[13] Newspapers ran advertisements for slaves.[14] Unwilling to surrender the city it had ruled since 1855, the Know-Nothing administration also called forth its old allies, the gangs that had long done battle for the Know-Nothings in the city streets.

The mob proved to be the Confederate leaders' most potent weapon, and it was in its element in the largely lawless days between Farragut's arrival and the restoration of order by Butler's troops on May 1. In those five days, the mob ruled the streets, and most witnesses saw them as the agents of the city's leadership. The mob's Confederate patriotism, in other words, was born to a large extent of political favors and patronage, not just a love of secession. A reporter for the *Philadelphia Press* described the mob as an "organized band of Thugs" whose stock in trade—assassination—received no check from law enforcement. He reported that the police ignored the mob's murders because the thugs were the "useful instruments of the secret vigilance committee," a group that targeted "men suspected of Union proclivities."[15] In addition to intimidating and killing Unionists, the mob also illegally destroyed private property to prevent it from falling into Union hands. At least one letter writer claimed that the destruction that greeted the Federal fleet was the work of the mob, not of the real owners of the burning ships, cotton, molasses, and sugar. "In no instance did the owner of property apply the torch," he wrote, calling into question the claim that southerners willingly sacrificed their possessions for their new country.[16]

Union soldiers provide the most interesting evidence that the mobs were called forth by the mayor instead of arising spontaneously from an outraged people. Union soldiers encountered a surprisingly passive crowd during their first landing on May 1. Accounts written by soldiers right after they set foot in New Orleans depict the city's people as quiet and orderly. In other words, subsequent angry protests against the soldiers began only after the city's leadership summoned the mob, not as soon as people first saw blue uniforms. Upon landing, an eyewitness with the 31st Massachusetts saw a crowd of several thousand men and women at the wharf but wrote that "the people were all very quiet, and appeared like curious gazers at some unusual advent," like the arrival of a large steamship or of the Japanese ambassador. Some quiet threats were issued, he admitted, but there was "not the slightest demonstration or disturbance." Another person who was with the first troops saw "no disturbance. I think the people were taken aback."[17] The people seemed so harmless that U.S. brigadier general John Phelps spent the night wandering the city alone, pausing occasionally to talk with people and even asking for directions. They were, he said, "very polite to him."[18] Admittedly, there was some opposition, but Frank Harding of the 4th Wisconsin noted, "We were hissed

The Many Fates of the Fort Jackson Garrison

and gronned [*sic*] at but after arresting a few they have become quite peaceble [*sic*]."[19] Far from hostile to the United States, the people of New Orleans reacted with equanimity to the arrival of Butler's troops.

Even though New Orleans could still be a dangerous (or even deadly) place for Unionists and northern troops during the first week of May, many northern men quickly took to sightseeing about the city. One sailor, Edward Bacon, spent May 2 touring the city with a son of the poet Henry Wadsworth Longfellow. Edward Bacon was himself the son of a well-known New Haven clergyman, Leonard Bacon. The two young men ambled about the city, taking in the Custom House and the closed St. Charles Hotel. They were often treated rudely, but Bacon noted that "some few were glad to see us and talked as if they had just come out from under a featherbed." The two youths hired horses and, complacent in their apparent safety, eventually found themselves "outside of all pickets and in a lonely neighborhood, one of us in uniform, but armed only with a pocket-knife." Turning around, they had no trouble returning home.[20] That the unarmed sons of a clergyman and a poet could carelessly amble about the city on the day after their arrival testifies to the calm with which much of New Orleans greeted the arrival of U.S. troops.

As Bacon's story suggests, Union soldiers grew comfortable in New Orleans very quickly. Within days, they had made themselves at home. On May 3, Brigadier General Thomas Williams felt obligated to issue orders designed to keep his men from loitering about the city. He told his officers to keep the soldiers busy "in cleaning their persons, clothing, arms and accoutrements." He issued his orders because cleaning was a good way to fill up the men's spare time, not because they were especially dirty. "Much time can be profitably employed in this way," he admonished, and it will stop the men from "lounging in the street."[21] The presence of relaxed soldiers suggests that tensions between soldiers and citizens had abated sharply within a matter of days, and testimony from the 4th Wisconsin confirms that impression. George Hughes wrote on May 5, "The citizens are gradually becoming acclimated to us and respect us more than they did when we first landed," and Newton Chittenden wrote three days later that the people of New Orleans had been "so far tamed" that soldiers (with guns) could safely tour the city in pairs.[22]

While the New Orleans mob had been very active against Farragut's vastly outnumbered officers, it played a less conspicuous role once Butler's

The Many Fates of the Fort Jackson Garrison

troops landed. Butler's men faced only a few whispered threats as they marched through the streets of New Orleans on May 1. The mayor did summon his mob once more on May 2, in the hope of sending a message to Butler, but its failure to stand up to the Union military that day marked its end as an effective tool. Its weakness suggests that the citizenry did not fully endorse its politics. Certainly in other cities along the Mississippi where there was no history of mob violence, whites often greeted Farragut's ships with quiet reserve or even apparent relief. Despite a brief Federal bombardment of the city, Baton Rouge's Unionists publicly welcomed Farragut. According to one eyewitness, "The greatest enthusiasm prevailed among the inhabitants, who rushed down to the river and greeted them with cheers, and waving hats and handkerchiefs. One of the leading men of the town rode down on horseback, and cried out, *'Hurrah for Lincoln, bread and meat.'*" Continuing, the man reported that "the Union sentiment [was] overwhelming all sympathy with the rebellion." Sailor Oscar Smith recorded that the people of Baton Rouge "seemed very quiet and contented" when he arrived on May 10. As historians Lawrence N. Powell and Michael S. Wayne have noted, people in the lower Mississippi River valley often equated the return of the U.S. flag with the resumption of trade and prosperity. Without a mob organized to stifle their pursuit of self-interest, many people from Baton Rouge to New Orleans seemed "quiet and contented" when the Union warships arrived, signaling as they did the restoration of the Union and the end of the blockade.[23]

The New Orleans mob, however, did exist, and its fearsome reputation kept Unionists underground for much of May. Unionists emerged only gradually through May, and only when they sensed that their security was guaranteed. A correspondent for the *Boston Courier* noted that Unionist presidential candidates in 1860 had swept the city but that Unionist voters would not soon appear because they had been "so long under the military domination of the rebels." Others pointed to tangible evidence of Confederate oppression, including the release of between twenty and thirty "political prisoners" from the parish prison. As one New Orleans native wrote to Union general George Shepley, the mob and "their murderous deeds have kept the loyal citizens at home."[24]

It seems that every newspaper correspondent and Union soldier had stories to tell about their encounters with frightened Unionists. Their stories are too long and too numerous to give in full, but their frequency

The Many Fates of the Fort Jackson Garrison

"'Do you see me?'—General Butler defying the rebels at New Orleans," a northern depiction of Benjamin Butler facing down a particularly ugly mob. Such portrayals captured the northern heart but did little to capture the truth about what was happening on the streets of New Orleans. (The Historic New Orleans Collection)

indicates how many Unionist southerners had been kept quiet through coercion. W. P. Moore, an officer in the 4th Wisconsin, wrote home that many men in New Orleans had "a lurking love for the Union." Nevertheless, he said,

> The Union men are so cowed down that they dare not speak to a soldier by daylight, and then only in corners where they will not be disturbed by citizens. Some men came along by the side of me this evening, and talked in a low tone, and said they were glad that we were here—that they were Union men, but did not dare to have it known. One man today passed along by some officers, and without turning his head or looking toward them, said—"I am a Union man from Massachusetts, but dare not let it be known"—and kept up a running conversation in such a manner that outsiders did not know that he was talking to them. It shows what has been the domineering spirt [*sic*] of these southern lords. The Union men are fast discovering themselves.

Other men derived similar conclusions from similar stories. Captain Elliott of Massachusetts thought that there were "many good Union men here," but their timidity proved to him that "fear has carried much of the secession in New Orleans." After telling a long story about a Unionist who talked secretly with him while "he tremblingly clung to the elbow of a friend, feeling as though wolves' eyes were upon him in the crowd," northern correspondent A. G. Hills vented his anger at the rebellion that had driven patriots to fear for their lives. Had you seen this American patriot cowering in fear, he wrote, "you would acknowledge to have seen one thing that would make you swear eternal hatred for this accursed rebellion. I have spoken of one case," he continued, but "I know of a hundred, of my own personal knowledge."[25]

The arrival of Union troops did not automatically make Unionist civilians feel safe, perhaps for good reason. Many Unionists worried that the army might retreat. In this regard, the Union army's withdrawal from Jacksonville, Florida, cast a long shadow over New Orleans Unionists. In Jacksonville, Unionists had emerged from hiding shortly after the arrival of Union troops in March 1862. The Union army's retreat on April 9, 1862, however, left Unionists with the choice of remaining behind at the mercy of the returning Confederates or of evacuating and giving up their homes. With this event fresh in their memory, New Orleans Unionists worried that

Federal forces might soon leave. None of the Unionists relished having their political allegiances known to a resurgent Confederate government or mob. Future U.S. naval hero George Dewey, who served on board the USS *Mississippi* in 1862, assured his father that "there are plenty of Unionists in the South" and that they would "make themselves heard" just as soon as they "feel there will be no change" in troop deployments. Soldier Orange Smith found this fear still very much alive as late as August, noting that "there was a great many afraid to come out for the Union fearing that our armies might leave and they would be left at the mercy of the rebels."[26] Taught by long experience that political dissent could be dangerous—many of the Unionists having experienced repression not just in New Orleans but by European monarchs—Unionists often thought it wise to keep quiet.

Despite all the dangers, however, some Unionists publicly showed their pleasure at seeing the United States regaining control of their city. Perhaps exhibiting Unionism was not the wisest course to follow, but these people took the opportunity to rejoice and even gain a measure of satisfaction for the way they had been treated over the past year. Surprisingly, despite the massacre on the levee, some Unionists made contact with the Union fleet even during the interim period before Butler's infantry arrived in the city. On board the USS *Hartford* one day after it arrived at New Orleans, a man remarked that "as we passed along the levee in the upper part of the city, *considerable Union feeling* was manifested by all classes." Even as the ships lay off New Orleans, civilians came alongside in small boats to visit with the crews. Some came to trade, telling everyone how close to starvation the Confederate experiment had brought them. Others wanted only a sympathetic ear to hear about the tensions they had experienced over the past year. One woman relayed the intelligence that the Confederates had evacuated Forts Pike and Livingston.[27] Even in the midst of the most famous Confederate mob of all, the one that encircled Captain Bailey as he conveyed Farragut's demands to the mayor, Bailey heard whispered words of encouragement such as "Glad to see you" and "Why didn't you come before?"[28]

Unionists did not always need Farragut's fleet right behind them to taunt their foes. Germans took the fore in efforts to harass Confederates. The diary of Ann Penrose, an ardent Confederate, relates stories about how German Unionists had embarrassed her relatives. Her diary shows that Confederate women, even in the days before Butler's troops landed, lived in an uncertain world in which their social place was called into question. Penrose and her relatives detested the Germans who challenged their status, and the Unionists' public actions horrified them. While the mob was turned out to stand up to Bailey and Butler, it did not control the streets.

Ann Penrose wrote her first diary entry about a trip made by two of her relatives on either the day the fleet "arrived in the city, or the day after." Her relatives, Rebecca and Anna, were riding a city streetcar when they arrived at their stop. Ringing the bell for the car to stop, the women were surprised when the car kept moving. "The driver (a German)" ignored two more rings of the bell, moving the women farther away from their stop. Finally, Penrose wrote, "he condescended to stop, & as they got [off] told them, 'if they wanted to get out, they had no business to get in.'"[29] One wonders whether the driver was speaking metaphorically about the war, saying that if they did not like the war's egalitarian results, they should not have started it by seceding from the Union. Whatever he meant, such backtalk from a German streetcar driver infuriated Ann Penrose, and it must have smarted especially for being such a novel experience.

To drive home her point that the Germans were no longer to be trusted, Ann Penrose followed her streetcar story with a second one, this time about an aunt's experiences in New Orleans. Again, German disloyalty to the Confederacy surfaces soon after the fall of Fort Jackson. In this story, her aunt is concerned because an acquaintance had been involved in the fighting at Fort Jackson. Hearing nothing about his welfare, she enlisted Anna and Rose to accompany her on a visit to a man who had been in the forts. Returning from their visit, the three women were confronted by a German Unionist. This one, Penrose wrote, had "a horn in his mouth, was dancing & skipping along singing, 'Yankee Doodles that's the tune, Yankee Doodles that's the tune.'" She could dismiss his harassing behavior as the product of drink, but she could not avoid the conclusion that his politics were Unionist. "It proved not the less, their sentiments in favor of our enemies." In fact, she had to admit that "nearly all Dutch or Germans . . . have turned against us."[30] These accounts suggest that some Unionists staked a claim to the city's streets even in the earliest days of the transition from Confederate to Union control. The mob, therefore, hardly spoke for all the white people of New Orleans. Sometimes Unionists only waved at

The Many Fates of the Fort Jackson Garrison

the fleet or visited the sailors, but at other times they could be loud and unruly enough to make Confederates uncomfortable. Although these Unionists have been written out of the history of New Orleans, they could not be ignored in 1862. As Butler's troops moved in, the Unionists became an even larger force.

Butler's administration of the city sought to help Unionists gain control over public spaces and civic discussion. By taking over the municipal government, Butler removed the patronage jobs and legal protections that had spurred and enabled the mob. His new political machine clamped down on members of the mob who terrorized Unionists. Within two weeks of his arrival, for example, Butler had successfully prosecuted two men whom he accused of using violence against Unionists. On May 12, a man named Benzic was sentenced to hard labor for "his natural life" at Fort Jackson for threatening to kill a Unionist; two days later George Reed was convicted of murdering a Union man and "extorting money from loyal citizens."[31] On May 20, George F. Shepley, a Maine general appointed military commandant of New Orleans, issued orders promising "speedy and effectual" punishment of anyone found guilty of denouncing or threatening "any civilian of the United States for the expression of Union or loyal sentiments." Journalists celebrated the arrest of four prominent "Thugs" in early June, presumably under these regulations. Reinforcing the notion that the Confederate mob had been both dangerous and an artificial product of municipal corruption, the New Orleans True Delta described the men as "the leaders of thugs, the friends of Aldermen, [and] the social companion[s] of every mayor who has cursed the city for ten years back."[32] Busting up the mob and its organization no doubt encouraged Unionists to enter the city's public life. Success soon greeted Butler's and Shepley's efforts to bring calm to the city.

Union soldiers marveled at how quickly the Crescent City became peaceful. Reading their letters and diaries, one senses that they thoroughly enjoyed coming into a city where they often were made to feel welcome. While the men give different dates for when they first felt at home in the city, their happy letters come shockingly early to anyone familiar with the histories that have painted the city as a hotbed of secession. On May 12, Rufus Kinsley of Vermont remembered what he had seen as his ship pulled up to the wharf at sunset. "The levees were crowded with thousands of people from all countries," he wrote in his diary, "and in all costumes;

some giving us a most hearty welcome, and singing Union songs; and some others demonstrating their displeasure, and singing the songs of secession. Our splendid brass band played for their benefit Yankee Doodle, Columbia, John Brown, and others." Three days later, Justus Gale of the 8th Vermont wrote home that "the people here seem to be very friendly to us so far although there are many that are rebels as much as ever. Stephen and I went out yesterday into the City and had quite a walk through the City; we traveled [sic] about three hours through the heart of the City and met no one that done or said a word to us but what was all propper [sic] and right."[33] Although not everyone was won over to the Union cause overnight, there can be no doubt that many whites quickly adjusted back to life in the United States.

The Confederate mob seems to have evaporated as quickly as the city's rebel government. This is probably not a coincidence. Once men in the mob sensed that their patrons no longer controlled the resources of city hall, they stopped obeying their orders. With the mob's disappearance came a period of increasing calm in the city as civilians and soldiers grew accustomed to each other. Local Unionists, gaining confidence, became more assertive as the summer wore on. The people's smiling faces, Union songs, and generally relaxed mood are a far cry from our picture of Civil War New Orleans, but they were the historical reality within a fortnight of the arrival of U.S. troops. The society and politics of New Orleans were far more complicated than our myths suggest, and it was into this uncertain, changing atmosphere that the veterans of Forts Jackson returned in the days and weeks after their mutiny.

THE FORT JACKSON GARRISON AFTER THE MUTINY

Mutiny is a dangerous business when it is going on, and the risks persist long after the incident is over. Fort Jackson's mutineers faced an especially uncertain future after handing themselves over to the Federal army. From this point onward, the Confederacy represented a mortal threat to any of the mutineers it was able to capture, as Thomas Graham's life and death demonstrate. Still, the mutineers had several options, and the choices they made tell us a great deal about what the Civil War meant to them. The men could choose to give their parole, then wait to be exchanged as prisoners of war and continue their Confederate service. This option was taken by the

The Many Fates of the Fort Jackson Garrison

Saint Mary's Cannoneers, many of whom served in the Confederate army for the rest of the war. Another option for mutineers was to swear a Federal oath of allegiance and return to New Orleans; having taken the oath, they would never be exchanged back to the Confederacy. This choice was made harder by the city's stagnant economy, which threatened any working family with starvation. But the mutineers had the comfort of knowing, within a week or two, that they could receive charitable relief from either the Union or the Confederacy. Some Unionist men from the fort's garrison chose a third option. They avoided New Orleans and worked as laborers for the Union army near Fort Jackson. Others enlisted in "northern" regiments. The willingness of so many of the mutineers to work for, or serve in, the Union army suggests that many of them endorsed the goals and visions of the United States.

Mutineers who chose to return to New Orleans put themselves at considerable risk by doing so. For the first days of May, the city's newspapers incited the mob by running stories about how "traitors" had betrayed the gallant officers of Fort Jackson.[34] Fanning the flames, the board of aldermen praised General Duncan for his "noble deeds," in effect absolving him of responsibility for the fort's surrender. On May 2, General Duncan used the pages of the *Daily Picayune* to call his loyal soldiers "brave men" while condemning the rest as "traitors" and "renegades."[35] In the turbulent atmosphere of early May, such words served as official license to exact revenge against the mutineers.

Looking back, the reporter for the *Boston Journal* recalled that "it is a desperate game that has been played here." Perhaps remembering Duncan's words in the *Picayune*, he wrote that "there is talk of 'traitors at Fort Jackson.' It is true," he wrote, "there were 'traitors' to the cruel rule that put men into an army to fight a people from whose firesides they had not been separated three years."[36] Still, the mob responded to the talk of "traitors." At least one man from the Fort Jackson garrison was "set upon by the rowdies" on May 7, only barely escaping to Union lines.[37] He stands as another example of the dangers the mutineers faced if they returned to the city.

Confederate leaders knew, however, that they needed more than threats if they wanted to regain the lost allegiance of the fort's garrison. No longer able to compel obedience, they looked for ways to keep men from defecting to the Union. As his first blush of anger passed, General Duncan realized that perhaps he had erred by insulting his rebellious men. Could he win them back, or at least keep them out of blue uniforms? Duncan soon began to do everything he could to ensure that starvation did not push men into the Union ranks. He even arranged to give them the back pay they were due as Confederate soldiers. Duncan ordered Captain M. T. Squires, who had commanded Fort St. Philip, to set up an office in the city from which he could pay men their overdue money. In addition, Duncan coordinated an effort by the city authorities and "the city safety committee to have [the forts' garrisons] boarded and lodged temporarily, all with the view of preventing them from going over to the enemy through distress and starvation." Duncan's efforts to establish a welfare system that could retain or regain the loyalties of Confederate soldiers were supported by Pierre Soulé, one of the city's leading politicians. Soulé had complained on May 8 that the city was teeming with "the scattered remnants" of the Confederate army, men who were "prowling about in the streets asking for their pay, and having no bread to put in their mouths or to give to their families, and exposed to the temptations which the enemy fails not to hold out to them, to entice them into the Federal ranks."[38] Confederates did what they could, in other words, to make sure that desperation did not drive the men into blue uniforms. As we will see in the next chapter, Benjamin Butler also made sure that the mutineers and their families could draw rations even if they did not enlist in Union regiments. While no member of the garrison ever explained why he later fought for the Union, the men who made this choice clearly were not motivated by hunger.

Not every Confederate agreed with Duncan, Squires, and Soulé that the mutineers and deserters could be won back with food, lodging, and money. Lieutenant Colonel Edward Higgins, late of Fort Jackson, protested to Richmond that these payments "reward the scoundrels and traitors who have inflicted such a dreadful blow." He wrote on May 21, "Many of these men have already enlisted with the enemy and it is my belief that nearly all will do so when their money is spent."[39] Nor was Higgins alone in his bleak assessment. A staff officer complained that five companies of the 22nd Louisiana Regiment had been taken prisoner (two at Fort Jackson) and "have not since been exchanged + it is understood that they dont [sic] wish to be." Even Duncan himself admitted defeat as early as May 13. Having done what he could to buy the loyalty of his former soldiers, he realized that money would not make them Confederates. "Notwithstand-

The Many Fates of the Fort Jackson Garrison

ing that they were thus amply provided for," he wrote, "scores of them have been daily going over to the enemy and enlisting since, until now there are but a few left from either fort not in the ranks of the enemy." He continued his grim report: "Although I really did think at the time of the surrender that some few of the men were loyal, the facts which have since come to light have perfectly satisfied me that nearly every man in both forts was thoroughly implicated and concerned in the revolt on the night of April 27, with the exception of the company of Saint Mary's Cannoneers, composed mostly of planters."[40] Faced with a variety of ways to earn money, most of the garrison chose to stay in New Orleans either as Union citizens or soldiers. In those ways, they reaffirmed the allegiance that they had adopted on the night they mutinied.

The historical record reveals only glimpses of what the men in the Fort Jackson garrison did after the mutiny, but it is certain that they no longer acted as a group. Rather, the men appear to have pursued a variety of courses. Some aimed to get out of a war in which they may never have felt much interest. These men tried to enter the civilian economy, a tough mission in a moribund economy. Among this group of men were fifteen veterans of Forts Jackson and St. Philip, who petitioned General Butler for steamship tickets to a northern port. Willis Reynolds and Alexander Ashton, both of whom had been temporarily sentenced to death for their plot to desert from Fort Jackson, placed their names at the head of the petition. Hoping for free "passage out of the Southern states," the men warned Butler that some of them might be driven by desperation "to enlist in the Southern Army," though it seems unlikely that Reynolds and Ashton, at any rate, would want to go down that road again. Also in May, a group of Fort St. Philip veterans said in a petition that they could not "get employment in the city" and therefore had "no chance of paying for there [sic] support." Claiming to be facing eviction, the men asked Butler for "some means of subsistence" so that desperation would not drive them to break their "*Parole* of *Honor*" and reenlist in the Confederate army.[41] Whether they hoped to escape from New Orleans or accept charity from General Butler, these thirty-seven petitioners hoped to stay out of the war. That they were willing to work with Federal authorities to accomplish that goal indicates how indifferent they were to the Confederate cause.

Other men from Fort Jackson allied themselves more closely with the Union cause. These Unionist southerners defected to the U.S. military in

The Many Fates of the Fort Jackson Garrison

one form or another. Confederate officers knew that some of their men had never returned to New Orleans. Wary of going home, many of the mutineers stayed near the Quarantine Station and Fort Jackson throughout May and probably even longer. Even several days after the surrender, men in the 26th Massachusetts at the Quarantine Station were still being ordered to "disarm all that may come" into their lines. However, their orders hinted that many of the Confederates who surrendered would harbor Unionist sympathies. The men on the picket line were told to "pass such as will take the oath of allegiance."[42] Once passed into Union lines, the men soon found work helping to rebuild Fort Jackson.

Presumably, these men appreciated the irony of their situation. Many of them had worked on Fort Jackson for the past year, including making emergency repairs while under Union mortar fire. Now, men who gave their oath of allegiance to the United States could do the same work, though for the same people who had sent the mortar shells screaming at them for much of April. But it is also likely that the men enjoyed working for the United States more than they did for the Confederacy. Certainly, their wages improved. A reporter who interviewed Colonel E. F. Jones, commander at Fort Jackson, thought that the men who worked there fared well. By his count, "at least 200" of the men "who had mutinied and deserted to the woods and swamps in the vicinity of the forts, have been gradually dropping in" to find work. Carpenters and masons, he noted, were "in great demand" and were paid $2.50 per day plus a soldier's ration of food. Unskilled laborers, so large a part of the garrison, also found work, wages, and food. The correspondent, no doubt reflecting the colonel's assessment, wrote that "all, without exception, on reaching the fort, expressed an ardent desire to take the oath of allegiance to the United States, which was administered, and will, I venture to affirm, be most religiously kept."[43]

Despite good wages and relative safety, life at Fort Jackson still had its drawbacks. Mosquitoes bothered everyone, and the heat and hard work were unpleasant. It is hard to know how men reacted to the orders requiring them to bathe twice a week—"using soap." But for former Confederates, the isolation they had known may have lessened. It is possible, though not documented, that the wives of the former Confederates, many of whom had been laundresses at the Quarantine, found their way into the Union camp as workers. Certainly, the Union commanders welcomed es-

The Many Fates of the Fort Jackson Garrison

Many former members of the Confederate garrison were hired by the United States to help repair Fort Jackson, shown here by Daniel Nestell as needing work after the battle. (Special Collections and Archives Division, Nimitz Library, U.S. Naval Academy)

caping slaves into their lines as laundresses to help with the cleanliness campaign.[44] By restoring families, the Union commanders may have gone another step toward securing the loyalties of their new allies.

Many of the mutineers did more than just try to escape the war or find jobs with the Union army. Like Thomas Graham, some members of the Fort Jackson garrison volunteered for the U.S. military. They did so, in some cases, quite soon after the mutiny. Letters from General Duncan and other Confederates suggest that this trend was visible by the middle of May. Union documents reinforce this impression. An official U.S. recruiting station opened in New Orleans on or before May 12, about the time that the streets came under full Union control. By May 24, 1862, Benjamin Butler ordered "a detachment of Loyal volunteers" to Fort Livingston to help drive off nearby Confederate troops. His orders included a warning that the men were "to be treated and respected as in the service of the United States."[45] Union muster rolls and regimental books provide more evidence of early enlistments. They indicate that New Orleans residents began enlisting as early as May 2, the day after Union troops landed in the city. The first week of May saw quite a few recruits come into "northern" regiments looking to make good losses they had suffered from disease, and the volunteers kept coming in throughout the month. Richard Elliott's Massachusetts unit recruited twelve Germans from New Orleans, all "fine musicians," to form a regimental band. Homer Sprague's 12th Connecticut had lost 220 men but found an equal number waiting to enlist in the Crescent City. A cavalry captain promised Butler that "recruits can easily

The Many Fates of the Fort Jackson Garrison

be procured." Former Confederate sailors also began joining Union ships' crews by the middle of May.[46] The speed with which these volunteers acted suggests that they welcomed the opportunity to fight for the Union, even though they could draw upon Union and Confederate charities in this period.

By September, Benjamin Butler reported that "more than 1,200" Loui- siana men had been enlisted in his "northern" regiments.[47] Although many of the Union regimental books and muster rolls have been lost, an examination of the records of seven Union infantry regiments and one artillery battery reveals some characteristics of the 503 New Orleans recruits who joined these particular "northern" units. Almost all the men volunteered before the end of September, when most of the units moved up the Mississippi River toward Vicksburg. The men who enlisted in New Orleans came from a range of occupations. Regimental books reveal the past jobs of many of the 503 volunteers: 198 (50.8 percent) held skilled positions, 72 (18.5 percent) were in semiskilled jobs, and the remaining 120 (30.8 percent) were unskilled. Records also give the place of birth for 455 of the 503 men. Not surprisingly, immigrants made up the majority of the volunteers. Irish (32.1 percent) and Germans (31 percent) each made up almost a third of the 455 volunteers. Other European nations, ranging from Sweden to Italy, supplied an additional 15.8 percent of the enlistees. In all, 373 immigrants (including men from Canada, Mexico, and the West Indies) were among the 455 men (82 percent) who enlisted in New Orleans that summer. The remaining 82 volunteers (18 percent) had been born in the United States; more than half of the native-born men (48, or 58.5 percent) were born in northern states. The remaining 34 men (7.5 percent) were born in slave states. Of these, 14 (3.1 percent) were born in New Orleans, 13 (2.9 percent) in the rest of the Confederacy, and 7 (1.5 percent) in border slave states and the District of Columbia. Clearly, the Union volunteers in New Orleans came from immigrant and northern communities. Still, the presence of 34 southerners (7.5 percent of enlistees) among these recruits suggests that not all southern whites embraced the Confederacy.[48] This was not really a war of "North against South," and not just because about 100,000 blacks from the Confederate states enlisted in the Union army. It was a war between the United States of America and the Confederate States of America. At least some native-born southerners and many foreign-born men who made their home in New Orleans—possibly for

The Many Fates of the Fort Jackson Garrison

much of their young lives—chose to support the United States and its laws, government, and values.

Nor were these recruits the only white men in New Orleans to enlist in the Union army. In July, pressured by New Orleans natives such as Charles May, Bernhard Becker, Joseph P. Murphy, and C. Renaud, Benjamin Butler asked the War Department to fund recruiting expenses for Union regiments from Louisiana. The first regiment, as one Massachusetts soldier reported, "was raised very quickly." Another soldier wrote that the 1st Louisiana Volunteers was "nearly or quite raised" by July 23, meaning that about 1,000 men had enlisted in it in less than a month. Recruiting for the 2nd Louisiana Volunteers began shortly thereafter. Among the recruits were "white slaves," men who had been born to enslaved mothers but who could pass for whites. Bolstered by these men, the regiment had about 400 recruits by early September. In late October, Charles J. Paine happily told his father that the regiment had gained enough strength to be mustered in, although it was not yet at full strength. Meanwhile, recruiting for the 1st Louisiana Cavalry Regiment had begun. In all, more than 5,000 men would serve in "white" Louisiana regiments.[49]

But what of the men of the Fort Jackson garrison? Did they, as Duncan and others thought, enlist in Union regiments? Here the evidence is less clear. John W. De Forest of the 12th Connecticut agreed with Duncan's assessment. He wrote in July that "probably half the fellows who defended the forts against us are already wearing our uniform," with some serving in the 12th Connecticut and "many more in the Ninth [Connecticut]."[50] But this is hard to prove. Union regimental books are often incomplete. In addition, both Confederate and Union records often spell the same man's name several different ways, which baffles efforts to determine whether a person listed on Confederate muster rolls subsequently enrolled in a Union regiment. The attempt to match up names is sometimes aided by muster rolls that list a recruit's age, since two people who have very similar names and are the same age are likely to be the same person. For example, John Christonia of the 1st Louisiana Heavy Artillery and John Chrystona of the 12th Maine (who joined in New Orleans) are the same age, thereby increasing the likelihood that they are the same person. But there is a larger problem with matching up names from Confederate and Union muster rolls. Men seem to have often used aliases when they enlisted, presumably to avoid identification by Confederates if they were captured. There is, of

The Many Fates of the Fort Jackson Garrison

course, no way to determine how many men fought under an alias, but the practice could have been quite common. The entry for Daniel Bernhardt in the 30th Massachusetts's Descriptive Book records that he "enlisted under assumed name." His "real" last name may well have been Levy. Serving under an alias had been a widespread practice among Anglo-American sailors in the War of 1812 and earlier, especially among men who had deserted from English ships and who would be hanged if they were recaptured and recognized.[51] Men who abandoned the Confederacy to fight for the Union ran similar risks. Using an alias could at least offer a first line of defense in the event of capture, but it means that historians cannot easily trace men from Fort Jackson into Union ranks.

Despite these problems, the names of thirty-one men from the Fort Jackson garrison can be found in "northern" regiments. This is a small fraction of the garrison, a bit less than 5 percent. It is hard to determine whether these men enlisted out of necessity or out of sympathy with the Union cause. Some evidence suggests that the men enlisted because it was a job, perhaps one with which they were already familiar. These veterans of other armies may have enlisted with the Union because it was convenient at the time. Jeremiah Coffee, for example, had lived a military life long before the American Civil War started. Coffee was 31 years old when he volunteered for the 13th Connecticut on May 20, 1862; he was remembered by a regimental officer as clean and "soldierly," perhaps because of his prior service "before Sebastopol" in the Crimean War. In October, Coffee became the regiment's first casualty, suffering a head wound at Georgia Landing. He recovered, only to be killed at Irish Bend in December.[52] Two other men from Fort Jackson, Peter Gurnett and James McDonald, later transferred to the U.S. Regular Army, a move that meant that they would stay employed in the military after the war ended.[53] For these men, military service probably looked like a good career.

However, the men may have genuinely favored the Union cause. Again, the evidence is sketchy but significant. Many of the men enlisted in the Union cause very soon after they returned to New Orleans. Of the thirty-one men, twelve (38.7 percent) joined in May, with Louis Freedman, a 21-year-old Polish huckster, leading the way on May 6. With only one exception, the men had joined up by the end of August. Such speed suggests a motive other than food and shelter, both of which were made available by Union and Confederate commanders at this point. Nor were the volunteers

The Many Fates of the Fort Jackson Garrison

necessarily the poorest men in the old garrison. Only six of the thirty-one men were listed as "laborers" by their recruiting officers, a slightly lower figure than in the old garrison as a whole. Finally, only three of the men subsequently deserted from the Union army.[54] Although a 10 percent desertion rate sounds high, the men served close to New Orleans for several

years and therefore had a good chance to flee and lose themselves in the city if they so chose. Many Civil War soldiers deserted under far less favorable circumstances, often traveling hundreds of miles before reaching home. Indeed, Union recruits enlisted in New Orleans gained a solid combat record and a reasonably low desertion rate.[55] As one Union veteran wrote, "These New Orleans men were a valuable accession to our ranks, many of them being brave men, experienced in war."[56]

Working-class people do not always have many options in their life, but the men who had been stationed in Fort Jackson did have some choices in the late spring of 1862. Men from St. Mary's Parish chose to return to their homes and by doing so made themselves available for prisoner exchange and further Confederate military service. But other men did not make that choice, even though they certainly could have. Even the soldiers who had passively watched as the mutiny took place seem to have returned to Union-held New Orleans. Though General Duncan offered them lodging and food, very few accepted his offer. Instead, they turned to the United States, thereby cementing the allegiance they had made clear when they refused to obey orders in the isolated brick fort far down the river. Some put on civilian clothes and tried to earn a living, often with the Union's help. Others took jobs working for the United States at Fort Jackson. And others—no one can know how many—donned Union uniforms and fought against the Confederacy at Irish Bend, Port Hudson, and across the bayous of southern Louisiana. These men's decisions tell us that immigrants and native-born Americans alike faced complicated choices about which nation they would support for the rest of the war. That so many chose the most hazardous of the options open to them and backed the United States means that that country appeared to be worth the risk of their lives.

The lives of these men tell the story of a Civil War that was not one of North against South. Historians have known that many southerners—the ones who were enslaved when the war started—almost always acted decisively to ensure Union victory when they could. The role of white southerners who endorsed the Union remains less well known. Even recent

The Many Fates of the Fort Jackson Garrison

scholarship about Unionist whites has looked for them in the South's poorer, rural regions. The non-slaveholding people of the Appalachian Mountains have attracted the most attention, along with those living in the piney woods regions of the Confederacy. Finding Unionists in the urban South complicates our understanding of who the white Unionists were and how they came to their beliefs. Rather than coming from economically backwards parts of the South, New Orleans Unionists were deeply immersed in regional and global trade networks. Like the most modern of people, they worked for wages in jobs at least once removed from agriculture. As immigrants who had already chosen the United States as their home, they pursued their Unionism out of a variety of motives that had little in common with their peers in eastern Tennessee or northern Alabama. Hurt by the Confederate experiment's ruinous economy, discriminatory politics, and anti-immigrant culture, many whites in the Crescent City eagerly embraced a return of the U.S. flag to New Orleans. The city's working-class Unionists found a strong champion in the administration of General Benjamin F. Butler.

benjamin f. butler and unionist new orleans

New Orleans experienced dramatic changes after the arrival of U.S. troops. Slavery, not yet dead, nevertheless cracked as enslaved people sought even a tenuous freedom behind Union lines. Whites also adjusted to life under the "Old Flag." They did this far more quickly than we might have supposed; Union troops moved easily about the city soon after their arrival. After about six months, the United States held congressional elections, and loyal white men cast ballots to determine who would represent them. The transformation into a Union city did not, of course, happen by accident. The commander of the Department of the Gulf, Major General Benjamin F. Butler, worked with New Orleans Unionists to organize already loyal citizens and rally additional men and women to the United States. Working both on the streets and in the halls of power, Benjamin Butler and local loyalists managed to make the city safely Unionist by the end of 1862.

Benjamin F. Butler has perhaps the worst reputation of any Union general in the Civil War. Loathed by Confederates, their descendants, tour guides, and many historians, he rarely receives praise even from northerners. He is condemned as a "political general," a politician who received his high rank solely on the basis of his ability to inspire fellow Democrats to enlist. He was handicapped by a lack of military training, especially during his service in Virginia and North Carolina during the war's final year. His mistakes there make it easy for historians to discount his largely successful administration of New Orleans from May until December 1862. The United States, forced to govern a city of 170,000 people, needed a skilled urban politician to do the job. Butler proved to be just the man for the job.

Benjamin Butler could not have accomplished what he did in New Orleans without the political training he had received in Lowell, Massachusetts. While Lowell had only about a quarter of New Orleans's population, its emergence as an industrial city meant that Butler had grown up in a capitalist economy like that of the Crescent City.[1] Lowell's diverse population also made him comfortable around working men and women, whether they were immigrants or native-born, Catholics, Protestants, or freethinkers. Such workers had been Butler's most reliable constituents. Once in Louisiana, he could recognize the hostility many wage workers felt toward the Confederate elite. He also knew how to secure their allegiance to the Federal government. Butler had spent his Lowell years learning the value of street theater and patronage in building a political movement.

Charlotte Butler moved to Lowell with her son when Ben was about 12 years old. Charlotte, a widow, had kept the family afloat by opening a boardinghouse that served as Butler's introduction to working-class life. Even though he eventually owned a large share of the Middlesex Mills, Butler never felt any passion for Lowell's factories. Convinced that long hours, hard manual labor, and rushed meals injured many workers, he looked to politics for a remedy. Beginning in 1840, he became one of the city's leading proponents of the ten-hour work day.[2] Within a year, the young attorney helped to start *Vox Populi*, a newspaper that embraced a wide range of labor reforms.[3] Butler also tried to help his poorer constituents by calling attention to the conditions in the state's almshouses. During 1858, he said, 666 of the 2,700 inmates in the state almshouses had died, including 341 children. Never one to turn away from a controversial turn of phrase, Butler said that the children had "died like dogs in a kennel in our own almshouses."[4] Focused on improving the lives of the poor, he also routinely called for a tax code that would help the working class.[5] Unlike most of his contemporaries, he reasoned that since the rich benefited the most from the government's protection, they should pay a higher share of the tax burden.

Butler knew that the population of Lowell had become increasingly diverse, and he embraced this trend. He became one of the first of a long line of Massachusetts politicians to boast of his Irish ancestry. Speaking in the state senate in 1859, Butler proclaimed, "I thank God, sir, that in some far off degree the old Irish blood runs in my veins."[6] He also matched his words with legislative action. He urged the state to reimburse the Catholic Church after an Ursuline Convent was burned by a Charlestown mob in 1834.[7] Nor did he shy away from censuring England for causing starvation in Ireland in the late 1840s and 1850s.[8] Later, when the state's Know-Nothing governor disbanded militia companies made up of Irish immigrants, Butler, a militia officer, refused the direct order. The governor dismissed him, a serious blow to a man who so enjoyed serving in the militia. While his fellow officers responded by electing him to an even higher office, he had proved his willingness to stand up to nativist pressure.[9] Butler also spoke out in favor of making citizenship dependent on place of residence, not place of birth.[10] Butler's pro-immigrant stand made him a popular speaker at Democratic events. One correspondent wrote in 1853, "The Irish people are fast coming round to their support of the new [state] Constitution and you gave them a grand lift last night." If there was one thing he could not stand, it was a man who deserted the Democratic Party for the Know-Nothings.[11]

Butler's record in Lowell as a defender of black workers is much more varied, and this inconsistency, too, comes across in his administration in New Orleans. At times before the war, Butler worked with the antislavery movement; at other times he exploited racism as blatantly as any other politician of his time. Whereas his support of white workers proved almost automatic, Butler allowed his stand on black rights to be dictated by political expediency. In this, he mirrored the antebellum labor movement's ambivalent relationship with abolitionism.[12] He may have started with genuine antislavery leanings to match his democratic sentiments. In 1846, the

Benjamin F. Butler and Unionist New Orleans

Free Will Baptist Church of Lowell engaged Butler's services to settle a boundary dispute. It is hard to imagine that the Free Will Baptists, a denomination formed to denounce slaveholding, would have hired a lawyer with decidedly pro-slavery views.[13] During the early 1850s, he was part of a Democratic Party coalition with the antislavery Free Soil Party in Massachusetts. Gaining control of the state senate in 1851, the coalition elected the antislavery activist Charles Sumner to the U.S. Senate.[14] This coalition, however, was soon busted apart by the national Democratic Party, which was becoming more proslavery during the mid- and late 1850s. With national patronage now dependent on toeing a proslavery line, Butler changed his positions. He now mustered his rhetorical skills to keep black men out of the state militia and supported—quite adamantly—the proslavery administration of James Buchanan.[15] Butler's record in New Orleans reflected a similar pattern of political expediency. In 1862 he looked to the Lincoln administration for patronage, and he adhered to Lincoln's moderate policies by at times stifling subordinates who advanced black equality more quickly than the president thought prudent. At other moments, Butler promoted black rights when it suited Lincoln and the Union cause to do so. Through it all, however, he consistently supported white wage workers.

Inclined by his upbringing to support white workers, Butler also brought to Lowell's politics a fierce determination to succeed. The 1851 Lowell elections demonstrate his tenacity and also his early grasp of street theater. Butler's support of the ten-hour work day and of the secret ballot, which would protect wage earners from retribution by their employers, came to a head in 1851. Butler led a coalition ticket of Free Soilers and Democrats committed to capping an industrial work day at ten hours.[16] Nine of the ten coalition candidates won, only to have the mayor and city council invalidate the election because of allegations of voter fraud. A Free Soil newspaper in Lowell called it "CHEATING the people," but the decision stood.[17] Just before the rescheduled election, the owners of the Hamilton Mills warned that they would fire any employee who voted for a ten-hour day candidate. Before a packed crowd, Butler accused the Hamilton Mills of telling their employees to "vote as your masters permit you to do, and thereby become their slaves."[18] Such language was not unique to Butler during this election. The Democratic and Free Soil newspapers, such as the *Lowell Advertiser*, urged readers to "BE MEN, not serfs or slaves."[19]

Butler, however, went well beyond the rhetoric of his peers. His speech also included a rhetorical threat that presages his later warnings to the Confederates of New Orleans: "As God lives and I live, by the living Jehovah! if one man is driven from his employment by these men because of his vote, I will lead you to make Lowell what it was twenty-five years ago, —a sheep pasture and a fishing place; and I will commence by applying the torch to my own house. Let them come on. As we are not the aggressors, we seek not this awful contest."[20] The mill owners retracted their threat. The coalition won the election, and Butler's star rose in the party. In addition, Butler had learned the value of dramatic yet plausible threats of violence. As he would in New Orleans, he played on his opponents' worst fears about what he might do.[21]

Benjamin Butler's private life holds another key to the political education he would bring to the South in 1862. In 1844, he married Sarah Hildreth, the daughter of an established Democratic family in neighboring Dracut. At the time of their engagement, Sarah worked as a professional actress.[22] Although she quit the stage upon her marriage, she never lost her sense of herself as a public figure. On a visit to her husband during the war, Sarah wrote to her sister, "It was my duty to play the courtier to the people who have it in their power to send troops here and everything else that is wanted."[23] Transferring her stage experience to the parlor and headquarters where she "played" the part of "the courtier," Sarah would have been a knowledgeable person to whom Ben could turn for strategies on how to exploit the public arena.

While Butler's sense of the dramatic may have exceeded that of many of his peers, he also learned a more mundane political skill in Lowell. Patronage, the lifeblood of the country's fledgling democracy, became one of his most effective weapons, and he quickly learned how to translate federal jobs and money into political support. A political neophyte when he married into the Hildreth clan, Butler soon found himself working the patronage network of Middlesex County Democrats. Sarah's brother Fisher Hildreth owned the *Lowell Daily Advertiser*, which printed Butler's speeches verbatim and supported his positions through good times and bad. In return, Butler rewarded Fisher with the Lowell postmastership and helped him negotiate the tortuous shifts in Democratic Party politics in the 1850s. Indeed, patronage is a key to understanding Butler's racism in

Benjamin Butler, with his dog, in a prewar photograph. (Courtesy of the Massachusetts Historical Society)

this period. His need to please southern politicians who controlled federal patronage in the 1850s compelled him to take unpopular stands on slavery—even to the point of supporting Jefferson Davis for the 1860 Democratic Party presidential nomination. By the 1850s, Butler had learned the power of patronage, and he used it adeptly while he governed New Orleans.[24]

When Butler left Lowell with his beloved militia in the spring of 1861, he took with him a working-class outlook and a range of skills and tactics that he had honed in Lowell. His troops would be among the first to arrive in Washington, D.C., and Baltimore, securing those cities for the Union. One year later, he would find himself leading fifteen thousand U.S. troops into New Orleans. Throughout his time there, Butler would draw repeatedly on the political lessons and dramatic flourishes he had mastered on the banks of the Merrimac.

Benjamin F. Butler and Unionist New Orleans

When Benjamin Butler declared martial law in New Orleans on May 1, 1862, he assumed control of many of the functions of government. While he attempted briefly to work with the mayor and the city council, he gradually took over more and more control. As he had in Lowell, Butler rewarded his allies with patronage and issued threats (as well as punishments) to anyone who stood in his way. Through his reorganization of the city's police force, his partnership with the city's Union Association, his use of band music and flag raisings, his charitable works and his stern edicts, he demonstrated his power and won over people to the Union. His actions turned the city streets into a theater, and the play's plot revealed that the United States was more powerful and more benevolent than the Confederacy had ever been. Through his actions, he helped the white Unionist community become a viable political force in time for elections in December 1862. Confederates in and outside the city were forced to acknowledge that many of the city's whites had proclaimed their allegiance to the Union. In part, their vehement hatred of Butler—Confederate president Jefferson Davis declared him "an outlaw and a common enemy of mankind" and authorized his execution should he be captured—had its roots in Butler's ability to prove the single most damaging thing that could be said about the Confederacy: it did not enjoy the unanimous support of the white South.[25] To say that was to undermine the Confederacy's legitimacy as a nation, and Butler's New Orleans said just that every day.

Benjamin Butler arrived in Louisiana with a clear understanding of the tensions that existed between classes in an urban economy like that of New Orleans or Lowell. Almost immediately, he moved to exploit the alienation workers felt from the Confederate elite. By the time Confederate forces left the city, hunger and even starvation had become widespread. Union soldier J. E. Goodhue recalled the "great amount of suffering in the city of the poor" caused by high food prices.[26] On May 9, Butler responded by issuing General Order No. 25, which began by recognizing "the deplorable state of destitution and hunger of the mechanics and working classes in this city." Butler blamed the mayor and city council (holdovers from Confederate days) for having shipped as much food as possible *out* of the city with the retreating rebel army. The rich rebels, he said, cared not a bit about the starving poor they left behind. "The hunger does not pinch the wealthy and influential," he wrote. "The leaders of the rebellion, who have gotten up this war, . . . are now endeavoring to prosecute it, without regard to the starving poor, the working man, his wife and child." Now, the United States would distribute food "among the deserving poor of this city, from whom the rebels have plundered it."[27] Confident that honest workmen had been duped by the wealthy into supporting secession, Butler argued that they would now renew their former allegiance. After all, many people had already followed this course, some by mutinying, others by deserting, and still others by enlisting in the Union army.

The Union army began giving food to civilians on May 12, 1862, starting with fresh beef captured from the Confederacy. Crowds of city residents, mostly women, lined up to receive food from an office in the Custom House. Union soldiers were overwhelmed by the desperation they saw before them. The weather was sunny and very warm, but the people crowded together and pressed one another toward the door. Connecticut soldier H. W. Howe estimated that one thousand women showed up for food that day. A Vermont solider wrote that he "saw a large collection of women and children yesterday with their baskets pressing to get their share of the provisions as though they were pressed hard with hunger." A 21-year-old private, Charles Blake, was among the fifty soldiers detailed to distribute food. When he arrived, he "found a constantly increasing crowd, waiting our coming. We first cleared an open space in front of the door and then letting a few pass at a time, we endeavored to keep order outside," he wrote. "But it was striving against those who were starving. Three times they broke through our lines, and once broke the door down. We had to charge bayonets on them. They were nearly all women. . . . I never felt worse in my life." Even though many of Butler's soldiers came from cities where hunger was a fact of life for the poor, desperation on so large a scale clearly took them aback. Hunger, a soldier wrote, "stands guard at every door."[28]

Familiar with the press of people eager for food, a Louisville editor made the rather callous joke that while the people of New Orleans might not like Butler's martial law, they did "like its 'provisions.'"[29] Nor did the food lines go away, even after Lincoln reopened the port on June 1, 1862. During one week in October, the U.S. Relief Commission gave out food to

32,150 people in New Orleans. These recipients, like the ones in May, had had to take the oath of allegiance before getting in line. Although some desperate pro-Confederate civilians took the oath, the Relief Commission's statistics resemble the profile of volunteers for the Union army. Only 9.5 percent of food recipients had been born in the United States; Irish (37 percent), Germans (32.6 percent), and other Europeans (14.4 percent) constituted the majority. The parallel constituencies are not coincidental, since 1,052 of the *families* that received relief were the relatives of Union soldiers. Even though some Confederates took the oath to get food, Butler's food program mostly rewarded the Union's allies. With this relief, Butler helped to guarantee the continued loyalty of the people who had welcomed his arrival. He also reached out to people who had spent the first year of the war as passive Confederates.[30]

Benjamin Butler's efforts to aid Unionists went beyond passing out free food. Along with his military commander of New Orleans, George F. Shepley, Butler combined economic policy and personal charity to make life in the Union better than it had been under the Confederacy. Shepley fixed a maximum price for bread, a move favored by the city's poor. When bakers evaded the law, Shepley threatened to seize their bakeries and have them operated by Union soldiers.[31] The bakers backed down. Another part of the Union economic strategy was to replace Confederate currency with U.S. greenbacks. This policy, known as General Order No. 30, sought to redress the economic wrongs of the Confederacy. The discontinuation of Confederate currency could have hurt everyone who held those notes. Butler, however, sought to make banks feel all the pain. The losses entailed by the currency switch, he said, should fall "on those who have caused" the city's people such "great distress, privation, suffering, hunger, and even starvation." Since bankers had encouraged people to accept Confederate notes, Butler forced them to redeem Confederate notes in specie, U.S. money, or the current notes of the bank. Some banks failed as a result, but the order helped "the poor and unwary" to hold off utter ruin. General Order No. 30, in the eyes of the *New York Herald*'s reporter, "has already been productive of a vast amount of good in restoring the old spirit of attachment to the Union." He added that "the improvement in the feelings of the citizens has become a palpable thing within the past few days; one can see it in the people as they pass through the streets, and feel its influence pervading the atmosphere of public opinion. The citizens are no longer afraid to be seen near headquarters, or speaking with Union officers or soldiers, who can now walk singly and unarmed through the city as safely as they could in any Northern city." Businesses reopened; commerce picked up.[32]

To complete the picture of the United States as the champion of the poor, both Butler and Shepley made personal donations to New Orleans churches. In part, Butler may have given gifts to the Sisters of Charity and Catholic orphanages to help win over the Catholic hierarchy, which had vigorously supported the Confederacy. It seems more likely, however, that Butler and Shepley, who gave money to the Episcopal Church's Children's House, hoped to curry favor with the parishioners.[33] Gifts to nunneries and orphanages would appeal to a broad cross section of people.

Confederates tried to develop arguments against Butler's economic policies even as working-class people (and others) benefited from them. The Confederates condemned Butler's special tax on people and businesses that had donated money to the Confederate defense fund in 1861. Butler countered, however, that if they could afford to give money to the rebellion, they could now help buy food for the poor. But Confederates denounced Butler's use of the government to help the needy. The anonymous "President of the council of ten" threatened Butler "with the Corsican *Vendetta*" in a letter delivered to his headquarters. The writer complained, "It seems to be a settled purpose with you . . . *to rob us in the name of the poor*."[34] To this man, Butler's relief work boiled down to theft; while the author made other charges, this was the only one he underlined for emphasis. Other Confederates picked up the issue. A Mississippi editor said that Butler's "attempts to excite the poor against the rich, and to force the unfortunate population of [New Orleans], by the stern gnawings of hunger, to take up arms against their country, is truly a magnificent 'Yankee trick.'"[35] Eager to denounce Butler's policies, neither man explained why Butler's ideas would not work for most people in the city.

Louisiana's governor, Thomas O. Moore, tried to step into that breach. Elected governor in 1859, Moore was a wealthy sugar planter from Rapides Parish, and he was well versed in proslavery arguments. Aware that the Confederacy was losing the support of many people in New Orleans, he tried to explain how slavery benefited all whites. His words warrant attention, if only to demonstrate how hard he worked to construct his argument:

General Butler's attempt to incite the poor against the more wealthy is characteristic of the man, and is as mean as it is contemptible. He springs from a race [northerners] that has ever been purse-proud when fortune favored them, and idolatrous worshippers of the almighty dollar. He comes from a section of [the] country that has done more than any other to degrade and cheapen labor and reduce the laboring man to the condition of slave—a section that has warred against slavery because its natural tendency is to keep up the price of white labor, and elevate the white laborer—a section that has always contended that the government should take care of the rich and leave the rich to take care of the poor.

He continued:

The workingmen of the South know full well that this war on the part of the North is not so much against the institution of slavery as it is against its influence upon labor. Men get better prices for their services where slavery exists, than in the free states. Labor in the South is capital. Consequently it is the object of all who depend upon labor, directly or indirectly, for a support, to keep up its price. There are those in the South who have not sense enough to understand this question in its true light, hence we find a few, not natives, or to the manor born, however, who may be found affiliating with the invaders. If all such will only leave the South with the invaders, their coming will have done some good. We want no white men among us who would consent to take the negro's place.[36]

Moore's claim that slavery benefited white laborers has been widely questioned by historians, who have seen unpaid labor as exerting a general downward pull on wages in the slave states.[37] These historians use much the same logic as people who argue that low wages in China and elsewhere undercut pay scales in the United States and Western Europe. But whether Moore was correct is not really the point. It is Moore's attention to the issue that is so remarkable. Like the Mississippi editor, the governor was concerned that Butler had won the loyalty of many white southerners. Moore clearly felt the need to fight for the hearts and minds of many of Louisiana's citizens, and he had every reason to be concerned.

Butler also built a patronage network that would serve as the founda-

Benjamin F. Butler and Unionist New Orleans

tion for a Unionist political movement. In the middle of a broken economy, Butler found many men willing to take the oath of allegiance in order to be hired by his administration. In early June, he ordered the city council and the United States to hire 2,000 men to clean out stagnant drainage canals throughout the city, keeping them on the payroll for "at least thirty working days" at the generous wage of fifty cents per day, plus a full army ration of food.[38] Celebrated for making the city's water cleaner and thus protecting New Orleans from its seemingly annual yellow fever outbreak, Butler's bands of workers with hoses, rakes, and hoes did more than flush out the festering waterways. The employed men also learned that the United States had brought them work.

The men cleaning out the canals did not labor alone. Butler had begun the experiment of exchanging jobs for oaths of allegiance in the first week of his administration. On May 6, he granted Thomas Jones, a shipping pilot, permission to work in return for his allegiance.[39] In the middle of June, a group of impoverished former Confederate soldiers asked for jobs cleaning the streets; Shepley "instantly granted" the request as long as the men swore an oath of allegiance. By the end of the month, the United States employed 3,000 men cleaning the city's streets. Two hundred more men took the oath of allegiance before starting jobs under the Collector of the Port. Other men worked in miscellaneous, short-term jobs that nevertheless paid well; in one small example, 15 people shared the work of "repairing and cleansing the House and outbuildings" at 13 Prytania Street, earning two dollars a day.[40] Working for the government became a major part of the city's economy for the rest of 1862, and Butler and Shepley were kept busy answering inquiries for jobs and their accompanying declarations of loyalty.[41]

The most dramatic patronage showdown came in the wake of Butler's decision that every city police officer must swear an oath of allegiance to the United States. Because the Know-Nothings had handpicked policemen who would aid their party on election days, Butler had inherited a police force devoted to Mayor Monroe and the Confederacy.[42] As a result, his demand that officers take an oath of allegiance caused a nearly universal resignation from the department. Ann Penrose, a resident of New Orleans who backed the Confederacy, rejoiced that all but 2 officers had refused to swear the oath; the fact that 11 men actually continued in the force hardly matters. Penrose also reported that the Union would need 500 recruits to fill the vacated posts, and she happily doubted that they would find enough men willing to take the job.[43] In this, she was only partially correct. Within a month, the Union had added 370 new men to the force. The overwhelming majority of the recruits joined within a week.[44] Butler's public works projects helped to build a valuable patronage network for the United States.

Butler's public works program gave wage workers exactly what they wanted from city government. Throughout the antebellum era, many of the city's workers had supported the Know-Nothings because they had started large public works projects and paid decent wages.[45] Now, labor activists saw Butler's hiring spree and reconsidered their opposition to Union government. As a former ten-hour day activist, Butler would have known that labor movements could rally thousands of people to the Union cause. Labor activists in turn no doubt knew about Butler's background in labor politics and approved of it. Indeed, one petition sent to Butler, signed by twenty-five workers, closed by saying, "We hope your honour as you always was a friend of the working class and Poor you will see to us."[46] Workers may very well have expected a labor-friendly government from Butler, and he did not disappoint them. As a result, he would win the support of the labor movement, even if individuals did not personally get a patronage job.

Significantly, the vast majority of the public works jobs that Butler created kept workers outside and very much in public view. Whether they walked a beat, inspected ship cargoes, cleaned streets and drainage canals, or restored buildings, the men who worked for the Union administration did so in front of their friends and neighbors. This meant that everyone in the city knew who had accepted, either wholeheartedly, nominally, or somewhere in between, the advent of U.S. control. Employing Unionists, in that sense, was a kind of street theater, even as it cleaned the streets. In effect, Butler used the streets to display the thousands of men who had taken the oath of allegiance. This display not only demonstrated the size of the Unionist community but also presumably scared off many Confederates who would have taken the oath only because they wanted the paycheck. By having the men work where they would be seen, Butler made it impossible for any devoted Confederate to take his offer and still be true to his political loyalties. For people who might have been indifferent about the war, acceptance of Butler's jobs made them more committed to Union

Benjamin F. Butler and Unionist New Orleans

victory. Given that Confederates had jailed Unionists and seized their property before Farragut's arrival, anyone who now publicly sided with the United States would have to hope, and act, for Union military victory. By making the work so public, Butler both showed how many residents supported the Union and also made the workers more committed to Union victory.

In this and in other ways, Benjamin Butler turned New Orleans into a theater, with the exercise of power as the main action and the superiority of the Union as the moral of the story. The city's people filled in as the audience. Butler, of course, took a starring role. Many of his contemporaries and some historians have called this self-aggrandizement, suspecting that he took the lead role in order to advance his political career. Carl Schurz, a Republican politician and major general, saw Butler earlier in the war and commented that "General Butler thoroughly enjoyed his position of power." Butler, he said,

> keenly appreciated its theatrical possibilities. . . . While we were conversing, officers entered from time to time to make reports or to ask for orders. Nothing could have been more striking than the air of authority with which the General received them, and the tone of curt peremptoriousness peculiar to the military commander on the stage, with which he expressed his satisfaction, or discontent, and with which he gave his instructions. And, after every such scene, he looked around with a sort of triumphant gaze, as if to assure himself that the bystanders were duly impressed.[47]

In New Orleans, however, Butler's theatrical performance may have been helpful to the cause. As he had when he threatened to burn down Lowell in 1851, he understood the need for politicians to occasionally become larger than life. In this, his wife, Sarah Hildreth Butler, the former actress, no doubt helped. As her husband's companion from early May until she left New Orleans on June 11, Sarah sensed that her life was an ongoing public performance.[48] Now, with all eyes on them, the two put on a show, this time with a cast of thousands.

Former Confederate soldiers made up part of Butler's cast. Butler made sure that the thousands of Confederates who had deserted from their units as they withdrew through New Orleans were able to stay quietly in the city. His declaration of martial law on May 1 said that Confederate soldiers

who returned "to peaceful occupations" would not be disturbed. General George Shepley struck the same note in mid-June. His General Order No. 13 offered New Orleans citizens in the Confederate army the chance to come home if they took the oath of allegiance and registered with the Union government. The resulting "crowd of applicants" was so large that Shepley had to extend the deadline twice in order to handle the demand.[49] Butler and Shepley's success took men out of the Confederate army and showed New Orleans citizens that men from the city continued to abandon the rebellion.

Taking an oath of allegiance, so necessary to getting food, a job, or a ticket out of the war, proved to be the most important (and scripted) moment in many New Orleans citizens' lives. At first, Butler held out the

Benjamin F. Butler and Unionist New Orleans

promise of food and employment to those who took the oath. People who took the oath under these circumstances may well have been genuine Unionists, even if most of them had been hesitant to broadcast the fact before Butler's arrival. But by late September, Butler reserved the right to exile any individuals who refused to take the oath. The Union could then also seize their property in accordance with a congressional law passed in July. People with Confederate sympathies soon had to debate whether oaths sworn under duress would be taken at face value by God. Some probably convinced themselves that they could take such an oath without perjuring themselves. Given the powerful incentives to swear allegiance to the old flag, September oaths cannot be considered signs of true Unionist sympathies. Nevertheless, such oaths did mark a significant public concession by the people who swore them. By submitting to U.S. law, they recognized publicly that they were willing to obey (if only as a practical matter) in order to get along with their lives. Thus, Butler sought to publicize the names of not only the 14,500 citizens who took the oath before property confiscation became an issue but also the 46,500 more people who had done so by the end of September. (In contrast, 4,000 people decided that they could not swear their allegiance in good faith and faced the consequences.) The names of oath takers, now at least officially Unionists, were published in the newspapers. People could also see who was going in to swear the oath. One angry Confederate soldier complained in October that black Union soldiers "guard the Yankees who receive the oaths, + our ladies are obliged to pass up thro [sic] a file of them to take the Oath."[50] Not content with recovering or cementing individual loyalties, Butler wanted to make everyone swear the oath visibly in order to convince people that the United States was in charge.

In addition to helping Confederate soldiers ease out of the war, Butler's street show could provide dramatic entertainment. After six paroled prisoners were arrested and sentenced to death for secretly recruiting Confederate volunteers in New Orleans, Butler made a show of halting the executions. Wisely, he credited two native Unionists, J. A. Rosier and Thomas Durant, with convincing him to be lenient.[51] In another pointed demonstration of power, Ben (often with Sarah) took to riding through the streets in an open carriage, sometimes without guards. One staff officer who accompanied him, Robert Davis, confessed in July, "It seems strange to ride in the carriage with him backwards and forewards [sic] from the office to the house, as I do every day, and know and feel that two thirds of the people that we pass hate us as the devil, and would consider it a glorious act to shoot him if they only dared to: but I really think he and all of us are safe, the city is completely cowed."[52] Davis's letter points to the fishbowl in which the Butlers lived. But Davis also knew that no one had dared to kill Butler, a daily fact of life that showed everyone the rebellion's impotence. By risking his own life and living to tell the tale, the general put himself in the spotlight for a larger dramatic purpose. As one Confederate soldier complained, "How my heart aches when I think that in all that multitude of men not one has been found bold enough to attempt the Beast's life. . . . *I say that those cowards deserve* the treatment they are receiving at Butler's hands."[53]

Union leaders also made sure that they commanded the streets by making every day seem like the Fourth of July. Military bands playing patriotic music became a fixture in the city after May 1, and U.S. flags became points of contention between Confederates and Unionists. Patriotic music could both entrance and infuriate Confederate sympathizers. According to the *New York Times* correspondent, the band on the uss *Mississippi* managed to silence a pro-Confederate mob in Algiers on May 5. At the sound of "Hail Columbia," the men in "the rabble ceased howling." Then, "instinctively some of the old men in the throng raised their hats in acknowledgment of the strains which from their youth had inspired them." Patriotic music reminded some people of allegiances they had held as recently as eighteen months ago.[54]

But it did not always have this effect. At times, music provoked Confederate defiance, as when a Wisconsin soldier saw young women "stop up their ears with their fingers" when a band played "the star spangled banner."[55] The same Union band also started a confrontation between the mob and the army on May 2. On that eventful day, when the first New Orleans resident joined the Union army, Edward Bacon and his friend roamed the city alone and unarmed, and the mob harassed Somers, the Unionist recorder, a showdown took place at Butler's headquarters at the St. Charles Hotel. There, Mayor John Monroe summoned his mob while he and Butler negotiated for control over the city. Undaunted, Butler ordered the 4th Wisconsin's band to play from the hotel's portico. The mob, perhaps swayed by happy remembrances, stayed "very quiet" throughout "the Red White & Blue and the Star Spangled Banner," soldier Frank Harding recalled. But, he added, that was not the case when the band started into "Yankey Doodly," which caused "a great commotion in the crowd." On this, the second day of Butler's administration, anarchy loomed. Sarah Butler, an eyewitness, later recalled the uncertainty of the moment. She also spoke of the music's larger purpose. "We could not foresee what would be the result of this," she wrote, "but it was time the Federal power should be established and mob law suppressed."[56] With control of the city hanging in the balance, Butler deployed a battery of field artillery in the street. Reminiscent of Napoleon's then famous use of artillery to gain control over Paris, Butler's deployment of cannons where they could fire into the mob shocked the mayor. Assured by Butler that the cannons would be ordered to fire, Monroe and the mob backed down. From that point forward, neither the mayor nor his mob effectively resisted Union control. The 4th Wisconsin's band returned home late that night, having highlighted Butler's control of New Orleans in a language understood by all, regardless of their literacy or command of English.

If patriotic music spurred some conflicts between Unionists and Confederates (while perhaps dampening others), flags became the most important flash point. Butler still has a reputation for cruelly repressing the people of New Orleans, and almost all the charges brought against him involved his efforts to float U.S. flags and banish Confederate ones. For both sides, flags represented not only national authority but also honor, taking within their folds all the sacrifices and hopes of people at war. Already, Confederate sympathizers had killed Unionist civilians when they flew U.S. flags to welcome Farragut. Now Butler prepared to clear the streets of Confederate emblems.

When Benjamin Butler declared martial law, he ordered that Confederate flags be taken down throughout the city.[57] That order seems to have been followed; a naval officer arriving on May 8 saw no rebel flags anywhere in the city.[58] But the Confederates did not mean to abandon the flag war without a fight. When the Confederate flag flying over city hall was replaced during the first week of May, Clara Solomon reported that the new U.S. flag was greeted by "one deafening, rousing cheer for Jeff. Davis, & the Southern Confederacy." (This surprised Solomon, who curiously had expected to hear "cheers for 'Lincoln.' ")[59] Other Confederate women took to wearing their flag or dressing in Confederate colors to express their patriotism. But the most famous incident involved William Mumford, who had helped pull down the first U.S. flag Farragut had installed over the city.

Benjamin F. Butler and Unionist New Orleans

Storming into the Mint building, Mumford and his compatriots had removed the flag and torn it to shreds. A professional gambler, he then walked around the city for days with his tattered bit of the flag on his lapel.[60] Arrested by Butler, Mumford was sentenced to be hanged on June 7.

Mumford's execution was the hard edge of Butler's sense that he had to perform the United States' control over the city. In early May, Butler had written to the secretary of war about the need "to make some brilliant examples" in order to cow the mob and convince Unionists of their safety. Hanging William Mumford proved to be the most violent of these "examples," and it seems to have shocked a city that had hoped for clemency right up until the man was hanged at about 10:47 A.M. on June 7. The crowd was large, but it made not "the slightest demonstration" as the man was killed. Ever theatrical, Butler appears to have circulated the rumor that Mumford was hanged with rope that the Confederate authorities had planned to use to execute a Union spy on the day Farragut arrived. Twenty-five minutes later Mumford's corpse was cut down and hauled away.[61]

Mumford's death was only the first act of the day's performance. After what might be conceived of as a half-hour intermission, Butler's Unionist allies staged the second act, a presentation of national rebirth after the death of William Mumford and, through him, of the rebellion. At about noon, a thirty-four-member committee of the Union Association of New Orleans raised the U.S. flag over city hall. The Union Association made sure that it put on an entertaining show, with cannons firing salutes and a native New Orleans band playing patriotic songs. The president of the Union Association, Anthony Fernandez, delivered a speech, which was seconded by General Shepley. Throughout the show, the same message was emphasized: New Orleans men had arranged the event. Benjamin Morse, a soldier from Vermont, wrote home, "There [is] a union assosiation [sic] formed in New Orleans + they had a grate [sic] time raising the United States flag over the city Hall the other day it was the citizens that raised it." Union soldiers Melvan Tibbetts and Charles Boothby likewise credited the flag raising to "the Citizens of New Orleans" or "the loyal citizens."[62] That both of them linked the Union Association ceremony to the death at the Mint indicates that people on the streets were receiving a message about the permanence of the U.S. flag. The day closed with the Union Association making a "splendid procession through the different streets of the city."[63]

Reporters estimated that the crowd on St. Charles Street and in Lafayette Square that day reached between 10,000 and 20,000 people. While secessionists and scoffers appeared, most of the audience appeared appreciative. A Union naval officer closed his account of the ceremony by remarking that he had "never heard such enthusiastic cheering." The correspondent for the *New York Evening Post* wrote that "the whole affair was regarded as a complete Union success." The *New York Herald*'s reporter left no doubt that Unionism now thrived in the city. He claimed to see people cry tears of joy as they watched "Old Glory" rise over the city hall, and perhaps they did, just as Henry Snyder's wife, Phebe, had reacted strongly when she first saw the flag again. Indeed, some of the people at the event were women, who filled the windows of nearby buildings. Their faces "bore evidence of their joy at seeing the old flag restored," and they waved innumerable handkerchiefs in the breeze.[64] Although these newspaper accounts might be overly optimistic, the event must have been taken as a success by local Unionists; six days later, Unionists in the town of Gretna staged a similar flag raising, complete with artillery, bands, Unionist resolutions, and "rejoicing cheers."[65]

As we can see in the accounts of the June 7 ceremony, women played an important part in American flag culture during the Civil War. For this reason, they became central to Unionist and Confederate efforts to gain control over New Orleans. Americans generally believed that women's nationalism was purer than that of men, who too frequently allowed partisan politics to trump their love of country. Although women had become more partisan since 1840, the war seems to have momentarily driven women back into their role as apolitical nationalists. In both nations, women sewed flags for local military units and then presented them to the soldiers in public ceremonies. Confederate women had performed this function in New Orleans. Once the U.S. army arrived, many women wore small Confederate flags. Unionist women countered the Confederate women with their own flag-centered events. Women waved U.S. flags at passing warships and turned out to cheer the Union Association flag raisings.[66] Women also thronged into the galleries of Lyceum Hall on June 14 to listen to the speeches at the mass meeting of the Union Association.[67]

Unionist women also took center stage by presenting flags to the 13th Connecticut Volunteers on two separate occasions. In the first ceremony, held on May 17, Miss Angela Snyder "presented a beautiful silk guide

Benjamin F. Butler and Unionist New Orleans

color" to the unit's colonel, who in turn thanked her for the gift. Snyder was accompanied by a cousin, and both of the women were introduced to Benjamin Butler, who "chatted with them pleasantly for a few minutes."[68] By early July, New Orleans women had sewn a much larger banner, this time "the Star Spangled Banner," a light blue flag adorned with white stars. General Shepley made sure that the presentation ceremony would attract as much attention as possible by holding it up on the levee behind the centrally located Custom House. He also held the event on the Fourth of July, when the crowds would be larger. No one recorded the names of the women at this event or how many participated. Nevertheless, Union soldier Edwin Nickerson came away thinking that the ladies of New Orleans "seem to take quite a fancy to us."[69] That was exactly the impression that Unionists wanted to create. Confederates could no longer claim to have the exclusive loyalty of the city's white women, an important issue in terms of both women's real political influence and their symbolic value as moral judges.

The actions of Angela Snyder and her cousin on May 17 are all the more remarkable because they happened only two days after Benjamin Butler issued his "Woman Order." Like the hanging of William Mumford, the Woman Order reflects the harder side of Butler's battle to control the city's streets. Shortly after May 1, Confederate women had sought to delegitimize Union control and cut away at the morale of Union officers and men. Some women refused to sit in the same church pews as Union officers; others would not make eye contact, let alone small talk, with men in blue. Many women wore Confederate emblems or colors. Others took more extreme measures, exchanging hostile words or even spitting on Butler's troops.[70] Taken as a whole, these signs of defiance constituted a street theater campaign that rivaled Butler's ambitious productions. Unable to strike back, Union soldiers suffered these indignities in silence, and the displays of Confederate patriotism continued unabated. Butler had managed to get the mob off the streets, but the women's defiance effectively blocked his efforts to make Unionists feel safe by presenting New Orleans as fully under U.S. control.

Benjamin Butler's Woman Order, issued on May 15, was designed to stop Confederate women from challenging Union soldiers as they moved about the city. The order proclaimed that any woman guilty of showing "contempt for any officer or soldier of the United States . . . shall be regarded and held liable to be treated as a woman of the town plying her avocation."[71] Butler's phrasing prompted debate about what the order authorized soldiers to do. Would women who insulted Union troops now be solicited, assaulted, carted off to jail, or simply dismissed as unworthy of attention? Pro-Confederate commentators imagined the worst, and they ignited weeks of outrage in the Confederacy and Europe. Even some northerners wondered whether Butler had gone too far. But just what Butler had meant by his order is less important than the fact that it worked.

Although the order did not silence Confederate women, it worked well enough to enable the Union army and local Unionists to get on with the job of governance. A naval officer who had previously marveled at the "vulgarity" of Confederate women (especially at the words they had spoken to Union soldiers in front of their children) noted that "a marked change has been the result" of Butler's order. An amateur correspondent to the *New York Times* agreed. "The ladies themselves felt the justice of the rebuke," he wrote, "and have been in their hearts gratified at having the precipice upon which they stood fairly presented to them." In other words, Confederate women obeyed the order because they knew that they had overstepped the boundaries of female decorum by assuming too controversial a role. Shortly after Butler's order, a Confederate woman hastened to reassure her relatives that she would never "have compromised myself so far as to do anything rude or unladylike."[72] Respectable southern society frowned on women entering into politics (especially after the women's rights campaign started in 1848), and the growth of the Unionist movement made it appear that the secessionist women were lowering themselves into a brawl between a Union party and a Confederate party.[73] Caught between Butler's stiff penalties and the traditional restraints placed on women's conduct, most Confederate women became far less controversial. In early July, many women began wearing small Confederate flags, and secessionist women turned out in large numbers one day to cheer Confederate prisoners steaming by on a ship. Such conduct allowed women to retain a political voice, as historian Alecia Long has argued, but Butler's order stopped the open abuse of Union troops.[74] Wearing Confederate flags and waving handkerchiefs at prisoners did not violate the terms of Butler's order, which had banned only behavior that disrespected Union soldiers. Butler could declare his summer street theater a blockbuster success.

Benjamin F. Butler and Unionist New Orleans

In the end, Benjamin Butler's theatricals would not have worked unless there were Unionists, both white and black, willing to take jobs, raise flags, and do business with northern merchants. Butler raised several thousand troops from the city's population, but even with those Unionists away at the front, enough supporters remained to create a welcoming atmosphere for northern soldiers. Throughout 1862, Union soldiers and the city's civilians worked together to create new political structures, police the city, and invigorate the economy. All of this called for formal and informal contacts between civilians and soldiers, and these interactions usually satisfied both parties. Even in the midst of war, New Orleans became more and more peaceful as 1862 came to an end.

The image of troops from northern regiments policing the city's streets often conjures up draconian images for those who want to see Butler as a tyrant. While those regiments now included many New Orleans recruits, there can be no doubt that the soldiers arrested many men and women and took them to military courts (or Butler's headquarters), where those found guilty were sentenced to stays in military prisons at Fort Jackson or Ship Island. But that is only part of the story. Union troops also served as liberators, freeing Unionists imprisoned for their political beliefs. W. P. Moore, a captain in the 4th Wisconsin, was detailed to visit city jails on the night of May 1. At the "Calaboose," where prisoners were held on the first night after their arrest, they "liberated a Union man from confinement." Proceeding to the parish prison, the soldiers freed another man and made the guards swear oaths that no other political prisoners were being held.[75] The guards may well have lied to the Union soldiers. Five days later, a letter signed by "the Prisoners in the Parish Pris." was smuggled out and delivered to Butler's headquarters. The letter detailed, quite graphically, the abuse meted out by prison authorities to male and female prisoners, both white and black. Further, the letter asserted that men held because they were abolitionists were now having false larceny charges recorded against them. The petitioners admitted that "we were not all loyal citizens when this rebellion commenced" but argued that months in Confederate prisons had changed them. Now, they wrote, "the tiranny [sic], despotism, corruption and cruelty we have witnessed in this prison have made us all good Union men, and there is not one amongst us now, who would not gladly

Benjamin F. Butler and Unionist New Orleans

embrace the chance of fighting for the beloved stars and stripes." Not expecting universal clemency, they asked only that officers be sent to investigate conditions at the prison.[76] For the men and women held in New Orleans jails, Union patrols on the streets looked like an improvement over the old Know-Nothing police.

Ordinary civilians also found comfort in the Union patrols. Union soldiers policed the city in May, and their duties grew when Butler discharged the city's regular police on May 22 for failing to take the oath of allegiance. New Orleans Unionists took their place—a *Herald* reporter wrote the next day that Butler had 2,000 applications for 500 positions—but soldiers picked up the slack while the new policemen trained.[77] The soldiers soon won the regard and even the affection of people on the streets. Vermonter Benjamin Morse noted that the hostility of the earliest days of civilian-army relations had improved immensely. On June 14, he fondly remembered his old beat back in New Orleans, where "we met smiling faces and we could go where we pleased in perfect saf[e]ty[.] [T]here was one place that they would set up a cup of coffe [*sic*] + some biscuit in the window for me when I was on police in the city + I could eat + drink and not leave my beat." Having the Union patrols was clearly desirable enough to provide the men with incentives to visit; more to the point, whoever gave Morse coffee and biscuits must not have feared retaliation for feeding a Union soldier. Local residents wanted the soldier-policemen so badly that some complained to Massachusetts colonel N. A. M. Dudley when "no force of *any* kind passed through their street last night." General George Shepley was not idly boasting when he wrote a friend, "I have made it a *peaceful city where life* and property are *safe*." As historian Joy Jackson has concluded, the police and provost judge appointed by Butler did their jobs "in an overall fair and equitable manner."[78]

Soldiers and civilians also came together in less official capacities. Here again, relations seem to have been harmonious, even enjoyable, especially as the summer wore on and the chance of a Confederate return to power dwindled. Mutually beneficial business ties soon restarted between New Orleans and the Atlantic world. The revival of trade with the North and Europe thrilled merchants whose livelihood had been threatened by secession and war. Newspapermen in New Orleans and northern ports welcomed the news that people had resisted Confederate commands to burn all valuable commodities.[79] Rumors of a revival of commerce spread to the

Benjamin F. Butler and Unionist New Orleans

streets, where Wisconsin soldier Jerry Flint sensed that people were "elated to find their Port again opened."[80]

But it was the smaller commercial interactions between soldiers and civilians that may have mattered the most. Doing business brought the army into contact with the people of New Orleans. Many officers abandoned their quarters and rented rooms with Unionist families. Alfred Parmenter and a friend split a room, without board, for six dollars a month "in the house of a very intelegent [sic] German," and Frank Morse paid eight dollars a week for room and board "with a good Union family." Food also brought soldiers and civilians together; Parmenter bought pies from a "very strong union woman." But sometimes soldiers did not look into the politics of the people who sold them food, as long as it was tastier or fresher than their rations. Clark Carr of the 8th New Hampshire found a brisk commerce in food at Camp Parapet, the Union defensive line just north of New Orleans. Women visited the camp daily to sell "cakes, pies, milk, eggs, blackberries, onions, green corn, string beans, squashes, etc." Such abundance, plus "the sweet singing of birds," made Camp Parapet, he thought, vastly superior to Ship Island. Peddlers also sold seashells to soldiers as gifts to mail home, and local women cleaned clothes for Union soldiers. In fact, so many female peddlers and laundresses came into Union camps in July that Butler ordered the women to stay outside picket lines. Only that way, he thought, could the camps' military atmosphere be maintained. Nevertheless, he allowed men to transact business with women outside their camps, so the contacts between civilians and the soldiers continued.[81] Whether or not all the civilians engaged in this commerce were "very strong union" allies, many people in New Orleans learned that Butler's army paid its bills. Henry Snyder's former membership in the Confederate Guards did not stop him from doing a brisk business in fresh bread with the Union army after he returned from Camp Moore. Regular interactions no doubt helped to erase the worst stereotypes that each group may have had of the other.

Some civilians and soldiers even formed friendships. Residents sometimes invited Union soldiers into their homes. Some may have done so for Unionist company, as when John Guild began a letter home by saying that he was "in the sitting room of a Union lady" who bore the Confederacy "an honest hatred." Others, especially officers, started paying calls on people they had met. Charles Boothby found that he was "always very welcome"

Benjamin F. Butler and Unionist New Orleans

on his visits. The most vivid description of such social interaction comes from the diary of Charles Blake, the young man who had found the starving mass of women on May 12 so disturbing. By August, he and a friend had been invited to spend the evening in the home of a German family. There they sang and played the piano, accompanied by "a very pretty girl" named Louisiana Hawthorne. It hardly seemed to matter that she was "a strong, and decided secessionist." (With a states' rights name like Louisiana, that was probably not a surprise.) Everyone had "a very pleasant time," and the soldiers returned two days later for more singing. Later in the week, the two men, the German family, and a girl named Katrina went to the "German theatre" together. The playbill for the evening mixed classical music with knife throwers and fire-eaters (of the apolitical variety). While that blend of entertainment may seem odd, the sight of Union soldiers and New Orleans civilians spending the evening together seemingly struck no one as strange, and they had another fine evening.[82]

Courtship and dancing also helped to break down barriers between civilians and the Union military. From time to time, the city's Unionists staged dances and invited soldiers. The first "grand Union ball" was held at the Planters' Hotel on June 21, and it featured the 26th Massachusetts regimental band. While the event was a bust, band member Alfred Parmenter did not blame the low turnout (only ten tickets sold) on the ball's Unionist politics; rather, he thought that hot weather and the steep admission price of five dollars a person had kept people away.[83] Later Union balls were much more successful. John Purcell of New Orleans attended two Union dances at the start of 1863, and he found them to be "well attended by citizens, naval and land officers." The January ball, he thought, brought in between 400 and 500 people, some of whom stayed until 4:00 in the morning. Later, he estimated that "more than one thousand ladies and gentlemen" crowded February's Union ball at the Mason's hall.[84] In addition to forging personal contacts between civilians and the Union military, such well-publicized events heralded the existence of a cultured, well-connected Unionist leadership in the city. The days of finding Unionists hiding under featherbeds had ended.

Soldiers did not always need a Union ball to go dancing with local women or to start up romances. Although letters to parents and siblings understandably leave out romantic intrigues, some evidence suggests that such relationships started. While historians have focused on Confederate women, other New Orleans women appeared publicly on the arms of Union soldiers. One New Hampshire soldier wrote home to his sister that he had "fallen in love with a Creole girl." Together, they had gone to the city and had "pretty gay times." Stephen Spalding's long letter to a friend in Vermont—with whom he had shared many a hard-drinking carouse— relates his adventurous Fourth of July in New Orleans. Though refused a pass to leave camp, Spalding left anyway, visiting first a bar in which he drank "gin, whiskey, brandy, rum beer, [and] gin coctails (modesty prevents me from putting in the k)." He also drank "eleven other different kinds of coctails," as well as an impressive assortment of juleps and "smashes" before finding a "hospitable retreat" at the home of Miss Bianca Robbins, a lady "friendly to the Union." Still, his night was not over. He moved on to "Miss Burdell's" masquerade ball. Any party held on the nation's birthday must have had overtly Unionist overtones, but Spalding found there "the quintessence of beauty in the city." Soon he was dancing with a wealthy young Alabaman. The dance ended badly, but not because of sectional politics. The Alabaman was willing to be seen dancing with the young Vermont officer, but Spalding's drinking caught up with him. "Toes were broken, dresses torn," he wrote, relating the damage he had done to the people around him (hopefully with some exaggeration). Still, Spalding had one more success that evening. Staying despite his inability to polka, he soon saw two British naval officers arrive, each wearing " 'Secesh' badges" on their clothes. The music stopped, dancing ceased, and the partygoers began surrounding the new arrivals. Spalding and his friends then kicked and cuffed the two men out the door. As Spalding wrote, "40 boots assisted them in getting on to the side walk. They landed far out in the middle of the road, and with more quickness than grace 'Skedaddled.' " Clearly, Spalding had found a warm welcome in New Orleans on the Fourth of July. He had been entertained in a bar, invited into two Unionist homes, and survived the city despite being inebriated. He had seen Confederate sympathizers thrown out of a party, and he had danced with an Alabaman. Spalding's day may have cost him the staggering sum of fifty-seven dollars, but he concluded that it had been worth it. New Orleans, he wrote, "is a great place for fun."[85]

Union soldiers on the front line soon discovered that they had friends who could do more than dance. Local Unionists, both black and white, gave them vital information about Confederate military movements. A local Irishman helped a Maine regiment uncover hidden Confederate artillery, leading to a general rout of the rebels. But Unionists proved especially useful when they alerted Federal troops of imminent enemy attacks. Private Jonathan Allen wrote his sister that his regiment had been warned of rebel cavalry activity and that another sector of the unit's line was cautioned by "some union people" a few nights later. Realizing that slaves and free blacks could be relied upon, some northern soldiers became antislavery men. Others, like Rufus Kinsley, toured plantations "and saw enough of the horrors of slavery to make me an Abolitionist forever."[86]

Although some soldiers voiced a healthy skepticism about the sincerity of professed Unionists, most people recognized that New Orleans harbored a large and growing number of people who supported the United States.[87] The existence of southern white Unionists mattered deeply to the soldiers in blue. The frequency with which they speculated on the number of Unionists, debated the sincerity of their convictions, and hoped for even more friends to emerge indicated that they needed local support to validate their efforts. The importance of the Unionists to northern soldiers emerges in their letters home. John Carver Palfrey wrote a typical letter from Ship Island in August 1862. Palfrey had not yet set foot in New Orleans—he had yet to meet a resident of the Confederacy—and already he made authoritative declarations about how many Unionists he would find when he got there.[88] For the soldiers involved in the U.S. war effort, the presence of southern white Unionists gave them hope for an easier victory but also a reason to fight. They soldiered on, they could argue, because theirs was a war of liberation, an attempt to rescue those who loved the United States and its democratic experiment.

When these men looked at the people of New Orleans, they knew that they could count on the sympathy of an overwhelming majority of blacks, whether enslaved or free. But whites too, they found, were warming up to them, much faster than many of them had foreseen. A correspondent for the *New York Evening Post* was surprised by the change in public sentiment that occurred between May 2 and 3. On the third, he remarked that "a much better feeling exists." Yesterday, he wrote, people cheered for Jeff Davis, but today, after the troops made a small handful of arrests, the mob disappeared. Even the men arrested "begged to be let off—promised never to do so again." Still, he predicted that it would take a whole month for New Orleans to fully embrace the Union troops. Two days later, he filed a second dispatch: "I believe I shall have to reduce the time to two weeks. We are getting on famously. They no longer insult us on the streets. They begin to enter into conversations with us; make advances of various kinds; they throng to our reviews; the music of our Fourth Wisconsin band has great attractions for them." To find such a glowing report a week after Butler's regiments landed speaks to the speed with which the mob was vanquished and peaceful relations restored between the army and the city. But his report, though the earliest, was not alone. Soldiers reported warm welcomes too. A naval officer remarked later in the month that "reserve is fast wearing off, and people who would not speak to us on our arrival now tell us it is all up with the Southern Confederacy."[89]

By the end of the summer of 1862, the city that had provided most of the garrison for Fort Jackson seemed increasingly in the Union's pocket. Many northern soldiers looked around them and reported that Unionism was on the rise—slowly according to some, quickly according to others. The Reverend Joseph Colby of the 12th Maine, for instance, thought Unionism stirred "itself slowly," whereas Private E. Dane told his wife that it "is gaining ground here in new orleans very fast." Either way, most observers thought that among the citizens "the largest part of them are glad that we are here for the most of them are very quiet in + about the city."[90] Correspondents and soldiers even wrote about how much Benjamin Butler was loved by the Unionists and respected by everyone.[91]

Given the speed with which Unionism reasserted itself in the Crescent City, it is perhaps not surprising that some of the Confederate troops drawn from it had mutinied at the first opportunity. Allowed the chance to follow in the mutineers' footsteps by deserting the Confederacy, much of the city did so. Like the men in Fort Jackson, the people of New Orleans often chose the United States over the Confederacy as soon as the threat of the parish prison, or worse, was taken away. Benjamin Butler's ability to regard immigrants and the working class as equals, and to start municipal policies that gave people a chance to earn a decent living or get the food they so badly needed, benefited the Union enormously. His efforts also may have reminded immigrants of why they had chosen the United States in the first place. Native-born people, in turn, could remember why they had loved their country before secession. For so many of the people of New Orleans, the promise of America was ensured again by the restoration of the Union in May 1862. Once again, the city would enjoy religious tolera-

Benjamin F. Butler and Unionist New Orleans

tion, an open immigration policy, a functioning multiethnic society, and economic opportunity fostered by the government, not curtailed by it through war and legalized slavery. In Butler's aggressive use of the government to create jobs, relieve hunger and distress, and promote religious and ethnic cooperation, we find the key ingredients for what made the United States the attractive nation it was for so many of the world's people in the nineteenth century.

why the mutiny at fort jackson matters

For people living in 1862, the mutiny at Fort Jackson was big news. Even if its importance was only imperfectly understood at the time, the mutiny guaranteed success for the Union in its effort to retake New Orleans. With Forts Jackson and St. Philip passing out of their hands, the Confederates had no choice but to destroy the ironclad ram *Louisiana*, and with it their hopes for holding on to New Orleans. When General Duncan and the other Confederate officers realized on the morning after the mutiny that most of their remaining troops sympathized more with the mutineers than with their own wishes, the southern republic lost control of New Orleans. In addition, the Confederacy lost its grip on much of the Mississippi River. Baton Rouge, the capital of Louisiana, fell without resistance on May 9, less than two weeks after the mutiny. Four days later Natchez, Mississippi, surrendered to Union forces, and by May 18 (less than a month after the mutiny), Union ships and troops appeared off Vicksburg. As the Union ships moved farther north, they captured or forced the destruction of large amounts of cotton and other goods along the banks of the river. Perhaps all this would have happened without the mutiny, but it would not have occurred so quickly. Given more time, perhaps the Confederacy would have been able to patch together other defenses south of Vicksburg. With the fall of Memphis to southward-bound Union ships in early June, very little of the Mississippi remained to the Confederacy.

The successful mutiny also guaranteed other gains for the Union cause. General Duncan's surrender placed the garrisons of both forts, including loyal elements such as the St. Mary's Cannoneers, in Union hands. Together with the militia regiment that Farragut's fleet had captured at the Quarantine Station, David D. Porter could claim at an early date that the Union had captured seventeen hundred prisoners.[1] The view of New Orleans from the decks of Union ships revealed the further extent of Confederate losses. A Vermont soldier saw the wreckage of "scores of ships and steamers, some of them just completed, and seven 'rams,' which were almost ready to launch. On the levee for miles up and down the river, on both sides, were mounted guns of the heaviest caliber. . . . Many of these guns had just been made at two large establishments here, which are now in our hands. We find in them thousands of shells, and solid balls, of all sizes, and several unfinished cannon; besides everything for iron steamers. No expense had been spared for fortifying the city."[2] The destruction of the css *Louisiana* alone makes the mutiny important.[3] From a strictly military point of view, the New Orleans campaign was a decisive Union victory, resulting in the Confederacy's loss of prisoners, artillery, and shipping.

But the Confederacy lost more than just materials of war and miles of river when the mutiny opened the Mississippi to Union supply and troop ships. New Orleans itself was the main prize of the campaign, and its fall damaged the Confederacy's ability to make war. New Orleans had an industrial and financial capacity that much of the rest of the South lacked. While the evacuation of specie from the city's banks softened the blow to the young nation's financial stability, the loss of industrial enterprises such as the Leeds Foundry would be felt for the next three years.[4] One Union estimate of New Orleans's value to the Confederacy included "three large woolen mills" and "four large cotton mills." A shoe manufacturer, it continued, had produced an estimated twenty-six hundred pairs of shoes daily. Moving from clothing to armaments, the report mentioned that Cook and Brother had two steam-driven plants making rifles and that

Epilogue

An 1852 view of New Orleans, giving a sense of the city's vast scale.
(Library of Congress, Prints and Photographs Division)

Clark's two factories were turning out rifled cannons as quickly as they could. Other shops throughout the city produced knives and bayonets.[5]

The mutiny's most important damage to the Confederacy, however, was the loss of New Orleans as a potential recruiting station for Confederate armies. Historians have long recognized that New Orleans was the Confederacy's largest city, but that hardly does justice to the Crescent City's size. With 168,675 people in 1860, it was four times larger than the next largest Confederate city, Charleston, which had a population of only 40,578 people. New Orleans residents made up almost a quarter of Louisiana's population. Another way of stating the relative importance of New Orleans's population is to say that the city had 28,000 more people living in it than the state of Florida did in 1860.

Yet even these statistics underestimate the importance of New Orleans's people to the Confederate war effort. Because the Confederacy recruited only white people into its army, New Orleans was particularly central to its needs. Although the Confederacy had not been especially successful at gaining recruits from the Crescent City, the new national draft could have yielded a large number of conscripts. Because only about 25,000 people in the city were of African descent (free and enslaved), the city boasted a white population of more than 140,000 people. In comparison, South Carolina's white population was only 291,388. A solid 40 percent of Louisiana's whites lived in New Orleans.[6] This population constituted a large pool of po-

Epilogue

tential draftees for the Confederacy to lose. Instead of serving the Confederacy, the city's manpower resources, both black and white, were tapped by the Union, which gained just under 30,000 new soldiers for Lincoln's armies from Louisiana.[7] The Fort Jackson mutiny did not cause the fall of New Orleans all on its own, but it secured a military victory that had larger implications for the Union and Confederacy for the rest of the war.

The white Unionists visible at Fort Jackson and elsewhere in this study also served a critical function in wartime Reconstruction. Southern white Unionists undercut Confederate claims that it enjoyed the unanimous approval of its people. By the same token, white Unionists bolstered the U.S. claim that it was fighting against an illegal regime that oppressed American citizens. Lincoln also had more specific ideas in mind for Louisiana. With so many of the state's people loyal to their old allegiances, Lincoln decided to use it as one of the test cases for his Reconstruction plans. His idea was to welcome states back into the Union when 10 percent of the state's former voters had sworn an oath of allegiance to the Union. Their return would be heralded most dramatically by the election of new representatives to Congress, a formal step on the road back to full political integration into the United States. Given the large number of Unionists in Louisiana, it is not surprising that Louisiana served as one of the earliest Reconstruction experiments, with congressional elections held on December 2, 1862. The turnout at this election must have pleased both Lincoln and the state's Unionists. While the vote total of 7,760 votes was 41 percent lower than the turnout for the 1859 congressional election, Unionists could say that the glass was more than half full; even though men had to take the oath of allegiance before casting ballots, 59 percent of the old electorate had voted. And the election had been peaceful. A soldier in the 30th Connecticut noted that Union troops and the "absence of the 'Thugs'" had made it "the quietest election that has taken place for a great many of years." In addition to having a solid, peaceful turnout, Lincoln could also boast of the radical politics of the winning candidates, Michael Hahn and Benjamin Flanders. Both believed, in the words of historian Eric Foner, that the "Civil War was a genuine revolution that offered to overthrow a reactionary and aristocratic ruling class."[8] New Orleans's Unionists, then, not only helped to secure the city for the Union military but also provided the North with proof that there were southern whites who would happily lead their states back into the Union.

Epilogue

For people living today, the mutiny at Fort Jackson can teach many of the same things, but it also has other lessons. Civil War military historians have begun to consider the connections between the communities from which the soldiers came and the ways they acted in camp and on the battlefield. Certainly, the Fort Jackson mutiny confirms the necessity of this kind of inquiry. Knowing the background of a unit can tell us a great deal about how devoted to the cause it will be and how hard it might fight in battle. In the case of Fort Jackson, Confederate soldiers from St. Mary's Parish had more incentives to remain true to the Confederate cause than did men who enlisted on the streets of New Orleans.

But perhaps the most important reason to retell the story of the Fort Jackson mutiny is that it can serve as a necessary corrective to the way many Americans have come to remember the Civil War. When the journalist Tony Horwitz traveled across the contemporary American South (and he could have done so anywhere else in the country), he found that many people display the Confederate flag because they think it represents a rebellion of ordinary people against authority. As he writes about the Confederate flag, it seemed to "have floated free from its moorings in time and place and become a generalized 'Fuck You,' a middle finger raised with ulceric fury in the face of blacks, school officials, authority in general."[9] The Confederacy envisioned by people today represents poor, decent (white) people resisting an oppressive and entitled government. What happened at Fort Jackson and in New Orleans points to a different idea of what the Confederacy was all about.

In New Orleans, the Confederacy was the oppressive government. It was the established authorities. The Confederate leadership descended directly from antebellum politicians, typified by Know-Nothing–turned–Confederate Mayor John Monroe; former Democrat, now newly Confederate Governor John Moore; or even Second Lieutenant Olivier, the old planter and secessionist politician who served as an officer in the St. Mary's Cannoneers. The true rebels in New Orleans fought for the Union, whether they were inspired by abolitionism, racial equality, democracy, German or American revolutionary ideals, or their own poverty and class anger. Benjamin Butler sensed this dynamic when he wrote that "this rebellion was at first inaugurated for the purpose of establishing a landed aristocracy as against the poor and middling whites, who had shown some disposition to assert their equality with the planters." Nor did this dynamic vanish upon his arrival. Butler claimed that he "found that the aristocracy looked upon us as their enemies; and I found that the working and mid-dling classes looked upon us as their friends. . . . I found the working men true to the Union, and I found the slave owners false to the Union."[10] People on the street agreed with the Union commander. Sergeant Albert Krause wrote to his family in Germany that "rich, wealthy residents" seemed displeased at the mere sight of his uniform, while "the proletarians and the poorer classes favor the North." The elitist politics of the Confeder-ate movement in New Orleans became so notorious that slaves in St. Louis in 1862 sang that Butler "helped the poor and snubbed the rich."[11]

The Confederates' exclusionary politics hurt them on the battlefield. As historians, we need to recognize that nations and generals who choose to exclude people from their country or their military are responsible if they are then defeated because they are outnumbered. A historian has argued recently that Mansfield Lovell cannot be blamed for his loss of New Or-leans, saying that his "immediate problem was to acquire much-needed men, weapons, and ammunition." But some of Lovell's own policies, rein-forced by those of his political allies, limited the size of his force. Lovell has already been heard here disparaging the various ethnicities of southern Louisiana, but he also refused to arm, uniform, or call up the substantial number of free blacks in New Orleans who offered to serve the Confed-eracy as long as it offered them respect as men and citizens. Lovell first refused their help and then disbanded all free black militia units during the militia reorganization in February 1862.[12] While often protesting its need for more soldiers, the Confederacy snubbed potential recruits who lay within its grasp. This is most obvious in the case of the country's refusal to arm the people it held as slaves (40 percent of its population), but New Orleans also proves that the Confederacy was reluctant to welcome free blacks and many immigrants as warmly as it might have.

Immigrants came to the United States in the nineteenth century, as they do today, in the hope of improving their lives. Some part of their hopes were materialistic, but promises of equality and freedom also played their part. The Declaration of Independence and the rise of democracy in the United States appealed to many immigrants even as the new nation struggled to fulfill its egalitarian promise. The United States often fell short of living up to its ideals; the lives of many immigrants were exceedingly hard. Few cities or states treated all religions equally. In 1863 and beyond, some ethnic communities in the North fiercely resisted the draft and other U.S. wartime measures.[13] But for the men at Fort Jackson and their families, the sharpest ethnic tensions in the Civil War North lay in the unknown future. Their only point of comparison was between the antebellum United States and the Confederacy they had endured for the past year. Before the war, immigrants had met with some successes, though the extent of their prosperity depended on their luck, timing, ethnicity, skills, family connections, and any wealth they might have brought with them. Most had found at least a limited religious freedom, and many men had obtained citizenship and the vote, some very quickly. The point of this book is that the United States, despite its problems, would still have looked more prosperous than the Confederacy would have to the men stuck in Fort Jackson in April 1862. Neither wage labor capitalism nor the United States would have enjoyed an unblemished reputation for men in the urban working class—these men had worked hard and seen their fill of labor unrest before the war started. But they also knew that the Confederacy had made matters worse. The Confederacy's nativist local and state officials, antidemocratic tendencies, and devastated economy could not have looked promising to these men and their families. With the U.S. draft and the resulting ethnic conflicts yet in the future, the mutineers may well have been striking a blow for the side that they thought would give them the best chance for freedom, equality, and a decent wage. Prosperity for New Orleans's wage workers might come only through labor activism and unrest, but that struggle still offered a better chance for success than they saw in an economy dominated by slavery. In this campaign, the country that came closest to welcoming immigrants to the American dreams of prosperity and freedom would end up the victor.

We might well close this story with a small scene from Butler's headquarters after he had gained the city. Butler is meeting with a group of eight to ten women, all of whom need government relief from their poverty. One of the women speaks only German. She finds a willing and able ear in the person of Lieutenant Wiegel, "a good German scholar," who translates her story and enables Butler to direct her to the appropriate office.[14] New Orleans's immigrants had already chosen the United States once in their lives, having left their birth nationality in the hope of finding a welcome here. Given a new choice in 1862 as to what nation to choose, most once again picked the United States, much to its benefit and to the Confederacy's undoing.

Epilogue

notes

ABBREVIATIONS

AAS   American Antiquarian Society, Worcester, Mass.
Butler Papers   Benjamin F. Butler Papers, Library of Congress,
                        Washington, D.C.
CLH   Center for Lowell History, Lowell, Mass.
Goodhue   John E. Goodhue, "Civil War Correspondence,"
Correspondence   MS 81, Phillips Library, Peabody Essex Museum,
                        Salem, Mass.
Harding Papers   Frank D. Harding Papers, 1833–98, Wisconsin State
                        Historical Society, River Falls Area Research Center, River
                        Falls, Wis.
HNOC   Historic New Orleans Collection, Williams Research
                        Center, New Orleans, La.
Lawrence Diary   Henry Effingham Lawrence Diary, in Brashear and
                        Lawrence Family Papers, 1804–1982 (Series 3), in *Records
                        of Ante-bellum Southern Plantations from the Revolution
                        through the Civil War; Series J: Selections from the Southern
                        Historical Collection, Part 5: Louisiana* (Bethesda, Md.:
                        University Publications of America, 1996)
LC   Library of Congress, Washington, D.C.
LHAC   Louisiana Historical Association Collection, Civil War
                        Papers/New Orleans Papers, Howard-Tilton Library, Tulane
                        University, New Orleans, La.
LSU   Louisiana State University Libraries, Louisiana and Lower
                        Mississippi Valley Collections, Baton Rouge, La.
Massa Papers   Samuel Massa Papers, Syracuse University Library,
                        Syracuse, N.Y.
MassHS   Massachusetts Historical Society, Boston, Mass.

NA	National Archives and Records Administration, Washington, D.C.
NHCHS	New Haven Colony Historical Society, New Haven, Conn.
NHHS	New Hampshire Historical Society, Concord, N.H.
NOPL	New Orleans Public Library, New Orleans, La.
OR	*The War of the Rebellion: A Compilation of the Official Records of the Union and Confederate Armies*, 128 vols. (Washington, D.C.: Government Printing Office, 1880–1901)
ORN	*Official Records of the Union and Confederate Navies in the War of the Rebellion*, 30 vols. (Washington, D.C.: Government Printing Office, 1894–1922)
Parmenter Papers	Alfred Parmenter Papers, Howard-Tilton Library, Tulane University, New Orleans, La.
SCHS	South Carolina Historical Society, Charleston, S.C.
Shepley Papers	George F. Shepley Papers, collections 117, 1536, 1721, Maine Historical Society, Portland, Maine
TU	Howard-Tilton Library, Tulane University, New Orleans, La.
VtHS	Vermont Historical Society, Barre, Vt.
WSHS	Wisconsin State Historical Society, Madison, Wis.

INTRODUCTION

1 Apr. 25, 1862, in *New York Herald*, May 10, 1862.

2 Deck Log, USS *Brooklyn*, Apr. 25, 1862, NA; letter from Harris, Apr. 25, 1862, in *Chelsea (Mass.) Telegraph and Pioneer*, May 24 and 31, 1862, reprinted at <http://www.letterscivilwar.com/4-28-62a.html>; Samuel Massa Diary, Apr. 25, 1862, Massa Papers; G. M. Shipper to Benjamin F. Butler, July 23, 1862, Butler Papers, box 211; Farragut to Assistant Secretary of the Navy G. V. Fox, Apr. 25, 1862, Squadron Letters, Roll 185, NA.

3 Shipper to Butler, July 23, 1862, Butler Papers, box 211; report, Apr. 25, 1862, in *New York Herald*, May 10, 1862; Deck Log, USS *Richmond*, quoted in Hearn, *Capture of New Orleans*, 243 (and Dufour, *Night the War Was Lost*, 303); Deck Log, USS *Brooklyn*, Apr. 25, 1862, NA; Samuel Massa Diary, Apr. 25, 1862, Massa Papers.

4 *New Orleans Bee*, Apr. 26, 1862; another Confederate sympathizer claimed that only "two Dutchmen" were killed, and only after they imprudently proposed "three cheers for Lincoln." The two men were "promptly shot down" by "over twenty shots," he wrote. See two letters from New Orleans, Apr. 25 and 26,

1862, by "R. S." in the *Boston Journal*, May 24, 1862. The *Charleston Mercury* (May 5, 1862) quoted "an intelligent gentleman of character" from New Orleans as saying that "when the Yankee officers landed, five Sicilians, who cheered them, were shot down by the crowd. All who showed any signs of favor were knocked down as traitors." This supposed witness misplaced the time of the massacre, placing it when Union officers landed on the wharf, not when the ships first appeared on the river off the city. One also wonders if in the confusion he might have misunderstood the word "Silesians" as "Sicilians," thereby turning German victims into Italian ones. Anne Heard also placed the massacre at the time of the officers' landing: "several persons in the crowd who cheered for Lincoln, to give signs of joy upon the landing of the delegation from Commander Farragut, were shot down." Anne Brantley Heard letter, May 4, 1862, in Kagan, Hyslop, and Andrews, *Eyewitness to the Civil War*, 127.

5 *Journal of Commerce* story reprinted in the *New York Times*, May 25, 1862; Commander Emmons's report to Gideon Welles about his capture of the rebel schooner *Magnolia*, May 1, 1862, in *ORN*, ser. 1, vol. 18, 462. Emmons sarcastically wrote that the massacre was "another mode of 'firing the southern heart'" (462). The *Times* later printed a letter by a New Orleans Confederate who insisted that "not one of the seventy-five men said to be killed on the levee . . . was killed." See *New York Times*, June 19, 1862.

6 *ORN*, ser. 1, vol. 18, 231; Monroe's reply reprinted in *New York Tribune*, May 2, 1862. Confederate editors tried to divert attention from the massacre by emphasizing another shooting on the levee that day. A group of Confederate soldiers, the Pickwick Rangers, waved a Confederate flag on the levee and played Confederate songs. The editors complained that marksmen on the USS *Hartford* opened fire on the soldiers, killing a nearby male civilian. See *New Orleans Daily Picayune*, Apr. 27, 1862, and *New Orleans Daily Crescent*, Apr. 28, 1862.

CHAPTER ONE

1 More detailed chronicles of the campaign can be found in Dufour, *Night the War Was Lost*; Hearn, *Capture of New Orleans*; and Winters, *Civil War in Louisiana*, 71–102.

2 Clark H. Carr to "Dear Folks at Home," May 15, 1862, in Clark H. Carr, "Letters to His Wife," typescript, NHHS.

3 Sprague, *History of the 13th Infantry Regiment of Connecticut Volunteers*, 45; Jonathan Allen to mother, May 16, 1862, but from context probably Apr. 16,

1862, Allen Family Papers, VtHS; Alfred Parmenter to father and mother, Mar. 6, 1862, Parmenter Papers; Jerry E. Flint to brother, Apr. 14, 1862, Jerry E. Flint Papers, 1861–66, WSHS. See also Hollandsworth, "'What a Hell of a Place to Send 2000 Men 3000 Miles.'"

4 Melvan Tibbetts, letter, Apr. 11, 1862, Melvan Tibbetts Letters, HNOC; John E. Goodhue to mother and sister, Apr. 13, 1862, Goodhue Correspondence; Rufus Kinsley Diary, Apr. 11, 1862, VtHS.

5 Newton Culver Diary, Mar. 17 and Apr. 30, 1862, WSHS; for raccoons and birds, see report, Apr. 28, 1862, in *New York Evening Post*, May 10, 1862; river water in Freeman Foster Jr. to his father, Apr. 2, 1862, Freeman Foster Jr. Letters, LSU; Melvan Tibbetts, July 5, 1862, Tibbetts Letters, HNOC.

6 "Q. M.," letter, Apr. 22, 1862, in *Hartford Daily Courant*, May 24, 1862; report, Apr. 11, 1862, in *New York Times*, May 1, 1862. See also Alfred Parmenter, who later exclaimed: "Musquitos [*sic*]—O my—if you go into the swamps at *home* [Massachusetts] you will have no idea of them—and such large ones—tut-tut." Parmenter to his parents, May 1, 1862, Parmenter Papers.

7 *New York Times*, May 8, 1862. See also report, Apr. 25, 1862, in *New York Evening Post*, May 8, 1862, which also joked that "Birnam wood did come to Dunsinane." Eagle in report, Apr. 9, 1862, in *New York Herald*, Apr. 29, 1862.

8 Terrence Sheridan Diary, Apr. 20, 1862, NHCHS; Charles O'Neil Diary, Apr. 18, 1862, in Papers of Charles O'Neil, LC; Everett T. Manter to Eben Sherman, April 1862, recorded as "Plan of Fort Jackson," Record Group 45, NA.

9 Details about the mortars firing in report, Apr. 28, 1862, in *New York Evening Post*, May 10, 1862; dead fish from report, Apr. 21, 1862, in *New York Herald*, May 10, 1862; Richard S. Edes to his sister, Elizabeth C. Edes, Apr. 19, 1862, Edes Family Papers, MassHS.

10 *New Orleans Daily Picayune*, Apr. 23, 1862; second telegraph from Duncan to Lovell in *New Orleans Bee*, Apr. 24, 1862; letter from young officer in *New Orleans Bee*, Apr. 23, 1862. Duncan wrote, "We are all hopeful, in good spirits and very much in earnest. . . . I understand that some of the city papers have published alarming accounts, purporting to come from here. I wish it distinctly understood that all official dispatches are sent by myself. Private dispatches are all vised." Duncan to Lovell, Apr. 22, 1862, in *New Orleans Bee*, Apr. 24, 1862.

11 De Have Norton Diary, Apr. 25, 1862, De Have Norton Papers, 1861–65, WSHS.

12 George Davis to brother and sister, May 3, 1862, George H. Davis Letters, LSU. A Wisconsin soldier called it a ten-mile pull "waist deep, through water and mud, dragging small boats after them." See Chittenden, *History and Catalogue of the Fourth Regiment Wisconsin Volunteers*, 6. Butler's muddy marchers included the 26th Massachusetts and several companies from the 4th Wisconsin and the 21st Indiana Volunteers.

13 Farragut quoted in Dufour, *Night the War Was Lost*, 300; W. P. Moore, letter, May 3, 1862, in *Beloit (Wis.) Journal and Courier*, June 12, 1862.

14 Oscar Smith Diary, Apr. 25, 1862, LC.

15 Frank Peck to mother, Apr. 30, 1862, Peck-Montgomery Family Papers, LC; Frank Harding to father, May 3, 1862, Harding Papers; Shively, "USS Mississippi at the Capture of New Orleans."

16 Ripley, *Slaves and Freedmen in Civil War Louisiana*; Blassingame, *Black New Orleans*.

17 Sprague, *History of the 13th Infantry Regiment of Connecticut Volunteers*, 49; Taylor, *Notes of Conversations with a Volunteer Officer*, 22.

18 Report, May 1, 1862, in *New York Herald*, May 23, 1862; report, May 5, 1862, in *New York Times*, May 22, 1862; report, Apr. 24, 1862, in *New York Herald*, May 10, 1862.

19 Howe, *Passages*, 119.

20 George Hamilton Perkins, letter, Apr. 27, 1862, in Belknap, *Letters of Captain Geo. Hamilton Perkins*, 69.

21 Porter quotation from David Porter's official report, Apr. 25, 1862, Squadron Letters, Mortar Flotilla, NA; Benjamin Butler to "General," Apr. 26, 1862, unsigned draft of a letter, Benjamin F. Butler Papers, Boston Public Library, Boston, Mass. The argument concerning the threat posed by the *Louisiana* is also in Dufour, *Night the War Was Lost*, 337.

22 Strong, *Keystone Confederate*, 38–39.

23 Jones, *Civil War Memoirs of Captain William J. Seymour*, 32–33.

24 There are many statements about the number of mutineers who left Fort Jackson that night. The army correspondent of the *New York Herald* thought 300 men escaped, while the *Boston Courier* said that a "majority" had fled Confederate control. A bare majority would be just over 300 soldiers. Report, May 1, 1862, in *New York Herald*, May 23, 1862; *Boston Courier*, May 12, 1862. But Seymour's figure of about 250 also has considerable support. First Lieutenant John C. Palfrey of the U.S. Engineers reported that 250 men had mutinied, and Union soldier George Davis wrote that Butler's infantry captured about "two hundred prisoners." Palfrey's report, May 16, 1862, in *OR*, ser. 1, vol. 15, 428; George Davis letter, May 3, 1862, Davis Letters, LSU. Two statements illustrate the higher end of estimates, but neither comes from direct eyewitnesses. Two Confederate refugees from New Orleans told a North Carolina paper that the mutiny "*embraced nearly every company.*" The highest figure comes from Samuel Massa's diary. At the Quarantine Station on April 28, Massa wrote, "We found a body of rebel soldiers, five hundred, they had spiked some of the guns at the fort, killed one officer and deserted, the[n] gave themselves up to our men." *Wilmington (N.C.) Journal*, May 7, 1862, reprinted

in *New York Herald*, May 15, 1862; Samuel Massa Diary, Apr. 28, 1862, Massa Papers. Given the range of figures, historian John Winters estimates that about half the garrison, or 250 to 300 men, left the fort during the mutiny. Winters, *Civil War in Louisiana*, 100.

25 Edward Higgins to John Withers, undated, in David Dixon Porter Papers, General Correspondence, LC.

26 The army correspondent of the *New York Herald*, report, May 1, 1862, in *New York Herald*, May 14, 1862; Samuel Massa to Bessie, May 4, 1862, Massa Papers. See also report, Apr. 30, 1862, in *New York Herald*, May 10, 1862, which also notes that the mutineers reversed barbette cannons so that they could fire into "the unprotected casemates" where the officers were quartered.

27 *OR*, ser. 1, vol. 6, 531.

28 Holzman, *Stormy Ben Butler*, 65. See, for example, a four and a half column article by Butler attacking Porter in the *Boston Sunday Herald*, June 23, 1889, Butler Papers, box 193.

29 Porter to Meigs, May 14, 1862, David Dixon Porter Papers, General Correspondence, LC; Porter to Senator James Grimes, May 6, 1862, in *Chicago Times*, May 30, 1862; Porter to Gideon Welles, Apr. 30, 1862, in *OR*, ser. 1, vol. 15, 461.

30 Gerdes report to Bache, undated, in Squadron Letters, Mortar Flotilla, NA. Gerdes also spoke to the *New York Times* reporter, who wrote about the devastation wrought by Porter to the fort's drawbridges, cisterns, protective levees, and casemates. Report, May 5, 1862, in *New York Times*, May 22, 1862.

31 Alfred Parmenter to parents, May 7, 1862, Parmenter Papers; Deck Log, USS *Miami*, May 2, 1862, NA; Howe Diary, Apr. 29, 1862, in Howe, *Passages*.

32 Richard H. Elliott Diary, Apr. 28, 1862, CLH.

33 "Q. M.," letter, May 1, 1862, in *Hartford Daily Courant*, June 17, 1862.

34 All quotations from Horace Morse to mother and sister, Aug. 26, 1862, except second quotation about mosquitoes, which is from Horace Morse to mother and sister, Sept. 23, 1862, Frank Morse Papers, MassHS.

35 For food supply, see David D. Porter, official report of Apr. 25, 1862, Squadron Letters, Mortar Flotilla, NA, and report of Brigadier General J. W. Phelps, who commanded the initial occupation of the two forts, in *OR*, ser. 1, vol. 6, 509.

36 John Hart Diary, Apr. 29, 1862, HNOC.

37 Shively, "USS Mississippi at the Capture of New Orleans," 17; Lieutenant Roe's diary, in *ORN*, ser. 1, vol. 18, 772; Richard S. Edes to mother, May 2, 1862, Edes Family Papers, MassHS.

38 Richard S. Edes to mother, May 2, 1862, Edes Family Papers, MassHS.

39 Also, most Confederate soldiers remained loyal during the siege of Vicksburg, though a note threatening mutiny appeared at headquarters just before the surrender. See Robinson, *Bitter Fruits of Bondage*, 217–18.

40 Benjamin Butler to Edwin Stanton, June 1, 1862, in *OR*, ser. 1, vol. 15, 449; Sarah Butler to Harriet Heard, May 15, 1862, in Butler, *Private and Official Correspondence*, 1:488; see also Sarah Butler to Heard, May 1862, in Butler, *Private and Official Correspondence*, 1:532.

41 Palfrey quoted in Butler, *Private and Official Correspondence*, 1:430; Weitzel's report paraphrased in Sprague, *History of the 13th Infantry Regiment of Connecticut Volunteers*, 49–50; Manning's report, coauthored by Captain S. D. Shipley of Company C, 26th Massachusetts, and First Sergeant S. A. Perkins of Company B, 2nd Massachusetts Cavalry, Apr. 29, 1862, Butler Papers, box 11; William H. Smith to brother, June 30, 1862, William H. Smith Letters, LSU. Hans Trefousse regards Weitzel as Butler's "friend." Trefousse, *Butler*, 104.

42 Farragut to Fox, report dated Apr. 25, 1862, but clearly updated "this morning, the 29th," in *ORN*, ser. 1, vol. 18, 155; Bailey to Welles, May 7, 1862, in ibid., 173. Major Frank Peck of Butler's army explained that "the fact the [*sic*] Com. Farragut ran the gauntlet successfully + accomplished what he did afterwards will establish his deserts. . . . If when the bombardment was at a stand still on Friday + Saturday Gen. Butler had not conceived the idea of landing troops in the inter shore and cutting off communication with New Orleans—the men wading with the greatest difficulty through mud and marsh, I doubt whether the forts would have surrendered till this time. Nothing so dispirited them as I have been told by the Garrisoners themselves, and as the desertion of two hundred + forty six in one night proves." Peck letter, May 4, 1862, Peck-Montgomery Family Papers, LC. The *New York Tribune* correspondent thought that the forts' "fate was fixed the moment that Commodore Farragut had evaded them." *New York Tribune*, May 12, 1862.

43 Warley's testimony in John Kirkwood Mitchell Papers, in *Confederate Military Manuscripts: Series A*, frame 864; Read, "Reminiscences of the Confederate States Navy," 342.

44 *Franklin (La.) Weekly Junior Register*, Apr. 24, 1862; *New Orleans Daily Picayune*, Apr. 29, 1862 (report copied from the *New Orleans Bee* of Apr. 28, 1862); Higgins to Lieutenant William Bridges, Apr. 30, 1862, in *OR*, ser. 1, vol. 6, 549; *New Orleans Daily Picayune*, May 1, 1862. Lieutenant Colonel Higgins testified at Major General Lovell's court-martial that the forts had sixty days' provisions at hand. Colonel Szymanski, who commanded Confederate forces at the Quarantine Station, offered the only negative assessment of the forts' condition, stating that Fort Jackson was flooded with eighteen to twenty-four inches of water. *OR*, ser. 1, vol. 6, 580. For a report by Dr. Foster of the Fort St. Philip garrison and a list of the Confederate casualties on land and in the navy, see *New Orleans Daily Picayune*, Apr. 29, 1862.

45 Mitchell wrote to the Confederate navy secretary, Stephen Mallory, that "ser-

ious disturbances had occurred, and that the disaffection of the men was believed to be general, on account of what appeared to them to have become the desperate character of the defense of the forts." Mitchell's opinions and phrasing reappear in an 1877 account by another eyewitness to events, who wrote that "serious disturbances had occurred; and that the disaffection of the men was believed to be general on account of what appeared to them to have become the desperate character of the 'defense.'" See Commander Mitchell to Mallory, Aug. 19, 1862, in *ORN*, ser. 1, vol. 18, 298, and Wilkinson, *Narrative of a Blockade-Runner*, 53n.

46 Duncan's official report, Apr. 30, 1862, in *OR*, ser. 1, vol. 6, 531; Robertson, "Water Battery at Fort Jackson," 100; Read, "Reminiscences of the Confederate States Navy," 346; Lovell to Secretary of War Randolph, June 19, 1862, in *ORN*, ser. 2, vol. 1, 702.

47 Lovell to Samuel Cooper, May 22, 1862, in *OR*, ser. 1, vol. 6, 518.

48 Smith, *Between Mutiny and Obedience*, 176.

CHAPTER TWO

1 Russell, *My Diary*, 230; see also 229–30. For Russell's life, see Miller, *Reports from America*; Chapman, *Russell of the Times*; Hankinson, *Man of Wars*; and Furneaux, *First War Correspondent*. For Slidell's dinner, see Miller, *Reports from America*; mockingbird, see Russell, *My Diary*, 230.

2 Russell, *My Diary*, 239.

3 Russell, *Civil War*, 113, 128. Impressment of British subjects in Winters, *Civil War in Louisiana*, 34.

4 Russell, *My Diary*, 250. See also Russell, *Civil War*, 139. Cotton export figures in *Portland (Maine) Advertiser*, May 15, 1862.

5 Russell, *My Diary*, 231, 250. Russell noted that in Savannah Irish and German immigrants supported the Confederacy and were expected to fight for it. "There is a pressure brought to bear on them by their employers which they cannot well resist," he noted. Ibid., 158.

6 Russell, *Civil War*, 127.

7 For heat, see Russell, *My Diary*, 231, 238; Indian jungle, see ibid., 229. With up to three big fires a night, Russell became jaded despite the rumors that slaves set the fires. Near the end of his visit, he ended a diary entry: "more fires, the tocsin sounding, and so to bed." Russell, *My Diary*, 240. In his private diary, he wrote: "Incendiarism rife." Crawford, *William Howard Russell's Civil War*, 63.

8 Russell, *Civil War*, 129; Russell, *My Diary*, 239. As we will see below, the report of the six-month jail sentence is accurate, as other Unionists received that punishment. A Unionist refugee reports the confinement of a "poor old man, a

carpenter by trade," for six months for praising Lincoln at the expense of Davis. *New York Herald*, Apr. 26, 1862.

9   Russell, *My Diary*, 230; Russell, *Civil War*, 114.

10 Russell, *My Diary*, 243, 252. See also Crawford, *William Howard Russell's Civil War*, 63.

11 Russell, *My Diary*, 179.

12 Russell, *Civil War*, 127. Russell later toured the manufacturing center of Ellicott's Mills, Maryland, which he described as thoroughly Unionist. He concluded that "this is the case wherever there is a manufacturing population in Maryland, because the workmen are generally foreigners, or have come from the Northern States, and feel little sympathy with States' Rights doctrines, and the tendencies of the landed gentry to a conservative action on the slave question." Russell, *My Diary*, 492.

13 For the resources available at New Orleans, see Still, *Confederate Shipbuilding*, 29; Merrill, "Confederate Shipbuilding at New Orleans," 87.

14 Felix Senac, the navy paymaster, complained that he could not get a draft for seventy-five thousand dollars from the Treasury Department. *ORN*, ser. 2, vol. 1, 481. On Mar. 8, 1862, he noted that he still did not have the money to pay debts incurred in January. Such problems caused Secretary of the Navy Mallory to complain directly to the Treasury secretary in February 1862. "The credit of the government [is] damaged by the delays incurred in placing funds in New Orleans to meet expenditures," he noted. Senec on March 1862 shortfall and Mallory quotation from Still, *Confederate Shipbuilding*, 71.

15 *ORN*, ser. 2, vol. 1, 477. Hollins admitted, however, that his efforts proved useless because the money he borrowed showed up as bonds, which workers would not accept. Some people denied that work was ever delayed because of a shortage of funds. But even they usually hedged their testimony. For example, Captain W. C. Whittle, who had assumed command of the naval station in New Orleans, said that it did not happen on his watch. However, "I don't know whether or not it was the case [before I got there], but I heard so." Ibid., 444.

16 Still, *Confederate Shipbuilding*, 70–73.

17 *ORN*, ser. 2, vol. 1, 553.

18 Ibid., 771, 553.

19 Ibid., 771.

20 Testimony of Felix Senac, in *ORN*, ser. 2, vol. 1, 483. Senac's account of the strike concurred with that of the Tifts. For a brief account of the settlement, see *New Orleans Daily Picayune*, Nov. 14, 1861. The labor of enslaved ship carpenters also became more valuable. Diarist Henry E. Lawrence recorded that he had rented a *"ship carpenter"* named "Old Emanuel" for "$70 *per month*," a figure noteworthy enough for him to underline it. Lawrence Diary, Apr. 1, 1862.

21 Merrill, "Confederate Shipbuilding at New Orleans," 93.

22 *New Orleans Commercial Bulletin*, Aug. 3, 1861.

23 Nelson Tift and the locust pin in *ORN*, ser. 2, vol. 1, 537; Hollins in ibid., 473. Confederates turned the launch date of the *Louisiana* into a holiday, with the *New Orleans Daily Crescent* even giving directions to the shipyard. Diarist John Roy went to see the ship slide into the river but had to return the next day to see it happen. Given the failure on the first day, he "was somewhat surprised at the easey [sic] manner in which she slipped into the water." John Roy Diary, Feb. 5 and 6, 1862, LSU; *New Orleans Daily Crescent*, Feb. 6, 1862.

24 Dyer, *Secret Yankees*, 77–79; quotations on 79.

25 Moore to Jefferson Davis, June 2, 1862, in *OR*, ser. 1, vol. 15, 748.

26 *Burlington (Vt.) Free Press* story reprinted in *New York Evening Post*, May 15, 1862; report from Cairo in *New York Times*, Mar. 12, 1862, and *New York Evening Post*, Mar. 12, 1862. See also *New York Times*, Mar. 22, 1862, for "nightly" meetings of the "numerous 'Union Lodges.'" Radical abolitionists alone denied the existence of southern white Unionists. This denial enabled them to argue that all of southern society needed to be uprooted, starting with the immediate end of slavery.

27 *Portland (Maine) Advertiser*, Apr. 2, 1862; *New York Times*, Apr. 29, 1862. Chicagoan's story appears in the *New York Evening Post*, Apr. 2, 1862, and the *New York Herald*, Apr. 3, 1862. They copied it from the *Chicago Tribune*, Mar. 31, 1862.

28 *Hartford Daily Courant*, Apr. 30, 1862.

29 *Boston Courier*, May 3, 1862.

30 *Eastern Argus* (Portland, Maine), Apr. 29, 1862; *Portland (Maine) Advertiser*, May 3, 1862.

31 *New York Tribune*, Apr. 15, 1862.

32 Ibid., June 20, 1862; *New York Herald*, Apr. 3, 1862.

33 Confederates denied the existence of Unionists, since they undermined the legitimacy of their new country. Unanimity did not just raise morale—it meant that their country was the product of a popular uprising by a wronged people. In New Orleans, the *Daily Crescent* reported that "it is with feelings of the deepest pride that we point the Union officers to the fact that no union sentiment exists in our midst; that with almost one voice and one tongue this community entirely repudiates all allegiance to the old government, and warmly and devotedly adheres to the new." *New York Tribune*, May 12, 1862, from *New Orleans Daily Crescent*, Apr. 28, 1862.

34 Examples of this argument include Freehling, *South versus the South*; Current, *Lincoln's Loyalists*; Faust, *Creation of Confederate Nationalism*; Beringer et al., *Why the South Lost the Civil War*; and Stampp, *Imperiled Union*, 246–69.

35 The best overview of Unionism remains Tatum, *Disloyalty in the Confederacy*. For a broader chronological survey, see Degler, *Other South*. For rural Unionism, see Storey, *Loyalty and Loss*; Bynum, *Free State of Jones*; Inscoe and Kenzer, *Enemies of the Country*; Crawford, *Ashe County's Civil War*; Inscoe and McKinney, *Heart of Confederate Appalachia*; Pickering and Falls, *Brush Men and Vigilantes*; Sutherland, *Guerillas, Unionists, and Violence*; Paludan, *Victims*; Moneyhon, "Disloyalty and Class Consciousness"; Barnes, "Williams Clan"; Moore, "Sherman's 'Fifth Column'"; Auman, "Neighbor against Neighbor"; and Auman and Scarboro, "Heroes of America."

36 Varon, *Southern Lady, Yankee Spy*; Rogers, *Confederate Home Front*, 104–15; Dyer, *Secret Yankees*; Fitzgerald, *Urban Emancipation*, 37–41; Lack, "Law and Disorder in Confederate Atlanta"; Chesson, "Harlots or Heroines?"; Amos, "'All Absorbing Topics.'" For African Americans as Unionists, see Medford, "'I Was Always a Union Man.'" For Germans as Unionists, see Marten, *Texas Divided*.

37 Many of the works cited in the previous two notes include this interpretation, but it is advanced in convincing detail in Robinson, *Bitter Fruits of Bondage*; Williams, *Rich Man's War*; Escott, *After Secession*; and Escott, "Failure of Confederate Nationalism." Two other scholars argue that disloyalty to the Confederacy in Louisiana grew as hardships—and Confederate defeats—mounted. See Shugg, *Origins of Class Struggle in Louisiana*, 179, and Bragg, *Louisiana in the Confederacy*, 257–58.

38 See Rubin, *Shattered Nation*; Campbell, *When Sherman Marched to the Sea*; Blair, *Virginia's Private War*; Gallagher, *Confederate War*; Rable, *Confederate Republic*; and Bonner, "Flag Culture." Judkin Browning argues that many people in eastern North Carolina felt inclined toward the Union until the Emancipation Proclamation went into effect, at which point most became avid Confederates. See Browning, "Removing the Mask of Nationality."

39 *New Orleans True Delta* quoted in Dufour, *Night the War Was Lost*, 122. See also ibid., 121; *Algerine Newsboy* (Algiers, La.), Jan. 1, 4, and 11, 1862; *New Orleans Daily Picayune*, Dec. 29 and 30, 1861; and *New Orleans Commercial Bulletin*, Dec. 30, 1861. Between 1,000 and 15,000 pounds of gunpowder exploded. For the attempt to destroy the powder magazine, see *New Orleans Commercial Bulletin*, June 13, 1861.

40 *New Orleans Bee*, Mar. 28, 1862, quoted in *New York Times*, Apr. 20, 1862. The ship targeted was identified only as "the large vessel now building for our Government at Jefferson City." Both the *Mississippi* and the *Louisiana* were under construction there.

41 For Monroe presiding over hearings, see *New York Herald*, Apr. 26, 1862, and frequent references in the *New Orleans Commercial Bulletin*. Suppression of

dissent in Confederate New Orleans in Rousey, *Policing the Southern City*, 103–5.

42 This includes fifteen people mentioned in the City Intelligence column and four people listed in a story in the paper's editorial section on Sept. 6, 1861. The City Intelligence column missed three arrests for abolitionism in April 1862. New Orleans police records note the arrest of William Tellman "for being an abolitionist + a dangerous and suspicious character" on Apr. 22, 1862, and of August Franks "for being an abolitionist" on Apr. 24, 1862. "Reports of Arrests, Second District, 1862–1864," Department of Police Records, NOPL. The *New Orleans Daily Crescent* listed the arrest of Joseph Rousselion "on the serious charge of being an abolitionist" on Apr. 2, 1862. See also Dufour, *Night the War Was Lost*, 40–41.

43 *New Orleans Commercial Bulletin*, Oct. 7, 1861; all quotations about Drummond in ibid., Nov. 6, 1861; Reynolds in ibid., July 29, 1861.

44 Ibid., May 27, 1861; Lickenham in ibid., June 18, 1861.

45 Ibid., Apr. 24, Aug. 3, and May 11, 1861.

46 Ibid., May 11, 1861; F. Edwards, T. J. Edwards, William Davis, and D. Battelle to Benjamin Butler, June 3 and 6, 1862, Butler Papers, box 12; Ellis case in *New Orleans Commercial Bulletin*, Oct. 15, 17, and 25, 1861.

47 See, for example, the sentencing of John Hobson to be executed at Fort St. Philip "for desertion and assaulting an officer." *New Orleans Commercial Bulletin*, Jan. 30, 1862.

48 First quotation from Unsigned to Pa, Feb. 16, 1861, filed under "Republic of Louisiana," HNOC; Dostie letter included in Reed, *Life of A. P. Dostie*, 24; N. Maria Taylor to Benjamin Flanders, Aug. 14, 1862, Benjamin Flanders Collection, LSU.

49 *New Orleans Commercial Bulletin*, Aug. 24, 1861; Frenzel in ibid., Nov. 22 and 26, 1861.

50 Ibid., May 27, 1861; Dewey letter in ibid., Aug. 3, 1861.

51 Quotation from *New Orleans Commercial Bulletin*, Aug. 2, 1861. See also Winters, *Civil War in Louisiana*, 40.

52 For free market, see Bragg, *Louisiana in the Confederacy*, 89. For an example of set food prices, see *New Orleans Delta*, Apr. 4, 1862, reprinted in *New York Herald*, Apr. 23, 1862.

53 *New Orleans Daily Crescent*, Feb. 5, 1862; *Planters' Banner* (Franklin, La.), reprinted in *New Orleans Daily Crescent*, Jan. 13, 1862; Lovell's order in *New Orleans Daily Picayune*, Apr. 9, 1862. For stay laws in the Confederacy, see Rable, *Confederate Republic*, 36–37.

54 June 1861 order in *OR*, ser. 4, vol. 1, 752; Nov. 1861 order in ibid.; Lovell's January 1862 order in *New Orleans Daily Picayune*, Feb. 5, 1862. For trade with

enemy, see also Winters, *Civil War in Louisiana*, 47. For arrested fishermen, see the *New Orleans Commercial Bulletin*, July 6, Aug. 3, Oct. 15 and 16, 1861, and Feb. 3 and Apr. 29, 1862. Unionist refugee in *New York Herald*, Apr. 26, 1862. Final Lovell quotation in *New Orleans Daily Picayune*, Feb. 5, 1862. General Twiggs, Lovell's predecessor, complained that planters slipped their cotton into the city for export, even though this would "give aid and comfort to our enemies." *OR*, ser. 3, vol. 2, 726.

55 Lovell's arrests in *New Orleans Daily Picayune*, Apr. 22, 1862; report, Apr. 8, 1862, in *Boston Journal*, Apr. 29, 1862; Freeman Foster Jr., to father, Apr. 9, 1862, Freeman Foster Jr. Letters, LSU.

56 Four soldiers wrote about the refugees: Daniel Durgin to mother, Mar. 31, 1862, Daniel Veasey Durgin Letters, NHHS; Richard H. Elliott Diary, Mar. 24, 1862, CLH; George R. Hughes Diary, Mar. 26, 1862, WSHS; Terrence Sheridan Diary, Mar. 26, 1862, NHCHS. Freeman Foster Jr. to father, Apr. 2, 1862, Freeman Foster Jr. Letters, LSU.

57 *Springfield (Mass.) Daily Republican*, Apr. 29, 1862.

58 Lovell to Judah P. Benjamin, Mar. 22, 1862, in *ORN*, ser. 2, vol. 1, 692; for complaints, see Radley, *Rebel Watchdog*, 190–92; final Lovell quotation and text of the decree in *New Orleans Bee*, Mar. 15, 1862.

59 Earlier figure from *New Orleans True Delta*, Apr. 6, 1862, reprinted in *New York Herald*, May 14, 1862; second figure from *New Orleans Bee*, Apr. 14, 1862.

60 Winters, *Civil War in Louisiana*, 32; see also 74–75. Edward Murphy to W. H. Renaud, Aug. 16, 1861, Murphy Family Papers, HNOC. See also Shugg, *Origins of Class Struggle in Louisiana*, 176.

61 *New Orleans Daily Crescent*, Apr. 14, 1862; ibid., Mar. 1, 1862; *New Orleans Bee*, Feb. 22, 1862. The parishes that it said had failed to raise a company were Calcasieu, St. Bernard, St. Charles, St. John the Baptist, St. Tammany, and Vermillion. The parishes that had raised only one company included Assumption, St. Martin, Terrebone, Lafouche, Ascension, Lafayette, Plaquemine (home of Forts Jackson and St. Philip), and Jefferson.

62 Winters, *Civil War in Louisiana*, 31, 58; Shugg, *Origins of Class Struggle in Louisiana*, 173; quotation in Grivot in *OR*, ser. 4, vol. 1, 753.

63 The January 1862 law is discussed in Robinson, *Bitter Fruits of Bondage*, 155–56, and Winters, *Civil War in Louisiana*, 72–74; *New Orleans Bee*, 24 Feb. 1862.

64 Report, June 4, 1862, in *New York Times*, June 17, 1862; fifteen-year-old boy's story in letter by Morris Fyfe from Camp Boardman, Oct. 14, 1861, Fyfe Family Papers, 1848–69, in *Confederate Military Manuscripts, Series B*; Brooklyn man's story in John David to Benjamin Butler, June 19, 1862, Butler Papers, box 13; vigilance committee mentioned by a "foreign resident" of New Orleans who had fled to Cincinnati, *Portland (Maine) Advertiser*, Apr. 18, 1862; Butler

about the sheriff in undated fragment/draft in Butler's hand, Butler Papers, box 12.

65 *New Orleans Bee*, Feb. 11, 1862; *New Orleans Daily Crescent*, Feb. 20, 1862; *New Orleans Daily Crescent*, Feb. 24, 1862.

66 Lewis's order reprinted in *New Orleans Commercial Bulletin*, Nov. 27, 1861; *New Orleans Daily Crescent*, Jan. 10, 1862; Crescent Blues broadside in LHAC, box 9; Plaquemines Parish observer quoted in Robinson, *Bitter Fruits of Bondage*, 50; Dick Corbett quoted in "Q. M." of the 12th Connecticut Volunteers, letter, Apr. 21, 1862, in *Hartford Daily Courant*, May 24, 1862.

67 State militia law in Robinson, *Bitter Fruits of Bondage*, 155–56. For national draft law, see ibid., 152–62; quotation on 153.

68 *Manasses* diary copied in report, Apr. 25, 1862, in *New York Evening Post*, May 8, 1862; report of mutinies at Memphis and Grand Junction in *New Orleans Commercial Bulletin*, Aug. 5, 1861 (copied from *Memphis Appeal*, Aug. 3, 1861); *New Orleans Daily Crescent*, Feb. 26, 1862. Replacement of Captain Stevenson with Lieutenant Warley discussed in Read, "Reminiscences of the Confederate States Navy," 334.

69 Officer quoted in Winters, *Civil War in Louisiana*, 66; Bragg quoted in Dufour, *Night the War Was Lost*, 179.

70 *OR*, ser. 1, vol. 6, 564, 561.

CHAPTER THREE

1 Lawrence Diary, Apr. 28 and 29, 1862.

2 *Franklin (La.) Weekly Junior Register*, June 21, 1862.

3 Boston Passenger Lists, 1820–1943, M277, reel 23, NA, for the arrival of the Ashtons on the *Astracan*. Alexander Ashton appears to have been counted twice in the U.S. Census of 1850, once in Philadelphia on Aug. 28, 1850 (by a census taker who got names and ages correct but misidentified the place of birth of everyone in the family), and once in Greenwood Township, Gloucester County, New Jersey. U.S. Bureau of the Census, Federal Manuscript Census, Population Schedule, 1850; Second Ward, Philadelphia, U.S. Bureau of the Census, Federal Manuscript Census, Population Schedule, 1860, both in NA.

4 Lovell's General Order No. 11, Dec. 11, 1861, in Forts Jackson and St. Philip Collection, HNOC; Duncan to "Sir," Oct. 5, 1861, in Post Letter Book, Forts Jackson and St. Philip, 1861–62, TU.

5 *ORN*, ser. 1, vol. 18, 390–92; Harris's letter copied in report, May 5, 1862, in *New York Times*, May 23, 1862.

6 Companies B, D, E, and H of the 1st Louisiana Heavy Artillery had been in Fort Jackson since at least November 1861. Company B had been briefly posted in

Fort St. Philip in March 1862 but appears to have been transferred back to Fort Jackson before the surrender. Muster Rolls, 1st Louisiana Heavy Artillery, November 1861–April 1862, NA.

7 Prokopowicz, *All for the Regiment*; Dunkelman, *Brothers One and All*. For company-level loyalties, see Piston and Hatcher, *Wilson's Creek*. This point is mentioned in relation to the Fort Jackson garrison in Bergeron, "'They Bore Themselves with Distinguished Gallantry,'" 261.

8 Duncan's letter about MacManus, undated, and Duncan to Moore, Aug. 4, 1861, both in Post Letter Book, Forts Jackson and St. Philip, 1861–62, TU.

9 Court-martial proceedings included in Lovell's General Order No. 11, Dec. 11, 1861, in Forts Jackson and St. Philip Collection, HNOC. General Duncan later transferred Brand out of Fort St. Philip to make sure that he did not command the post, commenting that "neither the officers nor men at Fort St. Philip have that confidence in Capt Brand which should exist at such times as these, and in which I agree with them entirely owing to the lack of earnestness in Capt Brand's character." Perhaps Duncan's doubts were justified. When Duncan left to inspect another part of the coastal defenses, Brand took three junior officers and a group of navy officers on a thirteen-hour jaunt to round up some vegetables. Captain Anderson had already left to visit his ailing wife. Duncan questioned Brand's judgment in leaving the fort so short of officers. Duncan to General David Twiggs, undated but apparently late September, in Post Letter Book; vegetable trip in Duncan to Twiggs, Oct. 6, 1861, Post Letter Book. Governor Moore appointed Frederick Brand and James Anderson to the rank of captain in March 1861. Brand served in the U.S. Navy before the war. *New Orleans Commercial Bulletin*, Mar. 15, 1861.

10 Brand's leave of absence extended by Lovell on Dec. 27, 1861, in Forts Jackson and St. Philip Collection; for Duncan on Brand's letters, see Duncan to Brand, Jan. 11, 1862, in Post Letter Book. Brand later served as a lieutenant colonel in Miles's Louisiana Legion during the 1863 siege of Port Hudson.

11 *Franklin (La.) Junior Register*, Feb. 6, 1862. Sugar constituted 67 percent of the agricultural production of St. Mary's Parish in 1849. See Pace, "'It Was Bedlam Let Loose,'" 407.

12 Sugar harvesting described in Dunn, *Sugar and Slaves*, 189–201.

13 Population statistics from U.S. Bureau of the Census, Federal Manuscript Census, Population Schedule, 1860, St. Mary's Parish. Church fund-raising in *Franklin (La.) Junior Register*, Dec. 26, 1861.

14 U.S. Bureau of the Census, Federal Manuscript Census, Population Schedule, 1860, St. Mary's Parish; *Attakapas Register* (Franklin, La.), May 30, 1861.

15 *Attakapas Register* (Franklin, La.), Jan. 24, 1861; *Franklin (La.) Junior Register*, Mar. 6, 1862.

16 Letter, May 10, 1861, in *Attakapas Register* (Franklin, La.), June 20, 1861. Some maps refer to the town as Jeannerette.

17 *New York Evening Post*, Jan. 31, 1862, copied from an unknown Chicago newspaper, which clipped it from an unknown New Orleans paper; Lovell to Judah Benjamin, Dec. 5, 1861, in *ORN*, ser. 2, vol. 1, 649.

18 *Attakapas Register* (Franklin, La.), June 20, 1861. The cannons, three six-pounders and one twelve-pounder, in ibid., July 18 and 25, 1861.

19 St. Mary's had sent Company G, 13th Louisiana Volunteers, to Tennessee. See *Franklin (La.) Junior Register*, Dec. 26, 1861. Olivier also ran for the Confederate Congress. He resigned his commission as a second lieutenant just weeks before the unit shipped out to Fort Jackson. For St. Mary's Cannoneers, see St. Mary's Cannoneers (1st Field Battery), reel 47, Compiled Service Records of Confederate Soldiers Who Served in Organizations from the State of Louisiana, M320, NA.

20 Drill schedule advertised in *Attakapas Register* (Franklin, La.), July 25, 1861.

21 In August 1862, four cannons of the same size as those given to the Cannoneers and that "belonged" to St. Mary's Parish were given to another unit. See Bergeron, "Yellow Jackets Battalion," 55.

22 Duncan's card in *New Orleans Daily Picayune*, May 2, 1862; *Franklin (La.) Weekly Junior Register*, June 12, 1862.

23 In two cases, slave ownership is inferred. For example, Henry T. Foote is not listed as the owner of any slaves in the slave census, but his occupation is listed as merchant and planter, and he shares a page with four other Footes, all slaveholders, including his next-door neighbor, the 76-year-old Henry Foote, who owned real estate and belongings (including people) worth well over a hundred thousand dollars. Also counted as a slaveholder is Minos Gordy, who lived with John Gordy, the owner of thirty-nine people. U.S. Bureau of the Census, Federal Manuscript Census, Free and Slave Schedules, 1860, St. Mary's Parish, NA.

24 Ibid.

25 U.S. Bureau of the Census, Federal Manuscript Census, 1860, St. Mary's Parish.

26 Ibid.

27 A Knights pamphlet published in the parish argued that Republican Reconstruction "can never break down the impassible partition walls which nature has placed between the Caucasian and African races." See "White Man's, or—Caucasian Club," 9. On Oct. 18, 1868, the Republican sheriff of St. Mary's Parish, Colonel Henry H. Pope, and a local judge named Chase were brutally killed by five men for their roles in local Reconstruction. Blackburn and Brown, *Franklin through the Years*, 35.

28 For James McDonald as captain of the *Jeff Davis*, see *Attakapas Register* (Franklin, La.), Apr. 11 and Sept. 5, 1861.

29 Ibid., June 20, 1861.

30 The parish issued at least seventy thousand dollars in bonds before the Cannoneers left the parish. See ibid., May 30, 1861, and *Franklin (La.) Weekly Junior Register*, Mar. 20, 1862; "Hard Times" story in *Attakapas Register* (Franklin, La.), May 23, 1861; Free Market in *Franklin (La.) Junior Register*, Jan. 30, 1862.

31 *Franklin (La.) Weekly Junior Register*, Apr. 24, 1862.

32 They should not be confused with the Confederate Regular Army created during the inaugural meetings of the Confederate States of America in Montgomery, Alabama. The 1st Louisiana Heavy Artillery was part of the Regular Army of the state of Louisiana, one of many regiments raised by states as part of a permanent army that mirrored the national Regulars. For the Confederate Regular Army, see Weinert, *Confederate Regular Army*. It is possible to make too much of the distinction between the state and national Regular Army units; Company C of the 1st Louisiana Heavy Artillery had been raised in Baton Rouge as part of the Confederate Regular Army, only to be folded into the state regiment before the battle. It served in Fort St. Philip. See ibid., 57–59. For haircuts in the Georgia Regulars, see Andrews, *Footprints of a Regiment*, 4.

33 Coffman, *Old Army*, 137. For the size of Jefferson's army, see Smelser, *Democratic Republic*, 55–56. For American distrust of standing armies in the Revolutionary period and early Republic, see Bailyn, *Ideological Origins of the American Republic*, 112–19, and Banning, *Jeffersonian Persuasion*, 259–64.

34 Coffman, *Old Army*, 137–48; statistics on 141. See also Foos, *Short, Offhand, Killing Affair*, 13–30.

35 1st Louisiana Heavy Artillery, Compiled Service Records of Confederate Soldiers Who Served in Organizations from Louisiana.

36 Discharge papers and other information found in ibid. A member of the 1st Georgia Regulars remembered that his regiment included "a good many Irish." See Andrews, *Footprints of a Regiment*, 20. For the social and economic status of clerks, see Luskey, "Jumping Counters in White Collars," 173–219.

37 1st Louisiana Heavy Artillery, Compiled Service Records of Confederate Soldiers Who Served in Organizations from Louisiana.

38 Way, *Common Labor*. Immigrant background of most canallers, 76–104; for work conditions, 131–62; worker-community relations, 163–99.

39 1st Louisiana Heavy Artillery, Compiled Service Records of Confederate Soldiers Who Served in Organizations from Louisiana. For an introduction to Jacksonian era almshouses, see Rockman, *Welfare Reform in the Early Republic*.

40 For 1837–60, see Way, *Common Labor*, 205–64. 1st Louisiana Heavy Artillery, Compiled Service Records of Confederate Soldiers Who Served in Organizations from Louisiana.

41 Paperwork for wages in 1st Louisiana Heavy Artillery, Compiled Service Records of Confederate Soldiers Who Served in Organizations from Louisiana. Officers, unlike common soldiers, paid for their own uniforms, however.

42 Ibid.

43 Ibid.

44 Way, *Common Labor*, 200–264; gunpowder on 221, quotation on 214. Management tried several tactics to stop collective labor activism such as strikes and violence against representatives of the corporation. One practice was to employ Catholic priests on the company payrolls. Priests would serve the men's religious needs but would also oblige their corporate employers by preaching against labor activism. As Way notes, "bringing in a priest was often the only way to head off bloodshed and get the men back to work at times of labor unrest." Viewed against this historical backdrop, the appearance of Father Nachon alongside the Confederate officers during the mutiny is unsurprising. Ibid., 187–92; quotation on 191. For Father Nachon's appearance, see Jones, *Civil War Memoirs of Captain William J. Seymour*, 33.

45 There are no definite figures on how many men in any given command mutinied and left the garrison that night. The figures given here, stated as a percentage of the command's strength, are arrived at using the following methodology: Union officer Harris reported on the number of musicians, privates, and noncommissioned officers from each company surrendered at Fort Jackson on April 28. Since most, if not all, of the mutineers would have remained with Butler's troops at the Quarantine Station on that date, Harris's figure is then compared with the most recent muster roll of that company. The four Regular companies had a known strength of 288 men, of whom 187 remained in the fort. This methodology is hardly exact, since recruits could have been added to the companies before the attacks, some casualties were taken, and lists and figures can contain mistakes. Interestingly, if we factor out the St. Mary's Cannoneers and the officer corps, we find that 216 of 517 men (42 percent) in the garrison mutinied, a figure only somewhat below the estimates of 250 or perhaps 300 mutineers that appear in contemporary accounts. Harris's report, Apr. 28, 1862, in *New York Times*, May 23, 1862.

46 1st Louisiana Heavy Artillery, Compiled Service Records of Confederate Soldiers Who Served in Organizations from Louisiana. In Fort St. Philip's Company C of the 1st Louisiana Heavy Artillery, only one private went on to serve in the Confederate military after the surrender. See Weinert, *Confederate Regular Army*, 59.

47 For a chapter on the concept of "coerced" volunteers during the Mexican-American War, see Foos, *Short, Offhand, Killing Affair*, 61–81.

48 For the percentage of men who mutinied, see note 45 above. Information regarding men in these units from 22nd/21st Louisiana Volunteers, reels 318–21, and 23rd/22nd Louisiana Volunteers, reels 322–26, both in Compiled Service Records of Confederate Soldiers Who Served in Organizations from Louisiana. Note that the unit numbers of these two regiments were changed after Fort Jackson. The 22nd Louisiana became the 21st, and the 23rd became the 22nd. I will refer to them by their designations at the time of the battle. They are also known by the names of their regimental commanders. Thus, the 22nd is often known as "Patton's," and the 23rd is called "Theard's." For brief unit histories, see Bergeron, *Guide to Louisiana Confederate Military Units*, 125–27. Crule, *Units of the Confederate States Army*, 153–54. See also Bergeron, "'They Bore Themselves with Distinguished Gallantry,'" 253–82.

49 23rd Louisiana Volunteers, Compiled Service Records of Confederate Soldiers Who Served in Organizations from Louisiana.

50 Muster Rolls, 22nd Louisiana Volunteers, 1861–62, NA.

51 For the percentage of men who mutinied, see endnote 45 above. For further service, see 22nd/21st Louisiana Volunteers, reels 318–21, Compiled Service Records of Confederate Soldiers Who Served in Organizations from Louisiana.

52 Population figures in Lonn, *Foreigners in the Confederacy*, 481.

53 Marten, *Texas Divided*, 113–21; quotation on 107. See also Bailey, "Defiant Unionists," 208–28; Lonn, *Foreigners in the Confederacy*, 421–38; and Smyrl, "Texans in the Union Army," 234–50.

54 Kattner, "Diversity of Old South White Women"; quotation on 308.

55 See Lonn, *Foreigners in the Confederacy*, 417, and for Louisiana, Current, *Lincoln's Loyalists*, 89.

56 *New Orleans Daily Crescent*, Apr. 14, 1862; Lonn, *Foreigners in the Confederacy*, 481; *New Orleans Bee*, Feb. 20, 1862.

57 For Hessians, see *New Orleans Daily Crescent*, Feb. 10, 1862; Hirsch story in ibid., Jan. 20, 1862; Lieutenant Colonel Palfrey quoted in *OR*, ser. 1, vol. 6, 620.

58 *New York Herald*, May 3, 1862; ibid., Apr. 26, 1862; Henry A. Sa[torn page] to Shepley, June 2, 1862, Shepley Papers, collection 117; Pilot Town report, May 5, 1862, in *New York Times*, May 22, 1862.

59 Ernest Wench to Benjamin Butler, May 1862, Butler Papers, box 12. See also R. B. Nay to Butler, June 13, 1862, Butler Papers, box 12, for Nay's claim that the consul for Hanover, Prussia, formed a "battalion or Regiment of foreigners" for local defense, only to find themselves shipped out to the front in time for Shiloh. Once at Corinth, the unit became "dissatisfied," at which point "a

portion of them were placed in the *forts* here." The remainder of the unit, Nay continues, fought at Shiloh only because the Confederates placed a regiment of cavalry behind them to keep them from fleeing.

60 Soulé, *Know Nothing Party in New Orleans*, 52, 65. See also Carriere, "Anti-Catholicism, Nativism, and Louisiana Politics in the 1850s."

61 Soulé, *Know Nothing Party in New Orleans*, 84. John M. Sacher also discusses the party's use of "intimidation and violence on election days to rule virtually unchallenged." See Sacher, *Perfect War of Politics*, 259. The best study of the relationship between Know-Nothing politicians and gang leaders is Towers, *Urban South and the Coming of the Civil War*, 112, 121–36.

62 Towers, *Urban South and the Coming of the Civil War*, 146–47; Soulé, *Know Nothing Party in New Orleans*, 94–105. For Duncan's role in the vigilance committee, see report, May 5, 1862, in *New York Times*, May 23, 1862, and report, June 14, 1862, in *New York Times*, June 23, 1862. This report mentions that George B. McClellan helped Duncan hold the arsenal.

63 Johnson, "Slave Trader," 13–38.

64 For the Know-Nothing economic agenda in New Orleans, see Towers, *Urban South and the Coming of the Civil War*, 2–3, 111, 195. Studies of the national Know-Nothing movement include Voss-Hubbard, *Beyond Party*; Levine, "Conservatism, Nativism, and Slavery"; Formisano, " 'Party Period' Revisited"; Anbinder, *Nativism and Slavery*; Mulkern, *Know-Nothing Party in Massachusetts*; Baker, *Ambivalent Americans*; Holt, "Politics of Impatience"; and Gienapp, *Origins of the Republican Party*.

65 Faust, *Creation of Confederate Nationalism*, 32–39, 49, quotation on 35; Rable, *Confederate Republic*, 48, 54–56, 62, 122–23; Towers, *Urban South and the Coming of the Civil War*, 1, 7–8, 15–36. Anti-immigrant feeling is explored in Lonn, *Foreigners in the Confederacy*, 417–38. See also Marten, *Texas Divided*, 107–22.

66 *OR*, ser. 3, vol. 2, 280.

CHAPTER FOUR

1 Snyder's advertisement in the *New Orleans Daily Picayune*, Feb. 6, 1862. This appears to be the only information about him besides his 1862 diary. He is not listed in city directories, credit books, or the 1860 federal census.

2 Henry A. Snyder Diary, Jan. 2, 1862, LSU.

3 Ibid., Jan. 13, 17, and 27 and Feb. 7 and 10, 1862.

4 For reorganization, see ibid., Feb. 24, 1862. For calls to serve in Tennessee, see Feb. 25 and 26 and Mar. 1, 1862. Departure of volunteers for Columbus, Mar. 4, 1862.

5   Caly Nevins to "My dear Sister," Mar. 2, 1862, Edward Clifton Wharton Family Papers, in *Confederate Military Manuscripts, Series B*; *New York Herald*, Apr. 26, 1862. See also *New York Times*, Mar. 22, 1862. Both newspapers cited refugees as their source.

6   Snyder Diary, Mar. 11, 1862, LSU.

7   Initial camp described in ibid., Mar. 16, 1862; move to Lafayette Square, Mar. 24, 1862; permission to leave camp, Mar. 30, 1862.

8   *New Orleans Delta*, May 4, 1862, reprinted in *Kennebec Journal* (Portland, Maine), June 6, 1862.

9   Snyder Diary, Apr. 7, 1862, LSU.

10 Ibid.

11 *OR*, ser. 1, vol. 6, 564.

12 All quotations from Snyder Diary, Apr. 25, 1862, LSU. Train ride detailed in Winters, *Civil War in Louisiana*, 97. The *New Orleans Bee* (Apr. 26, 1862) also noticed that members of the Confederate Guards deserted as they pulled out of the city. It observed that after striking their tents in Lafayette Square "several of them were joining their families" as others "prepared to go" north on the trains.

13 All quotations from Snyder Diary, Apr. 26, 1862, LSU.

14 Ibid., Apr. 29 and May 1, 1862. Reference to unit being paid in S. M. Westmore to "Sir" (presumably Shepley), June 16, 1862, Shepley Papers, collection 117. Snyder does not mention being paid.

15 Snyder Diary, May 2, 1862, LSU.

16 Ibid., May 6, 1862.

17 For bread, see ibid., June 26, 1862; Mrs. Plumb in ibid., June 17, 1862. A second-class ticket cost only twenty-five dollars. See *Boston Courier*, June 24, 1862, copied from the *New Orleans Daily Picayune*.

18 Bonney's escape, background, and attire drawn from "Agaius," letter, Apr. 24, 1862, in *Boston Journal*, May 8, 1862; report, Apr. 20, 1862, in *New York Herald*, May 10, 1862; and Oscar Smith Diary, Apr. 20, 1862, LC. Date of enlistment from Muster Roll, Company I, 23rd Louisiana Volunteers, Feb. 28, 1862, NA.

19 Samuel Massa Diary, Apr. 20, 1862, Massa Papers; Richard Edes letter, Apr. 20, 1862, Edes Family Papers, MassHS; and reports from David Porter, including Apr. 25, 1862, report citing "a deserter who can be relied on." See Porter, Squadron Letters, Mortar Flotilla, NA. See also report, Apr. 27, 1862, in *New York Herald*, May 8, 1862.

20 See report, Apr. 23, 1862, in *New York Herald*, May 10, 1862, and Samuel Massa Diary, Apr. 21, 1862, Massa Papers.

21 See report in the *Chicago Times*, May 12, 1862; report, Apr. 18, 1862, in *New*

York Times, May 8, 1862; report, Apr. 10, 1862, in *New York Herald*, Apr. 29, 1862; and reports, Apr. 20, 22, and 24, 1862, in *New York Herald*, May 10, 1862.

22 Lawrence Diary, Apr. 30, 1862.

23 Report, Mar. 15, 1862, in *New York Herald*, Apr. 29, 1862; "Agaius" report, Apr. 8, 1862, in *Boston Journal*, Apr. 29, 1862; on bottled intelligence from the fort, see report, Apr. 27, 1862, in *New York Herald*, May 10, 1862; Confederate authorities complained about Unionists in New Orleans throwing bottles "containing newspapers and memorandums in writing, giving information to the blockaders." *New York Times*, Mar. 16, 1862.

24 Jones, *Civil War Memoirs of Captain William J. Seymour*, 26. For Duncan's request for "fire-barges," see Johnson K. Duncan to Captain Mitchell, Apr. 24, 1862, Johnson Kelly Duncan Letters, MS 109, HNOC. Duncan's official report blamed Mitchell for not illuminating the river. See *OR*, ser. 1, vol. 6, 534.

25 Report, Apr. 25, 1862, in *New York Times*, May 8, 1862; William Waud Papers, MS 106, folder 40, HNOC. Waud's note is on the back of a business card from a Newark clothier. On gunsmoke, see also Read, "Reminiscences of the Confederate States Navy," 344. The *New York Times* correspondent H. J. W. discusses the boat he shared with Mr. Hills of the *Boston Journal* in the *New York Times*, Apr. 29, 1862.

26 *Chelsea (Mass.) Telegraph and Pioneer*, May 24, 1862; Read, "Reminiscences of the Confederate States Navy," 343; Jerry Flint to brother, June 12, 1862, Jerry E. Flint Papers, 1861–66, WSHS; Frank Peck letter, May 4, 1862, Peck-Montgomery Family Papers, LC.

27 Quotation from Joseph S. Harris's report to F. H. Gerdes of the U.S. Coast Survey, May 4, 1862, in correspondent's report, May 5, 1862, in *New York Times*, May 23, 1862.

28 Muster Rolls, Company I, 23rd Louisiana Volunteers, Dec. 31, 1861, Feb. 28, 1862, and Mar. 29, 1862, NA.

29 *New York Times*, May 23, 1862; Lawrence Diary, Apr. 30, 1862.

30 *OR*, ser. 1, vol. 6, 544.

31 Fleet disobedience in ibid., 542; Read, "Reminiscences of the Confederate States Navy," 342; Samuel Massa Diary, Apr. 26, 1862, Massa Papers; report, Apr. 30, 1862, in *New York Herald*, May 10, 1862; Zerah Getchell to George Shepley, May 21, 1862, Shepley Papers, collection 117.

32 *OR*, ser. 1, vol. 6, 531.

33 The Confederate veteran's story in Frank Harding to his father, May 3, 1862, Harding Papers; report, May 5, 1862, in *New York Times*, May 23, 1862.

34 George Davis to brother and sister, May 3, 1862, George H. Davis Letters, LSU; Szymanski's biography in *OR*, ser. 1, vol. 6, 580; Samuel Massa Diary, Apr. 24, 1862, Massa Papers (Massa came away from the Quarantine with souvenirs,

including a homespun Confederate uniform, a rifle, a bayonet, and an "ugly looking" weapon called an "Arkansas tooth pick" that had a nearly foot-long blade); report, Apr. 24, 1862, in *New York Herald*, May 10, 1862; estimate of number of Confederates surrendered at Quarantine in report, Apr. 27, 1862, in *New York Times*, May 11, 1862; quotations describing Chalmette Regiment in Oscar Smith Diary, Apr. 24, 1862, LC.

35 Deployments described in Chittenden, *History and Catalogue of the Fourth Regiment Wisconsin Volunteers*, 7.

36 Presence of women at the Quarantine when Butler's troops arrived in George Davis to brother and sister, May 3, 1862, Davis Letters, LSU; bribery quotations from *New York Tribune*, May 14, 1862, and also paraphrased in *Eastern Argus* (Portland, Maine), May 10, 1862. Both papers probably copied the story from the *Memphis Avalanche*. Jones, *Civil War Memoirs of Captain William J. Seymour*, 32; stench on river from report, Apr. 30, 1862, in *New York Herald*, May 10, 1862. For women visiting the fort, see also Rowland and Croxall, *Journal of Julia Le Grand*, 42–43, and *ORN*, ser. 1, vol. 18, 342.

37 For time of surrender, see Deck Logs, USS *Kennebec, Miami*, and *Winona*, NA, as well as Herrman, *Yeoman in Farragut's Fleet*, 27; Richard H. Elliott Diary, Apr. 28 and 29, 1862, CLH; and Chittenden, *History and Catalogue of the Fourth Regiment Wisconsin Volunteers*, 7. For occupying forces, see Chittenden, *History and Catalogue of the Fourth Regiment Wisconsin Volunteers*, 7; Deck Logs, USS *Winona*, Apr. 28, 1862, and USS *Wissahicken*, Apr. 28, 1862, NA. For shipping out of the Cannoneers, see Deck Log, USS *Kennebec*, Apr. 28 and 29, 1862, NA, and report, Apr. 29, 1862, *New York Herald*, May 10, 1862.

38 For an account of the mutineers who left the fort being housed at the Quarantine, see Samuel Massa Diary, Apr. 28, 1862, Massa Papers.

39 Report, Apr. 30, 1862, in *New York Evening Post*, May 22, 1862; Frank Harding to father, May 3, 1862, Harding Papers; report, May 1, 1862, in *New York Herald*, May 14, 1862.

40 Report, May 5, 1862, in *New York Times*, May 23, 1862; Alfred Parmenter to father and mother, May 1, 1862, Parmenter Papers; Howe, *Passages*, 119.

41 Report, Apr. 30, 1862, in *New York Herald*, May 10, 1862.

42 Goodhue to mother, Apr. 29, 1862, Goodhue Correspondence; Phelps in *OR*, ser. 1, vol. 6, 510; Porter in *ORN*, ser. 1, vol. 18, 371.

43 H. W. Howe to parents, Apr. 29, 1862, reprinted in Howe, *Passages*, 119; Frank Harding to father, May 3, 1862, Harding Papers.

44 Alfred Parmenter to father and mother, May 1, 1862, Parmenter Papers.

45 For Fort Jackson workers, see report, Apr. 30, 1862, in *New York Evening Post*, May 22, 1862; for Quarantine, see George Davis to brother and sister, May 3, 1862, Davis Letters, LSU.

46 Farragut to Welles, Apr. 25, 1862, Squadron Letters, Roll 185, NA; Boggs in report, Apr. 25, 1862, in *New York Times*, May 8, 1862; Duncan in *New Orleans Bee*, May 2, 1862.

47 For Fort Jackson volunteers, see report, Apr. 30, 1862, in *New York Evening Post*, May 22, 1862; for men who desired to enlist at the Quarantine, see George Davis to brother and sister, May 3, 1862, Davis Letters, LSU; Duncan in *OR*, ser. 1, vol. 6, 533.

48 Quotation is Morse paraphrasing what he had been told; misspellings in original. Benjamin Morse to Rosina, May 22, 1862, Gale-Morse Family Papers, VtHS.

49 *OR*, ser. 1, vol. 6, 553. Report, Apr. 25, 1862, in *New York Herald*, May 10, 1862.

50 *Chelsea (Mass.) Telegraph and Pioneer*, May 24 and 31, 1862, from <www.letter-scivilwar.com/4-28-62a.html>; Deck Log, USS *Oneida*, Apr. 25, 1862, NA; John Roy Diary, Apr. 25, 1862, LSU. A Confederate soldier at Chalmette had called it "well fortified." See Durgin letter, Dec. 18, 1861, James and John Durgin Papers, in *Confederate Military Manuscripts, Series B*.

51 Report, Apr. 25, 1862, in *New York Herald*, May 10, 1862. Smith's casualties reported in *OR*, ser. 1, vol. 6, 553.

52 Farragut to Navy Department, Apr. 29, 1862, reprinted in *Eastern Argus* (Portland, Maine), May 10, 1862.

53 *OR*, ser. 1, vol. 6, 515. Lovell repeated this assertion at his court-martial. See ibid., 567.

54 Ibid., 656.

55 Lewis W. Pennington, commander of USS *Henry Janes*, report, Apr. 28, 1862, Squadron Letters, Mortar Flotilla, NA; Tower Dupres in Stanyan, *History of the Eighth Regiment of New Hampshire Volunteers*, 101–2.

56 Edward Butler to mother, Jan. 19, 1862, Edward J. Butler Letters, LSU; Snyder Diary, Mar. 17, 1862, LSU; Edward Butler to mother, Apr. 28, 1862, Butler Letters, LSU; desertion figures taken from Muster Rolls, Company I, 23rd Louisiana Volunteers, March and April 1862, NA. The April roll was taken on May 20, 1862; Lovell in *OR*, ser. 1, vol. 6, 567. For a Confederate soldier's description of Fort Pike, see Anonymous to Ann E. Spears, July 23, 1861, Ann E. Spears Papers, in *Southern Women and their Families in the Nineteenth Century*.

57 *OR*, ser. 1, vol. 15, 424; report, May 11, 1862, in *Beloit (Wis.) Journal and Courier*, May 15, 1862; for 20th Louisiana, see Bartlett, *Military Record of Louisiana*, 25; dissolution of state militia brigades in *OR*, ser. 1, vol. 15, 733, and vol. 6, 620; report, June 8, 1862, in *New York Evening Post*, June 26, 1862.

58 Edward Stewart letter, May 1, 1862, in John W. Gurley Papers, in *Confederate Military Manuscripts, Series B*.

59 *New Orleans Commercial Bulletin*, Apr. 28, 1862; *New Orleans Daily Picayune*, Apr. 29, 1862, which also includes a clipping from the *Algiers Newsboy*.

60 Unsigned to "Dear Francis," Apr. 29, 1862, LHAC, Jan. 2, 1862, through June 30, 1862, box 18, folder 2. Julia Le Grand recorded an abbreviated version of the same story. Rowland and Croxall, *Journal of Julia Le Grand*, 42.

61 Unsigned to "Dear Francis," Apr. 29, 1862, LHAC; Anne Peyre Dinnies to sister, May 18, 1862, Porcher-Dinnies Family Papers, 1820–1957, SCHS; ibid., Jan. 30, 1863; ibid., May 18, 1862.

62 *New York Tribune*, May 24, 1862.

CHAPTER FIVE

1 Stephen Spalding to James, July 8, 1862, Stephen F. Spalding Letter, VtHS. Enlistment records for the 8th Vermont are incomplete, but materials about fifty-three Louisiana volunteers are included in 8th Vermont Regimental Books, Record Group 94, NA. Orders issued between June 2 and Oct. 9, 1862, pertaining to the distribution of New Orleans recruits among the different companies can be found in the Regimental Order and Guard Report, 8th Vermont Volunteers, NA.

2 Justus Gale to sister, July 18, 1862, Gale-Morse Family Papers, VtHS. Captured recruiter in Justus Gale to father, July 10, 1862, in ibid.

3 For the number of men captured, see McFarland, *Some Experiences of the Eighth Vermont*, 12; massacre is described in, and quotation is taken from, Sprague, *History of the 13th Infantry Regiment of Connecticut Volunteers*, 56; list of names in Carpenter, *History of the Eighth Regiment Vermont Volunteers*, 64–65. Of the seven men, only Deidrich Bahne's Confederate service can be traced. He served as a private in the 30th Louisiana Volunteers as late as Mar. 20, 1862. See Booth, *Records of Louisiana Confederate Soldiers*. Writing about the grave site, a Connecticut veteran asked: "Will not the great republic some day rear a monument to mark the last resting place of the seven martyrs who died for her at Bayou des Allemands in the summer of '62?" Sprague, *History of the 13th Infantry Regiment of Connecticut Volunteers*, 56.

4 "General Order Number 43, Department of Mississippi and East Louisiana, Feb. 25, 1863, Court Martial at Vicksburg," pp. 1–4, NA.

5 J. A. Wilson to father (?), Mar. 6, 1863, MS 271, HNOC.

6 Gordon, "'In Time of War,'" 45–58.

7 For O'Neil's death, see Terrence Sheridan Diary, May 3, 1862, NHCHS; Murray, *History of the Ninth Regiment*; and report, May 4, 1862, in *New York Herald*, May 23, 1862. Quotation from report, May 6, 1862, in *New York Tribune*, May 26, 1862.

8 John Goodhue to mother, May 3, 1862,Goodhue Correspondence; George R. Hughes Diary, May 1, 1862, WSHS.

9 Report, May 8, 1862, in *New York Herald*, May 23, 1862; Hughes Diary, May 5, 1862, WSHS.

10 Report, Apr. 30, 1862, in *New York Herald*, May 10, 1862; *New Orleans Daily Picayune*, Apr. 29, 1862.

11 Unsigned to "Dear Francis," Apr. 29, 1862, LHAC, box 18, folder 2; report, May 5, 1862, in *New York Times*, May 22, 1862; report, May 2, 1862, in *New York Herald*, May 23, 1862.

12 *Chicago Times*, June 21, 1862, reprinted from *New York Herald* report dated May 31, 1862.

13 *New Orleans Daily Crescent*, May 3, 1862, reprinted from *Algerine Newsboy* (Algiers, La.); *New Orleans Daily Picayune*, Apr. 29, 1862.

14 For example, see *New Orleans Daily Picayune*, Apr. 27, 1862, for an advertisement offering thirty people for sale by Joseph Bruin at the corner of Chartres and Esplanade streets.

15 *New York Evening Post*, June 24, 1862, reprinted from *Philadelphia Press*.

16 *Chicago Times*, June 20, 1862, reprint of private letter dated May 23, 1862.

17 Report, May 1, 1862, in *New York Herald*, May 23, 1862; report, May 1, 1862, in *New York Evening Post*, May 22, 1862.

18 Phelps's travels in report, May 1, 1862, in *New York Herald*, May 23, 1862.

19 Frank Harding to father, May 3, 1862, Harding Papers. Other accounts mention a vocal opposition, including one Wisconsin soldier who described the crowd as "very noisy last night while we were coming up from the landing." Newton Culver Diary, May 2, 1862, WSHS. The most violent description comes from after the war, and its author may have been influenced by the growing mythology surrounding New Orleans's resistance to Union forces. Newton Chittenden says that the 4th Wisconsin marched "through a menacing mob, amidst the wildest confusion, the jeers, taunts' [*sic*] horrible threats and vilest abuse traitors can invent." Chittenden, *History and Catalogue of the Fourth Regiment Wisconsin Volunteers*, 7.

20 Edward Woolsey Bacon to father, letter in two parts, May 1 and 5, 1862, Edward Woolsey Bacon Papers, 1861–65, folder 12, AAS.

21 Orders Received, Fourth Wisconsin Cavalry, Book Records of Volunteer Union Organizations, vol. 11 of 15, Regimental Books, NA. The 4th Wisconsin was an infantry regiment in 1862 but converted to cavalry before the end of the war.

22 Hughes Diary, May 5, 1862, WSHS; Chittenden, *History and Catalogue of the Fourth Regiment Wisconsin Volunteers*, 7.

23 *New York Times*, May 25, 1862, report copied from *Boston Journal*, May 7, 1862. The Boston correspondent had talked with "an intelligent Scotchman" who

had seen events in Baton Rouge; Oscar Smith Diary, May 10, 1862, LC; Powell and Wayne, "Self-Interest and the Decline of Confederate Nationalism," 29–45. For another account of Baton Rouge's fall, see *Albany (N.Y.) Atlas and Argus*, June 25, 1862, copied from *New Orleans National Advocate*, May 31, 1862.

24 *Boston Courier*, May 14, 1862; report, May 4, 1862, in *New York Herald*, May 23, 1862; Emile Angard to George Foster Shepley, May 22, 1862, Shepley Papers, collection 117.

25 Letter, May 3, 1862, in *Beloit (Wis.) Journal and Courier*, June 12, 1862; Richard H. Elliott Diary, May 14, 1862, CLH; *Albany (N.Y.) Atlas and Argus*, June 10, 1862, copied from *Boston Journal*, report dated May 14, 1862. Hills's account was also reprinted in *New York Tribune*, June 5, 1862, and *New York Evening Post*, June 4, 1862. Similar stories about Unionists afraid of violent reprisals can be found in *Algiers (La.) Hoosier Newsboy*, May 27, 1862; *Milwaukee Sentinel*, May 30, 1862; report, May 5, 1862, in *New York Herald*, May 23, 1862.

26 George Dewey to father, July 15, 1862, in George Dewey Family Papers, VtHS; Orange Smith to brother, Aug. 6, 1862, Orange Smith Papers, LC. Other stories that mention a feared repeat of the Jacksonville evacuation appeared in the *New York Evening Post*, June 19, 1862; *New York Times*, May 21, 1862; *New York Tribune*, May 26, 1862 (report dated May 6, 1862); and *New York Herald*, May 14, 1862.

27 Report, Apr. 26, 1862, in *New York Herald*, May 10, 1862; sales to the fleet in report, May 5, 1862, in *New York Times*, May 22, 1862; visitors to fleet in report, undated, in *New York Evening Post*, May 31, 1862, and report, May 7, 1862, in *Boston Journal*, May 22, 1862; military intelligence in report, undated, in *New York Evening Post*, May 10, 1862; report, Apr. 28, 1862, in *New York Herald*, May 10, 1862. The USS *Cayuga* also took on board a young black man named Aristides, who asked for the fleet's protection. Deck Log, USS *Cayuga*, Apr. 27, 1862, NA.

28 *New York Tribune*, May 10, 1862. Another eyewitness, Lieutenant George Perkins of the USS *Cayuga*, remembered landing with Bailey. He wrote that the mob was "all shouting and hooting as we stepped on shore, but at last a man, who, I think, was a German, offered to show us the way to the council-room, where we should find the mayor." See Belknap, *Letters of Captain Geo. Hamilton Perkins*, 68.

29 Ann Penrose Diary, May 29, 1862, LSU.

30 Ibid.

31 Both cases recorded in reports, May 12 and 14, 1862, in *New York Herald*, May 30, 1862.

32 "Proclamation," May 20, 1862, Shepley Papers, collection 117; *New York Times*, June 13, 1862; *New York Tribune*, June 16, 1862, both copied from *New Orleans True Delta*, June 1, 1862.

33 Rufus Kinsley Diary, May 12, 1862, VtHS; Justus Gale to his sister Almeda, May 15, 1862, Gale-Morse Family Papers, VtHS.

34 See *New Orleans Daily Crescent*, Apr. 30, 1862, and coverage of a rally hosted by the mayor for Duncan and Seymour in *New Orleans Daily Picayune*, May 1, 1862.

35 *New Orleans Daily Picayune*, May 1, 1862; ibid., May 2, 1862.

36 *Albany (N.Y.) Atlas and Argus*, June 10, 1862, from *Boston Journal*, report dated May 14, 1862.

37 Hughes Diary, May 7, 1862, WSHS.

38 *OR*, ser. 1, vol. 6, 535; ibid., 887.

39 Edward Higgins to Samuel Cooper, May 21, 1862, Letters Received by the Confederate Adjutant and Inspector General, M410, NA.

40 Edward Palfrey, letter, undated, in Letters Received by the Confederate Adjutant and Inspector General, M410, NA; Duncan in *OR*, ser. 1, vol. 6, 535.

41 Petition to Major General Butler, May 12, 1862, Butler Papers, box 12; petition to Butler, May 21, 1862, in ibid.

42 26th Massachusetts Regimental Headquarters to Lieutenant Frost, Apr. 30, 1862, 26th Massachusetts Regimental Books, Record Group 94, NA.

43 Report, June 4, 1862, in *New York Times*, June 23, 1862.

44 For bathing with soap, see Colonel E. Jones, order dated May 16, 1862, 26th Massachusetts Regimental Book, NA; on escaped slaves, see Colonel Gooding, order dated Oct. 10, 1862, 31st Massachusetts Regimental Books, Record Group 94, NA.

45 *New York Tribune*, June 3, 1862, copied from *Philadelphia Evening Bulletin*, May 12, 1862. The office was at 105 St. Charles Street. Butler's order, May 24, 1862, Butler Papers, box 12. The troops were commanded by John P. Dasenbur and A. Costello.

46 Elliott Diary, May 31, 1862, CLH; Sprague, *History of the 13th Infantry Regiment of Connecticut Volunteers*, 55; Captain J. M. Magee to Butler, May 26, 1862, Butler Papers, box 12; Freeman Foster to father, May 15, 1862, Freeman Foster Jr. Letters, LSU.

47 *OR*, ser. 1, vol. 15, 559. Writing to Stanton, Butler reported that "large numbers of Union men, American, German, and French have desired to enlist in our service. I have directed the Regiments to fill themselves up with these recruits. I can enlist a Regiment or more here . . . of true and loyal men." Butler to Stanton, May 16, 1862, in Butler, *Private and Official Correspondence*, 1:494.

48 Regimental books of Manning's 6th Massachusetts Light Artillery and the fol-

lowing infantry regiments: 8th Vermont; 12th Connecticut; 4th Wisconsin (Regimental Books cataloged as 4th Wisconsin Cavalry); 12th Maine; 26th, 30th, and 31st Massachusetts, Record Group 94, NA. G. Howard Hunter's study of the ethnic origins of men who joined the 2nd Louisiana Infantry (Union) finds much the same composition in that regiment. In the 2nd Louisiana, Germans made up 27 percent of the regiment and the Irish 26 percent. Other foreign-born men filled an additional 24 percent of the ranks. Of the remaining 23 percent who were native-born, northerners appear to have predominated. See Hunter, "Politics of Resentment," 185–210, esp. 195. Homer Sprague of Connecticut notes that twenty-four men volunteered for Company H of his regiment in May. Of those, twelve had been born in Ireland, ten in Germany, and two in northern states. Sprague, *History of the 13th Infantry Regiment of Connecticut Volunteers*, 55.

49 Charles May and Bernhard Becker to Butler, May 12, 1862, Butler Papers, box 12; Joseph P. Murphy to Butler, May 12, 1862, in ibid.; C. Renaud to Benjamin Butler, June 27, 1862, in ibid., box 13; Butler to Stanton, July 13, 1862, in ibid., box 13; Charles J. Paine to Charles C. Paine, Sept. 7, 1862, Charles J. Paine Letters, 1856–69, MassHS; J. V. Allen to parents, July 23, 1862, Allen Family Papers, VtHS; Charles J. Paine to Charles C. Paine, Oct. 23, 1862, Paine Letters, MassHS; Edward W. Bacon to Kate, Aug. 1, 1862, Edward Woolsey Bacon Papers, AAS. For enlistment figures in Union Louisiana regiments, see Current, *Lincoln's Loyalists*, 216.

50 De Forest, *Volunteer's Adventures*, 31.

51 30th Massachusetts Descriptive Book, Regimental Books, NA; Glenn, "Troubled Manhood in the Early Republic," 59–93, esp. 92, 84.

52 13th Connecticut: Book Records, Order, Descriptive and Morning Report Book, Regimental Books, NA.

53 Gurnett served in Company B of the 1st Louisiana Heavy Artillery before enlisting in the 31st Massachusetts Volunteers. James McDonald served in the Louisiana Regulars, Company H, before joining the 30th Massachusetts.

54 For sources of statistics, see note 48 above.

55 For their combat record, see Hunter, "Politics of Resentment," 196–97. A unit drawn at random, Company I, 13th Connecticut, provides information about desertion rates. Of the 122 men of Company I, 90 joined in Connecticut and 32 in New Orleans. During the course of the war, 28 of these men deserted, a figure inflated by the 12 Connecticut men who managed to slip off the boat before it left for the war. Of the remaining 16 deserters, we have no information about 6 of them. The last 10 deserters left in two distinct groups. Five New Orleans recruits deserted together on July 23, 1864, while 5 men from New Haven escaped service on Aug. 27, 1864. Although a higher percentage of New

Orleans recruits deserted, it can be argued that they also had more opportunities to leave safely than did their Connecticut peers. 13th Connecticut: Order, Descriptive, and Morning Report Book, Regimental Books, NA.

56 Sprague, *History of the 13th Infantry Regiment of Connecticut Volunteers*, 55.

CHAPTER SIX

1 In 1860, Lowell was the second-largest city in Massachusetts, with a population of 36,827. New Orleans's population was 168,675 in 1860.

2 Butler also disliked the "pass system," which required workers to present references from former employers in order to obtain jobs elsewhere in the city. Butler, *Butler's Book*, 89, 91.

3 Trefousse, *Butler*, 30.

4 Charlestown speech, Oct. 10, 1859, Butler Papers, box 258.

5 Letter accepting 1858 Eighth Congressional District nomination, Oct. 15, 1858, Butler Papers, box 258. See also Butler's letter accepting the Democratic nomination for governor, Sept. 26, 1859, in ibid.

6 Undated newspaper clipping of Senate speech, Feb. 18, 1859, in ibid.

7 Butler, *Butler's Book*, 113–14. On the destruction of the convent, see Schultz, *Fire and Roses*.

8 In an 1863 speech, Butler explained England's aid to the Confederacy by citing how earlier American generosity had embarrassed the English aristocracy. First, Butler noted the arrival of the USS *Macedonian* in 1847 with food for "the poor that England was starving." Second, he thought that the English elite had resented the arrival of the *George Griswold* of New York with food "to feed the starving poor of Lancashire." Butler, *Character and Results of the War*.

9 Butler, *Butler's Book*, 124–26.

10 Butler took an expansive view of American citizenship. In response to an 1859 Republican plan to delay voting by naturalized citizens, Butler questioned the usual assumption that citizenship should be based on where a person was born. Speaking in the state senate, he called for immigrants to "have the entire right [of suffrage] equally with American citizens." Further, he asked why citizenship was extended only to men born in the United States: "I don't like the amendment to the [Massachusetts] Constitution which makes a man's right depend upon the speed of the clipper that brought him to this country. . . . Was there ever anything so monstrous as that a man's rights should depend upon whether a ship is a steam vessel, a clipper, or a Dutch sailor?" Pushing his point further, he joked that even a child whose parents took a steamer fast enough to get to the United States in time for his or her birth had seen that "the beginning of things was on the other side of the water." Butler

state senate speech, Feb. 18, 1859, Butler Papers, box 258. For the Massachusetts suffrage debate, see Laurie, *Beyond Garrison*, 285–86; Anbinder, *Nativism and Slavery*, 248–53; and Foner, *Free Soil*, 250–51.

11 [Unidentified] to Butler, Nov. 2, 1853, Butler, *Miscellaneous Papers*. For Butler on a defection from his party to the nativists, see Pierson, "'He Helped the Poor,'" 45.

12 For labor and antislavery in Massachusetts, see Laurie, *Beyond Garrison*, esp. 65–74, 135–40, 145–47.

13 Butler Papers, box 173. On Free Will Baptists, see Filler, *Crusade against Slavery*, 125, and Quist, *Restless Visionaries*, 12, 262, 293, 444–45.

14 For more on the Free Soil and Democratic Party coalition, see Taylor, *Young Charles Sumner*, 328–35; Donald, *Charles Sumner*, 182–204; Sewell, *Ballots for Freedom*, 218–23, 249, 251; and Earle, *Jacksonian Antislavery*, 103–22.

15 From his place as a high-ranking militia officer, Butler called the idea of black military service "an insult to the men in the ranks." Butler, Charlestown speech, Oct. 10, 1859, Butler Papers, box 258. See also Butler's comment that the Republican Party had two parts, "one of which believes that the intelligent naturalized citizen, whether English, German, Irish, Pole or Hungarian, is not fit to bear arms in the militia; and the other that the full blooded Negro is eminently fit." Butler's gubernatorial nomination acceptance letter, Sept. 26, 1859, in ibid.

16 *Lowell (Mass.) Advertiser*, Nov. 4, 1851. Butler had earlier shared a podium with fellow Democrat Robert Rantoul, where they were scheduled to "address the people on the increase of hours of labor in the Mills, in this city." Ibid. For Butler on the coalition, see Butler, *Butler's Book*, 94–97.

17 *Lowell (Mass.) American*, Nov. 19, 1851.

18 Butler, *Butler's Book*, 103. Butler also used this rhetoric in his private correspondence during the crisis, saying that "the people are with us and the free heart beats freer and the firm hand holds firmer when we think of our wrongs determined to show the State that we are our own masters. The charm is broken. men [*sic*] can no longer be led up to the polls like sheep to the slaughter." Butler to "Dear Sir," Nov. 18, 1851, in Butler, *Miscellaneous Papers*.

19 *Lowell (Mass.) Advertiser*, Nov. 22, 1851. See also Roedigar, *Wages of Whiteness*, 65–92.

20 Butler, *Butler's Book*, 104. For a version of this speech that differs in words though not in tone or message, see Bland, *Life of Benjamin F. Butler*, 21.

21 A Nov. 21, 1851, letter from Roland Parks of Springfield congratulated Butler on his "victory in Lowell—God bless her Spartan Band the fearless Champions of Freedom who dared to nail their colors to the mast and spurn the Bribe of State street Webster Whigs, and stand by their Principles regardless of consequences." Butler, *Miscellaneous Papers*.

22 Trefousse, *Butler*, 24. Noted for her performance as Ophelia, Sarah was touring in Cincinnati when Ben traveled there to propose to her. See clipping from the *Indianapolis Sentinel*, May 26, 1890, Butler Papers, box 192.

23 Quoted in Holzman, *Stormy Ben Butler*, 43. For women in the parlors of power, see Allgor, *Parlor Politics*.

24 For Butler's patronage alliance with Fisher Hildreth, see Trefousse, *Butler*, 31, 41, 46–47, 260 (n. 27). For patronage in antebellum politics, see Altschuler and Blumin, *Rude Republic*, 37–46, 115, 117. In Butler's case, see the many letters from Hamilton to Butler included in Butler, *Miscellaneous Papers*.

25 On Jan. 13, 1863, the Confederate House of Representatives resolved to support Davis's proclamation of Dec. 23, 1862, declaring Butler an outlaw. See House Resolutions No. 24, P-Pam 973.71 1863, pp. 1–2, SCHS.

26 J. E. Goodhue to mother, May 3, 1862, Goodhue Correspondence; see also "A. C. B." of the 4th Wisconsin, letter, May 3, 1862, in *Milwaukee Sentinel*, May 26, 1862.

27 Order, May 9, 1862, in *Chicago Times*, May 29, 1862. This issue also includes reactions by the still pro-Confederate newspapers in the city.

28 Howe to parents and sibling, May 13, 1862, in Howe, *Passages*, 120; Justus F. Gale to Almeda, his sister, May 15, 1862, Gale-Morse Family Papers, VtHS; Charles Blake, May 28, 1862, Charles H. Blake Diary, HNOC; Rufus Kinsley Diary, Aug. 31, 1862, VtHS. See also report, May 12, 1862, in *New York Herald*, May 30, 1862, which discusses the weather. Vermont soldier Deming Fairbanks reported that "thousands of Women and Children are in want of bread." Deming Dexter Fairbanks to wife, May 12, 1862, Deming Dexter Fairbanks Letters, VtHS.

29 *Portland (Maine) Advertiser*, June 5, 1862, paraphrasing story in *Louisville Democrat*.

30 Lincoln issued a proclamation reopening the port of New Orleans on May 12, effective on June 1, 1862. *Eastern Argus* (Portland, Maine), May 17, 1862. Statistics regarding the Relief Commission in *OR*, ser. 3, vol. 2, 731–32. For a consideration of New Orleans Confederates and the oath of allegiance, see Rubin, *Shattered Nation*, 94–100.

31 *New York Evening Post*, June 14, 1862, copied from *New Orleans True Delta*; *Beloit (Wis.) Journal and Courier*, June 26, 1862.

32 General Order No. 30, May 19, 1862, in *Chicago Times*, June 18, 1862; report, May 23, 1862, in *New York Herald*, June 17, 1862.

33 Butler's charity in report, June 18, 1862, in *New York Herald*, June 23, 1862; Trefousse, *Butler*, 119; Shepley's donation discussed in Mary E. Randall to Shepley, July 10, 1862, Shepley Papers, collection 117; Catholic support of the Confederacy in *Catholic Standard* (New Orleans), Apr. 13, 1862, which de-

clared a *"Te Deum* of Thanksgiving" for the Confederate "victory" at Shiloh and urged enlistment in "Col. Smith's regiment."

34 Letter, July 13, 1862, Butler Papers, box 13.

35 *New York Times*, June 11, 1862, copied from *Jackson Mississippian*. A northern editor replied: "What a deep, designing, artful monster it is! He wants to 'incite the poor against the rich,' and so he feeds them. A more shallow fellow would have let them get hungry, and then told them to rob and steal from their rich neighbors." *New York Evening Post*, May 23, 1862.

36 Moore's address quoted in Butler, *Private and Official Correspondence*, 1:460, 462. For arguments similar to Moore's expressed across the Confederacy, see Robinson, *Bitter Fruits of Bondage*, 35–36. In a second address in this period, Moore wrote that Unionists "can be tolerated no longer." He claimed that although they were "few in number, they exist." "Address to the People of Louisiana," undated but after the fall of New Orleans, Thomas O. Moore Papers, LSU. Biographical details about Moore in Sacher, *A Perfect War of Politics*, 273–78.

37 Shugg, *Origins of Class Struggle in Louisiana*, esp. 171–82 for war years; Bolton, *Poor Whites of the Antebellum South*; Bolton and Culclasure, *Confessions of Edward Isham*; Robinson, *Bitter Fruits of Bondage*, 9–10, 67, 88, 272.

38 Butler, *Butler's Book*, 404.

39 "Special Order no. 4," Order Book, Company H, 26th Massachusetts Volunteers, Regimental Books, NA; two days later, pilot James Robinson accepted the same offer.

40 Confederates asking for jobs in report, *Stars and Stripes*, June 17, 1862, in *New York Times*, June 26, 1862; street cleaners in *New York Evening Post*, June 30, 1862; port collectors in report, June 15, 1862, in *New York Evening Post*, June 26, 1862; house cleaning in "Expense Account," July 2, 1862, Shepley Papers, collection 117. The men worked for between one and seven days on the project, earning a total of eighty dollars.

41 See, for example, E. B. Briggs to Shepley, June 6, 1862, and Thomas Laster to Shepley, May 21, 1862, both in Shepley Papers, collection 117; Joseph Dunn to Butler, May 17, 1862, and Nathaniel McCann to Butler, May 12, 1862, both in Butler Papers, box 12.

42 For Know-Nothings and the police, see Towers, *Urban South and the Coming of the Civil War*, 122.

43 Ann Penrose Diary, May 24, 1862, LSU. Of the two men who stayed on the job, a friend of Penrose's disregarded one because he was "a Dutchman" and the other, a Virginian, because he "had a family." Even so, the friend thought that now the wife of the Virginian was "in disgrace." For the changing police force, see Rousey, *Policing the Southern City*, 107–9.

44 Rosters for districts 1 through 4 in "Police Book," 1862, NOPL.

45 Towers, *Urban South and the Coming of the Civil War*, 111, 136–44.

46 Patrick Fitzgerrald et al. to Butler, May 10, 1862, Butler Papers, box 11.

47 Schurz quoted in Holzman, *Stormy Ben Butler*, 34.

48 Sarah's departure recorded in the *Boston Courier*, June 19, 1862.

49 Butler, *Private and Official Correspondence*, 1:434; General Order No. 13, June 14, 1862, followed by General Orders No. 14, June 17, 1862, and No. 19, July 8, 1862, extending the deadline, Shepley Papers, collection 117. See also *New York Herald*, June 29, 1862, copied from *New Orleans Commercial Bulletin*, saying that the extension was "in consequence of the crowd of applicants."

50 Quotation from unsigned letter, dated Oct. 23, 1863, but 1862 from context, since it refers to Butler's current administration, Walton-Glenny Family Papers, HNOC; statistics in Towers, *Urban South and the Coming of the Civil War*, 203, and Winters, *Civil War in Louisiana*, 136; publication of names in Hearn, *When the Devil Came Down to Dixie*, 167; congressional law in Bragg, *Louisiana in the Confederacy*, 135. On oath taking, see Rubin, *Shattered Nation*, 94–100.

51 The men arrested and pardoned included Ben Smith, a former sergeant at Fort Jackson, as well as other men assigned to Jackson and St. Philip. For arrest, see Howe, *Passages*, 121, and report, May 16, 1862, in *New York Herald*, May 30, 1862; execution order in Butler, Special Order No. 36, May 31, 1862, in *Chicago Times*, June 21, 1862; pardon in *Albany (N.Y.) Atlas and Argus*, June 25, 1862, copied from *New Orleans National Advocate*, and Butler, *Private and Official Correspondence*, 1:573.

52 Robert S. Davis to Mary, July 20, 1862, William H. Gardiner Papers, MassHS.

53 Unsigned letter, dated Oct. 23, 1863, but 1862 by context, Walton-Glenny Family Papers, HNOC.

54 *New York Times*, May 22, 1862, report dated May 5, 1862.

55 De Have Norton Diary, May 3, 1862, De Have Norton Papers, 1861–65, WSHS.

56 Frank Harding to father, May 3, 1862, Harding Papers; Sarah Butler to Harriet Heard, May 2, 1862, in Butler, *Private and Official Correspondence*, 1:439. See also George R. Hughes Diary, May 2, 1862, WSHS, and Chittenden, *History and Catalogue of the Fourth Regiment Wisconsin Volunteers*. Events of May 2 summarized in Hearn, *When the Devil Came Down to Dixie*, 81–89.

57 Bragg, *Louisiana in the Confederacy*, 113.

58 Deck Log, USS *Portsmouth*, May 8, 1862, HNOC.

59 Ashkenazi, *Civil War Diary of Clara Solomon*, 351.

60 For a largely sympathetic overview of Mumford's life, see report, June 7, 1862, in *New York Herald*, June 19, 1862.

61 Butler to Stanton, May 8, 1862, in Butler, *Private and Official Correspondence*,

1:455; time of execution and removal of Mumford's body in *New York Tribune*, June 19, 1862, copied from *New Orleans True Delta*, June 8, 1862; quotation about crowd behavior and rumor about rope from report, June 7, 1862, in *New York Herald*, June 19, 1862. Butler also ordered the hanging of several men, including crew members from Union ships, for theft. See *Boston Courier*, June 25, 1862; *New York Herald*, June 23 and 26, 1862; and *Chicago Times*, June 26, 1862.

62 Benjamin F. Morse to Rosina, June 14, 1862, Gale-Morse Family Papers, VtHS; Melvan Tibbetts to parents, brothers, and sisters, June 8, 1862, Melvan Tibbetts Letters, HNOC; Charles Boothby to Charles, his brother, June 8 and 9, 1862, Charles Boothby Papers, LSU. The deck log of the USS *Portsmouth* notes that the flag was raised "by the Loyal citizens of New Orleans." Deck Log, USS *Portsmouth*, June 9, 1862, HNOC.

63 Deck Log, USS *Portsmouth*, June 9, 1862, HNOC.

64 Ibid.; report, undated, in *New York Evening Post*, June 19, 1862; report, June 7, 1862, in *New York Herald*, June 19, 1862.

65 *New York Times*, June 23, 1862, copied from *New Orleans True Delta*, June 14, 1862.

66 Herrman, *Yeoman in Farragut's Fleet*, June 19, 1862, 34.

67 For accounts of the June 14 meeting, see report, June 15, 1862, in *New York Herald*, June 23, 1862; report by "x. y. z.," June 15, 1862, in *New York Times*, June 23, 1862; women's presence noted in *Boston Courier*, June 24, 1862. For a Confederate view of the Union Association, see Ann Penrose Diary, June 23, 1862, LSU.

68 Report, May 23, 1862, in *New York Herald*, June 17, 1862.

69 Flag described in Orange Smith to brother, July 14, 1862, Orange Smith Papers, LC; place of event in "Special Order no. 105," July 3, 1862, Shepley Papers, collection 1721, v. 1; Nickerson to sister, July 7, 1862, Edwin L. Nickerson Letters, LSU; see also Smith, *Leaves from a Soldier's Diary*, 24.

70 For the Woman Order, see Rable, "'Missing in Action'"; Faust, *Mothers of Invention*, 207–14; and Ryan, *Women in Public*, 142–46.

71 Winters, *Civil War in Louisiana*, 132.

72 Diary of Lieutenant Roe, in *ORN*, ser. 1, vol. 18, 772, 773. Report dated May 11, 1862, but should be dated June 11, 1862, in *New York Times*, June 19, 1862; Anne Peyre Dinnies to "My Dear Sisters," May 18, 1862, Porcher-Dinnies Family Papers, SCHS.

73 Note, for example, the disappearance of women from Tennessee politics after Seneca Falls, in DeFiore, "'Come, and Bring the Ladies,'" 209. We might also compare the editorial careers of Jane Swisshelm and other northern female editors with the career of Mississippi's Harriet N. Prewett, who by 1855 had to

hire men as her paper's "Political Editor." We could also note that Prewett, unlike so many women writers and editors in the North, upheld "white male patriarchy and sexual prejudice." See Olsen, "'Molly Pitcher' of the Mississippi Whigs," 237–54; I advance this thesis in regard to the debate over John Brown between L. Maria Child and Margaretta Mason in Pierson, *Free Hearts and Free Homes*, 182–84. Varon, *We Mean to Be Counted*, provides the most persuasive evidence for southern women's involvement in politics in the 1850s, though again one senses that they can be involved only by taking conservative positions. Their writings include, for example, proslavery responses to *Uncle Tom's Cabin*. Writing of women's antebellum works, Varon comments that they display "a fealty to the southern social system" (119). The collapse of Rebecca Brodnax Hicks's magazine soon after it criticized men's dominance speaks to the limits placed on southern women (119–23).

74 For further Confederate resistance, see Winters, *Civil War in Louisiana*, 135; De Forest, *Volunteer's Adventures*, 30; and Long, "(Mis)remembering General Order 28."

75 Moore's testimony in report, May 3, 1862, in *Beloit (Wis.) Journal and Courier*, June 12, 1862; see also report, May 1, 1862, in *New York Evening Post*, May 22, 1862, for an account by another journalist who accompanied the soldiers.

76 Prisoners in the Parish Pris. to Butler, May 6, 1862, Butler Papers, box 11; see also a letter presenting a "case of pistols" to Butler from a grateful man who claimed to have been liberated by the Union troops. Anonymous to Butler, June 26, 1862, in ibid., box 13.

77 Report, May 23, 1862, in *New York Herald*, June 17, 1862. For the 8th Vermont filling in for the fired police for nine days, see Kinsley Diary, May 22, 29, and 31, 1862, VtHS.

78 Benjamin F. Morse to Rosina, June 14, 1862, Gale-Morse Family Papers, VtHS; N. A. M. Dudley, "Special Order # 18," Shepley Papers, collection 1721, v. 1; George F. Shepley to "my Dear Friend," May 30, 1862, Shepley Papers, collection 1536; Jackson, "Keeping Law and Order in New Orleans," 67. A soldier in the 12th Maine said that two large all-night patrols made only one arrest. Charles H. Blake Diary, May 22 and 25, 1862, HNOC.

79 For reports of surviving crops such as cotton, sugar, and molasses, see *Boston Courier*, June 23, 1862; *Boston Courier*, July 12, 1862, copied from *New Orleans Delta*, June 26, 1862; Report of Com. McCinstry in *Eastern Argus* (Portland, Maine), June 16, 1862; and *Eastern Argus* (Portland, Maine), June 17, 1862, report copied from *New Orleans Delta*, undated.

80 Jerry Flint to Mira, June 8, 1862, Jerry E. Flint Papers, 1861–66, WSHS.

81 Alfred Parmenter to parents, June 14, 1862, Parmenter Papers; Horace Morse to Mom and sister, Aug. 26, 1862, Frank Morse Papers, MassHS; Clark Carr to

Caroline, June 15, 1862, and May 24, 1862, in Clark H. Carr, "Letters to His Wife," typescript, NHHS; seashells in Daniel Durgin to sister, Aug. 7, 1862, Daniel Veasey Durgin Letters, NHHS; Butler's Order No. 38, quoted in order of Colonel Stephen Thomas to his regiment, Book Records: Regimental Orders and Guard Report Book, 8th Vermont, Regimental Books, NA.

82 John H. Guild to sister, dated July 21, 1863, but 1862 from context, John H. Guild Letters, LSU; Charles Boothby letter, July 10, 1862, Boothby Papers, LSU; Blake Diary, Aug. 16, 18, and 21, 1862, HNOC.

83 Alfred Parmenter to parents, June 27, 1862, Parmenter Papers; *New York Evening Post*, June 28, 1862.

84 John Purcell Diary, Jan. 22 and Feb. 23, 1863, Louisiana Collection, box 3, folder 1, AAS.

85 Daniel Durgin to sister, Aug. 7, 1862, Durgin Letters, NHHS; Stephen Spalding to James, July 8, 1862, Stephen F. Spalding Letter, VtHS. The less rambunctious Charles Blake watched "Union citizens" raise a U.S. flag over the Mint before having a quiet rest of the day. Others spent the day on duty. See Blake Diary, July 4, 1862, HNOC; Justus F. Gale to brother, July 4, 1862, Gale-Morse Family Papers, VtHS; and Jonathan Allen to sister, July 7, 1862, Allen Family Papers, VtHS.

86 Quotation from Tibbetts letter refers to an earlier raid on the Gulf coast. Melvan Tibbetts to father, Apr. 6, 1862, Tibbetts Letters, HNOC. Also, a second letter reported that the "folks in the city has [*sic*] told us just where the rebels are and what they calculate to do," Tibbetts to father, 8 June 1862, Tibbetts Letters, HNOC; Jonathan Allen to sister, June 20, 1862, Allen Family Papers, VtHS; Kinsley Diary, June 17, 1862, VtHS.

87 Expressions of distrust can be found in Benjamin Morse to Rosina, May 13, 1862, Gale-Morse Family Papers, VtHS; Jonathan Allen to sister, Sept. 24, 1862, Allen Family Papers, VtHS; and Sprague, *History of the 13th Infantry Regiment of Connecticut Volunteers*, 54–55. These soldiers, however, often changed their mind about the constancy of the Unionist community. Horace Morse wrote in early June that "union sentiments and union men are on the increase," only to write at the end of the month that "we get acquainted with but few citizens and still fewer invite us to see them[.] [U]nion people here are still frightened almost out of their wits are [*sic*] are very cautious of speaking their sentiments, . . . but after the Southern armies are dispersed there will be a great change." Horace Morse to Rev. Frank Morse, June 2, 1862, and June 29, 1862, Frank Morse Papers, MassHS.

88 John Carver Palfrey to Frank, Aug. 30, 1862, John Carver Palfrey Papers, MassHS.

89 Reports, May 3 and 5, 1862, in *New York Evening Post*, May 22, 1862; Lieuten-

ant Roe's diary, May 17, 1862, in *ORN*, ser. 1, vol. 18, 773. Other reports that emphasize the strength of the Unionist community are a letter from New Orleans woman, May 11, 1862, in *New York Times*, June 12, 1862; *Chicago Times*, June 18, 1862, report copied from *New Orleans Delta*, May 25, 1862.

90 The Reverend Colby quoted in *Eastern Argus* (Portland, Maine), June 21, 1862; E. Dane to wife, Aug. 22, 1862, E. Dane Letters, LSU; Benjamin Morse to Rosina, July 4, 1862, Gale-Morse Family Papers, VtHS. See also Horace Morse to Frank, June 23, 1862, Frank Morse Papers, MassHS.

91 For example, Alfred Parmenter to unknown, June 14 and 15, 1862, Parmenter Papers; letter by "a lady," copied from *Boston Post*, in *Hartford Daily Courant*, June 9, 1862; and report, June 14, 1862, in *New York Herald*, June 23, 1862. The *Herald*'s correspondent called Butler "one of the most popular men in the state."

EPILOGUE

1 David Dixon Porter to Montgomery Meigs, May 14, 1862, David Dixon Porter Papers, General Correspondence, LC.

2 Rufus Kinsley Diary, May 13, 1862, VtHS. Kinsley had arrived in the city the day before.

3 See especially Dufour, *Night the War Was Lost*, 336–37.

4 Ibid., 337.

5 *New York Times*, Apr. 20, 1862, copied from the *Philadelphia Press*, Apr. 16, 1862. For an argument that New Orleans might have been more trouble to the Confederacy than it was worth by summer 1862, see Surdam, "Union Military Superiority and New Orleans's Economic Value to the Confederacy," 389–408. Surdam's case rests on the port's weak wartime economy but does not take into consideration the industrial capacity or the value of the city's population for recruitment.

6 Statistics drawn from Blassingame, *Black New Orleans*, 1; Long, with Long, *Civil War Day by Day*, 702–3; Bragg, *Louisiana in the Confederacy*, 34–36.

7 An estimated 24,052 black Louisianians and 5,224 white Louisianians served in the Union army. See Berlin et al., *Slaves No More*, 203, and Current, *Lincoln's Loyalists*, 216. Victory in New Orleans also encouraged white Unionist military activity elsewhere in the state. See Bergeron, "Dennis Haynes and His 'Thrilling Narrative,'" 37–49.

8 Charles Sherman to Cousin, Dec. 8, 1862, Charles Franklin Sherman Letters, HNOC; Foner, *Reconstruction*, 46. See also Towers, *Urban South and the Coming of the Civil War*, 204–5.

9 Horwitz, *Confederates in the Attic*, 102–3.

10 Butler to Stanton, June 28 and July 3, 1862, in *OR*, ser. 1, vol. 15, 503. Second Butler quotation from speech in Lowell, Massachusetts, undated clipping from *Boston Journal*, Butler Papers, box 258.

11 Jackson, *Story of Mattie J. Jackson*, 15; Albert Krause to "Dear parents and brothers and sisters," Feb. 27, 1863, in Kamphoefner and Helbich, *Germans in the Civil War*, 204.

12 Lovell is ably defended, especially against President Davis's accusations, in Sutherland, "Mansfield Lovell's Quest for Justice," 236. On free blacks, see Hollandsworth, *Louisiana Native Guards*, 1–11, and Lieutenant John G. Devereux to Major General J. L. Lewis, Sept. 29, 1861, in *OR*, ser. 4, vol. 1, 625.

13 See especially Palladino, *Another Civil War*, and Bernstein, *New York City Draft Riots*.

14 *Beloit (Wis.) Journal and Courier*, Aug. 14, 1862, copied from *Baltimore Clipper*, July 19, 1862.

bibliography

PRIMARY SOURCES

Manuscript Collections

Barre, Vermont
    Vermont Historical Society
        Allen Family Papers
        George Dewey Family Papers
        Deming Dexter Fairbanks Letters
        Gale-Morse Family Papers
        Rufus Kinsley Diary
        Stephen F. Spalding Letter
Baton Rouge, Louisiana
    Louisiana State University Libraries,
            Louisiana and Lower
            Mississippi Valley
            Collections
        Charles Boothby Papers
        Edward J. Butler Letters
        E. Dane Letters
        George H. Davis Letters
        Benjamin Flanders Collection
        Freeman Foster Jr. Letters
        John H. Guild Letters
        John C. Kinney Letters
        Thomas O. Moore Papers
        Edwin L. Nickerson Letters
        Ann Penrose Diary
        John Roy Diary
        William H. Smith Letters
        Henry A. Snyder Diary

Boston, Massachusetts
    Boston Public Library
        Benjamin F. Butler Papers
    Massachusetts Historical Society
        Edes Family Papers
        William H. Gardiner Papers
        Frank Morse Papers
        Charles J. Paine Letters, 1856–69
        John Carver Palfrey Papers
Charleston, South Carolina
    South Carolina Historical Society
        Porcher-Dinnies Family Papers,
            1820–1957
Concord, New Hampshire
    New Hampshire Historical Society
        Clark H. Carr, "Letters to His Wife"
        Daniel Veasey Durgin Letters
        John McDaniel Letters
Lowell, Massachusetts
    Center for Lowell History
        Richard H. Elliott Diary
Madison, Wisconsin
    Wisconsin State Historical Society
        Newton Culver Diary
        Jerry E. Flint Papers, 1861–66
        George R. Hughes Diary
        De Have Norton Papers, 1861–65

234

New Haven, Connecticut
  New Haven Colony Historical
    Society
  Terrence Sheridan Diary
New Orleans, Louisiana
  Historic New Orleans Collection,
      Williams Research Center
    J. L. Batchelor Letters
    Charles Bennet Letters
    Charles H. Blake Diary
    Deck Log of the USS *Portsmouth*
    Johnson Kelly Duncan Letters
    Forts Jackson and St. Philip
      Collection
    John Hart Diary
    Murphy Family Papers
    Charles Franklin Sherman Letters
    Melvan Tibbetts Letters
    Walton-Glenny Family Papers
    William Waud Papers
    J. A. Wilson Letter
  Howard-Tilton Library, Tulane
      University
    Louisiana Historical Association
      Collection, Civil War
      Papers/New Orleans
      Papers
    Henry D. Ogden Papers
    Alfred Parmenter Papers
    Post Letter Book, Forts Jackson
      and St. Philip, 1861–62
  New Orleans Public Library
    New Orleans Department of
      Police Records
    Police Book, Rosters for 1862
Portland, Maine
  Maine Historical Society
    Moses Mason Robinson Papers
    George F. Shepley Papers,
      collections 117, 1536, 1721

River Falls, Wisconsin
  River Falls Area Research Center of
    the Wisconsin State
    Historical Society
    Frank D. Harding Papers, 1833–
      98
Salem, Massachusetts
  Phillips Library, Peabody Essex
    Museum
    John E. Goodhue, "Civil War
      Correspondence"
Syracuse, New York
  Syracuse University Library
    Samuel Massa Papers
Washington, D.C.
  Library of Congress
    William A. H. Allen Papers
    Benjamin F. Butler Papers
    Charles O'Neil Diary, Papers of
      Charles O'Neil
    Peck-Montgomery Family
      Papers
    David Dixon Porter Papers,
      General Correspondence
    Orange Smith Papers
    Oscar Smith Diary
  National Archives and Records
      Administration
    Boston Passenger Lists, 1820–
      1943, M277
    Compiled Service Records of
      Confederate Soldiers Who
      Served in Organizations
      from the State of
      Louisiana, M320
    1st Louisiana Heavy Artillery,
      reels 34–45
    22nd/21st Louisiana
      Volunteers (Patton's),
      reels 318–21

Bibliography

23rd/22nd Louisiana
Volunteers (Theard's),
reels 322–26
St. Mary's Cannoneers (1st
Field Battery), reel 47
Deck Logs: USS *Brooklyn*,
Cayuga, Kennebec, Miami,
Oneida, Portsmouth,
Winona
Deck Logs: Mortar Schooners
USS *Arletta, O. H. Lee,*
Owasco, Wissahicken
"General Order Number 43,
Department of Mississippi
and East Louisiana,
Feb. 25, 1863, Court
Martial at Vicksburg"
Letters Received by the
Confederate Adjutant and
Inspector General, M410
Muster Rolls: 1st Louisiana
Heavy Artillery, November
1861–April 1862
Muster Rolls: 22nd and 23rd
Louisiana Volunteers,
1861–62
"Plan of Fort Jackson:
Bombardment of Forts
Jackson and St. Philip,"
Record Group 45
Regimental Books, Record
Group 94
12th Connecticut
Volunteers
13th Connecticut
Volunteers

12th Maine Volunteers
6th Massachusetts Light
Artillery Battery
26th Massachusetts
Volunteers
30th Massachusetts
Volunteers
31st Massachusetts
Volunteers
8th New Hampshire
Veteran Infantry
8th Vermont Volunteers
4th Wisconsin Cavalry
Squadron Letters, Mortar
Flotilla
Squadron Letters, Roll 185
Reports by Lewis W.
Pennington, David
Dixon Porter
U.S. Bureau of the Census,
Federal Manuscript
Census, Population
Schedule and Free and
Slave Schedules, 1850 and
1860
Worcester, Massachusetts
American Antiquarian Society
Edward Woolsey Bacon Papers,
1861–65
Edwin C. Bidwell, Medical
Records
Louisiana Collection
John Purcell Diary

Newspapers

Albany (N.Y.) Atlas and Argus
Algerine Newsboy (Algiers, La.)
Algiers (La.) Hoosier Newsboy
Attakapas Register (Franklin, La.)
Beloit (Wis.) Journal and Courier
Boston Courier
Boston Journal
Catholic Standard (New Orleans)
Charleston Mercury
Chelsea (Mass.) Telegraph and Pioneer
Chicago Times
Chicago Tribune
Eastern Argus (Portland, Maine)
Franklin (La.) Junior Register
Franklin (La.) Weekly Junior Register
Hartford Daily Courant
Kennebec Journal (Portland, Maine)

Lowell (Mass.) Advertiser
Lowell (Mass.) American
Milwaukee Sentinel
New Orleans Bee
New Orleans Commercial Bulletin
New Orleans Daily Crescent
New Orleans Daily Picayune
New Orleans Delta
New Orleans True Delta
New York Evening Post
New York Herald
New York Times
New York Tribune
Planters' Banner (Franklin, La.)
Portland (Maine) Advertiser
Springfield (Mass.) Daily Republican

Books, Articles, and Microfilm Collections

Andrews, W. H. *Footprints of a Regiment: A Recollection of the First Georgia Regulars, 1861–1865*. Atlanta: Longstreet Press, 1992.

Ashkenazi, Elliott. *The Civil War Diary of Clara Solomon: Growing Up in New Orleans, 1861–1862*. Baton Rouge: Louisiana State University Press, 1995.

Belknap, George E. *Letters of Captain Geo. Hamilton Perkins, U.S.N. Edited and Arranged: Also a Sketch of His Life*. Concord, N.H.: Rumford Printing, 1908.

Butler, Benjamin F. *Butler's Book: A Review of His Legal, Political, and Military Career*. Boston: A. M. Thayer, 1892.

——. *Character and Results of the War. How to Prosecute and How to End It*. New York: Wm. C. Bryant & Co., 1863.

——. *Miscellaneous Papers, 1835–1858*. Washington, D.C.: Library of Congress, 1959. Microfilm.

——. *Private and Official Correspondence of General Benjamin F. Butler during the Period of the Civil War*. Vol. 1, *April 1860–June 1862*. Norwood, Mass.: Plimpton Press, 1917.

Carpenter, George N. *History of the Eighth Regiment Vermont Volunteers, 1861–1865*. Boston: Deland & Barta, 1886.

Chittenden, Newton H. *History and Catalogue of the Fourth Regiment Wisconsin*

Volunteers, from June 1861, to March 1864. Baton Rouge: "Gazette and Comet" Book and Job Office, 1864.

Confederate Military Manuscripts, Series A: Holdings of the Virginia Historical Society. Edited by Joseph T. Glatthaar. Bethesda, Md.: University Publications of America, 1997.

Confederate Military Manuscripts, Series B: Holdings of the Louisiana and Lower Mississippi Valley Collections, Louisiana State University Libraries. Edited by Joseph T. Glatthaar. Bethesda, Md.: University Publications of America, 1997.

Crawford, Martin. *William Howard Russell's Civil War: Private Diary and Letters, 1861–1862*. Athens: University of Georgia Press, 1992.

De Forest, John William. *A Volunteer's Adventures: A Union Captain's Record of the Civil War*. Baton Rouge: Louisiana State University Press, 1996.

Herrman, E. C., ed. *Yeoman in Farragut's Fleet: The Civil War Diary of Josiah Parker Higgins*. Carmel, Calif.: Guy Victor Publications, 1999.

Howe, Henry Warren. *Passages from the Life of Henry Warren Howe, Consisting of Diary and Letters Written during the Civil War*. Lowell, Mass.: Courier-Citizen Co., 1899.

Jackson, Mattie J. *The Story of Mattie J. Jackson: A True Story*. Lawrence, Mass.: n.p., 1866. Reprint, New York: Oxford University Press, 1988.

Jones, Terry L., ed. *The Civil War Memoirs of Captain William J. Seymour: Reminiscences of a Louisiana Tiger*. Baton Rouge: Louisiana State University Press, 1991.

Kamphoefner, Walter D., and Wolfgang Helbich, eds. *Germans in the Civil War: The Letters They Wrote Home*. Translated by Susan Carter Vogel. Chapel Hill: University of North Carolina Press, 2006.

McFarland, Moses. *Some Experiences of the Eighth Vermont West of the Mississippi*. Morrisville and Hyde Park, Vt.: News and Citizen, 1896.

Murray, Hamilton. *History of the Ninth Regiment, Connecticut Volunteer Infantry, "The Irish Regiment," in the War of the Rebellion, 1861–1865*. New Haven: Price, Lee & Adkins, 1903.

Official Records of the Union and Confederate Navies in the War of the Rebellion. 30 vols. Washington, D.C.: Government Printing Office, 1894–1922.

Read, C. W. "Reminiscences of the Confederate States Navy." *Southern Historical Society Papers* 1 (May 1876): 331–62.

Records of Ante-bellum Southern Plantations from the Revolution through the Civil War; Series J: Selections from the Southern Historical Collection, Part 5: Louisiana. Bethesda, Md.: University Publications of America, 1996.

Reed, Emily Hazen. *Life of A. P. Dostie; or, the Conflict in New Orleans*. New York: Wm. P. Tomlinson, 1868.

Robertson, William B. "The Water Battery at Fort Jackson." In *North to Antietam: Battles and Leaders of the Civil War, Volume II*, edited by Robert Underwood Johnson and Clarence Clough Buel, 99–100. New York: Thomas Yoseloff, 1956.

Rowland, Kate Mason, and Mrs. Morris L. Croxall, eds. *The Journal of Julia Le Grand: New Orleans, 1862–1863*. Richmond: Everett Waddey, 1911.

Russell, William H. *The Civil War in America*. Boston: Gardner A. Fuller, 1861.

——. *My Diary North and South*. Boston: T. O. H. P. Burnham, 1863.

Shively, J. W. "The USS Mississippi at the Capture of New Orleans, 1862." Read at the States Meeting of December 6, 1893, of the Military Order of the Loyal Legion of the United States.

Smith, George G. *Leaves from a Soldier's Diary*. Putnam, Conn.: George G. Smith, 1906.

Southern Women and Their Families in the Nineteenth Century: Papers and Diaries. Series E. Holdings of the Louisiana State University, Louisiana and Lower Mississippi Valley Collections. Bethesda, Md.: University Publications of America, 1998.

Sprague, Homer B. *History of the 13th Infantry Regiment of Connecticut Volunteers, during the Great Rebellion*. Hartford: Case, Lockwood & Co., 1867.

Stanyan, John M. *A History of the Eighth Regiment of New Hampshire Volunteers*. Concord, N.H.: Ira C. Evans, 1892.

Taylor, Asher. *Notes of Conversations with a Volunteer Officer in the United States Navy, or the Passage of the Forts below New Orleans, April 24, 1862, and Other Points of Service on the Mississippi River during that Year*. New York: Printed for private circulation, 1868.

The War of the Rebellion: A Compilation of the Official Records of the Union and Confederate Armies. 128 vols. Washington, D.C.: Government Printing Office, 1880–1901.

"The White Man's, or—Caucasian Club. Organized the 22d May, 1867." Planters' Banner Job Office Print, Franklin, La., 1868.

Wilkinson, J. *The Narrative of a Blockade-Runner*. New York: Sheldon & Co., 1877.

SECONDARY SOURCES

Books and Articles

Allgor, Catherine. *Parlor Politics: In Which the Ladies of Washington Help Build a City and a Government*. Charlottesville: University of Virginia Press, 2001.

Altschuler, Glenn C., and Stuart M. Blumin. *Rude Republic: Americans and Their Politics in the Nineteenth Century*. Princeton, N.J.: Princeton University Press, 2000.

Amos, Harriet E. "'All Absorbing Topics': Food and Clothing in Confederate Mobile." *Atlanta Historical Journal* 22 (Fall–Winter 1978): 17–28.

Anbinder, Tyler. *Nativism and Slavery: The Northern Know Nothings and the Politics of the 1850s*. New York: Oxford University Press, 1992.

Auman, William T. "Neighbor against Neighbor: The Inner Civil War in the Randolph County Area of Confederate North Carolina." *North Carolina Historical Review* 61 (January 1984): 59–92.

Auman, William T., and David D. Scarboro. "The Heroes of America in Civil War North Carolina." *North Carolina Historical Review* 58 (October 1981): 327–63.

Bailey, Anne J. "Defiant Unionists: Militant Germans in Confederate Texas." In *Enemies of the Country: New Perspectives on Unionists in the Civil War South*, edited by John C. Inscoe and Robert C. Kenzer, 208–28. Athens: University of Georgia Press, 2001.

Bailyn, Bernard. *The Ideological Origins of the American Republic*. Cambridge: Harvard University Press, 1967.

Baker, Jean H. *Ambivalent Americans: The Know-Nothing Party in Maryland*. Baltimore: Johns Hopkins University Press, 1977.

Banning, Lance. *The Jeffersonian Persuasion: Evolution of a Party Ideology*. Ithaca, N.Y.: Cornell University Press, 1978.

Barnes, Kenneth C. "The Williams Clan: Mountain Farmers and Union Fighters in North Central Arkansas." In *Civil War Arkansas: Beyond Battles and Leaders*, edited by Anne J. Bailey and Daniel E. Sutherland, 155–75. Fayetteville: University of Arkansas Press, 2000.

Bartlett, Napier. *Military Record of Louisiana*. New Orleans: L. Graham & Co., 1875. Reprint, Baton Rouge: Louisiana State University Press, 1964.

Bergeron, Arthur W., Jr. "Dennis Haynes and His 'Thrilling Narrative of the Sufferings of . . . the Martyrs of Liberty in Western Louisiana.'" In *Louisianians in the Civil War*, edited by Lawrence Lee Hewitt and Arthur W. Bergeron Jr., 37–49. Columbia: University of Missouri Press, 2002.

———. *Guide to Louisiana Confederate Military Units, 1861–1865*. Baton Rouge: Louisiana State University Press, 1989.

———. "'They Bore Themselves with Distinguished Gallantry': The Twenty-second Louisiana Infantry." *Louisiana History* 13 (Summer 1972): 253–82.

———. "The Yellow Jackets Battalion." In *Louisianians in the Civil War*, edited by Lawrence Lee Hewitt and Arthur W. Bergeron Jr., 50–71. Columbia: University of Missouri Press, 2002.

Beringer, Richard E., Herman Hattaway, Archer Jones, and William N. Still Jr. *Why the South Lost the Civil War*. Athens: University of Georgia Press, 1986.

Berlin, Ira, et al. *Slaves No More: Three Essays on Emancipation and the Civil War*. New York: Cambridge University Press, 1992.

Bernstein, Iver. *The New York City Draft Riots: Their Significance for American Society and Politics in the Age of the Civil War*. New York: Oxford University Press, 1990.

Blackburn, Florence, and Fay G. Brown. *Franklin through the Years*. N.p., 1972.

Blair, William. *Virginia's Private War: Feeding Body and Soul in the Confederacy, 1861–1865*. New York: Oxford University Press, 1998.

Bland, T. A. *Life of Benjamin F. Butler*. Boston: Lee & Shepard, 1879.

Blassingame, John. *Black New Orleans, 1860–1880*. Chicago: University of Chicago Press, 1973.

Bolton, Charles C. *Poor Whites of the Antebellum South: Tenants and Laborers in Central North Carolina and Northeast Mississippi*. Durham, N.C.: Duke University Press, 1994.

Bolton, Charles C., and Scott Culclasure, eds. *The Confessions of Edward Isham: A Poor White Life of the Old South*. Athens: University of Georgia Press, 1998.

Bonner, Robert E. "Flag Culture and the Consolidation of Confederate Nationalism." *Journal of Southern History* 48 (May 2002): 293–332.

Booth, Andrew B. *Records of Louisiana Confederate Soldiers and Louisiana Confederate Commands*. New Orleans: n.p., 1920.

Bragg, Jefferson Davis. *Louisiana in the Confederacy*. Baton Rouge: Louisiana State University Press, 1941.

Browning, Judkin. "Removing the Mask of Nationality: Unionism, Racism, and Federal Military Occupation in North Carolina, 1862–1865." *Journal of Southern History* 71 (August 2005): 589–620.

Bynum, Victoria E. *The Free State of Jones: Mississippi's Longest Civil War*. Chapel Hill: University of North Carolina Press, 2001.

Campbell, Jacqueline Glass. *When Sherman Marched to the Sea: Resistance on the Confederate Home Front*. Chapel Hill: University of North Carolina Press, 2003.

Carriere, Marius M., Jr. "Anti-Catholicism, Nativism, and Louisiana Politics in the 1850s." *Louisiana History* 35 (Fall 1994): 455–74.

Chapman, Caroline. *Russell of the Times: War Despatches and Diaries*. London: Bell & Hyman, 1984.

Chesson, Michael B. "Harlots or Heroines? A New Look at the Richmond Bread Riot." *Virginia Magazine of History and Biography* 92 (April 1984): 131–75.

Coffman, Edward M. *The Old Army: A Portrait of the American Army in Peacetime, 1784–1898*. New York: Oxford University Press, 1986.

Crawford, Martin. *Ashe County's Civil War: Community and Society in the Appalachian South*. Charlottesville: University of Virginia Press, 2001.

Crule, Joseph H., Jr. *Units of the Confederate States Army*. Midlothian, Va.: Derwent Books, 1987.

Current, Richard Nelson. *Lincoln's Loyalists: Union Soldiers from the Confederacy*. New York: Oxford University Press, 1992.

DeFiore, Jayne Crumpler. "'Come, and Bring the Ladies': Tennessee Women and the Politics of Opportunity during the Presidential Campaigns of 1840 and 1844." *Tennessee Historical Quarterly* 51 (Winter 1992): 197–212.

Degler, Carl. *The Other South: Southern Dissenters in the Nineteenth Century*. New York: Harper & Row, 1974.

Donald, David. *Charles Sumner and the Coming of the Civil War*. New York: Alfred A. Knopf, 1961.

Dufour, Charles L. *The Night the War Was Lost*. Garden City, N.Y.: Doubleday, 1960. Reprint, Lincoln: University of Nebraska Press, 1994.

Dunkelman, Mark H. *Brothers One and All: Esprit de Corps in a Civil War Regiment*. Baton Rouge: Louisiana State University Press, 2004.

Dunn, Richard S. *Sugar and Slaves: The Rise of the Planter Class in the English West Indies, 1624–1713*. Chapel Hill: University of North Carolina Press, 1972.

Dyer, Thomas G. *Secret Yankees: The Union Circle in Confederate Atlanta*. Baltimore: Johns Hopkins University Press, 1999.

Earle, Jonathan H. *Jacksonian Antislavery and the Politics of Free Soil, 1824–1854*. Chapel Hill: University of North Carolina Press, 2004.

Escott, Paul D. *After Secession: Jefferson Davis and the Failure of Confederate Nationalism*. Baton Rouge: Louisiana State University Press, 1978.

——. "The Failure of Confederate Nationalism: The Old South's Class System in the Crucible of War." In *The Old South in the Crucible of War*, edited by Harry P. Owens and James J. Cooke, 15–28. Jackson: University Press of Mississippi, 1983.

Faust, Drew Gilpin. *The Creation of Confederate Nationalism: Ideology and Identity in the Civil War South*. Baton Rouge: Louisiana State University Press, 1988.

——. *Mothers of Invention: Women of the Slaveholding South in the American Civil War*. Chapel Hill: University of North Carolina Press, 1996.

Filler, Louis. *The Crusade against Slavery, 1830–1860*. New York: Harper & Row, 1960.

Fitzgerald, Michael W. *Urban Emancipation: Popular Politics in Reconstruction Mobile, 1860–1890*. Baton Rouge: Louisiana State University Press, 2002.

Foner, Eric. *Free Soil, Free Labor, Free Men: The Ideology of the Republican Party before the Civil War*. New York: Oxford University Press, 1970.

——. *Reconstruction: America's Unfinished Revolution, 1863–1877*. New York: Harper & Row, 1988.

Foos, Paul. *A Short, Offhand, Killing Affair: Soldiers and Social Conflict during the Mexican-American War*. Chapel Hill: University of North Carolina Press, 2002.

Formisano, Ronald. "The 'Party Period' Revisited." *Journal of American History* 86 (June 1999): 93–120.

Freehling, William W. *The South versus the South: How Anti-Confederate Southerners Shaped the Course of the Civil War*. New York: Oxford University Press, 2001.

Furneaux, Rupert. *The First War Correspondent: William Howard Russell of the Times*. London: Cassell & Co., 1944.

Gallagher, Gary W. *The Confederate War: How Popular Will, Nationalism, and Military Strategy Could Not Stave Off Defeat*. Cambridge: Harvard University Press, 1997.

Gienapp, William E. *The Origins of the Republican Party*. New York: Oxford University Press, 1987.

Glenn, Myra C. "Troubled Manhood in the Early Republic: The Life and Autobiography of Sailor Horace Lane." *Journal of the Early Republic* 26 (Spring 2006): 59–93.

Gordon, Lesley J. "'In Time of War': Unionists Hanged in Kinston, North Carolina, February 1864." In *Guerillas, Unionists, and Violence on the Confederate Home Front*, edited by Daniel E. Sutherland, 45–58. Fayetteville: University of Arkansas Press, 1999.

Hankinson, Alan. *Man of Wars: William Howard Russell of the Times*. London: Heinemann, 1982.

Harris, William C. "The Southern Unionist Critique of the Civil War." *Civil War History* 31 (March 1985): 39–56.

Hearn, Chester G. *The Capture of New Orleans, 1862*. Baton Rouge: Louisiana State University Press, 1995.

———. *When the Devil Came Down to Dixie: Ben Butler in New Orleans*. Baton Rouge: Louisiana State University Press, 1997.

Hollandsworth, James G. *The Louisiana Native Guards: The Black Military Experience during the Civil War*. Baton Rouge: Louisiana State University Press, 1995.

———. "'What a Hell of a Place to Send 2000 Men 3000 Miles': Union Soldiers on Ship Island during the Civil War." *Journal of Mississippi History* 62 (Summer 2000): 123–39.

Holt, Michael. "The Politics of Impatience: The Origins of the Know Nothingism." *Journal of American History* 60 (September 1973): 309–31.

Holzman, Robert S. *Stormy Ben Butler*. New York: Macmillan, 1954.

Horwitz, Tony. *Confederates in the Attic: Dispatches from the Unfinished Civil War*. New York: Pantheon, 1998.

Hunter, G. Howard. "The Politics of Resentment: Unionist Regiments and the New Orleans Immigrant Community, 1862–1864." *Louisiana History* 44 (Spring 2003): 185–210.

Inscoe, John C., and Robert C. Kenzer, eds. *Enemies of the Country: New*

Perspectives on Unionists in the Civil War South. Athens: University of Georgia Press, 2001.

Inscoe, John C., and Gordon B. McKinney. *The Heart of Confederate Appalachia: Western North Carolina in the Civil War*. Chapel Hill: University of North Carolina Press, 2000.

Jackson, Joy J. "Keeping Law and Order in New Orleans under General Butler, 1862." *Louisiana History* 34 (Winter 1993): 51–67.

Johnson, Walter. "The Slave Trader, the White Slave, and the Politics of Racial Determination in the 1850s." *Journal of American History* 87 (June 2000): 13–38.

Kagan, Neil, Stephen Hyslop, and Harris J. Andrews. *Eyewitness to the Civil War: The Complete History from Secession to Reconstruction*. Washington, D.C.: National Geographic, 2006.

Kattner, Lauren Ann. "The Diversity of Old South White Women: The Peculiar Worlds of German American White Women." In *Discovering the Women in Slavery: Emancipating Perspectives on the American Past*, edited by Patricia Morton, 299–311. Athens: University of Georgia Press, 1996.

Lack, Paul D. "Law and Disorder in Confederate Atlanta." *Georgia Historical Quarterly* 60 (Summer 1982): 171–95.

Laurie, Bruce. *Beyond Garrison: Antislavery and Social Reform*. New York: Cambridge University Press, 2005.

Levine, Bruce. "Conservatism, Nativism, and Slavery: Thomas R. Whitney and the Origins of the Know-Nothing Party." *Journal of American History* 88 (September 2001): 455–88.

Long, Alecia. "(Mis)remembering General Order 28: Benjamin Butler, the Woman Order and Historical Memory." Southern Association for Women Historians Convention, 2006, Baltimore.

Long, E. B., with Barbara Long. *The Civil War Day by Day: An Almanac, 1861–1865*. Garden City, N.Y.: Doubleday, 1971.

Lonn, Ella. *Foreigners in the Confederacy*. Chapel Hill: University of North Carolina Press, 1940.

Luskey, Brian P. "Jumping Counters in White Collars: Manliness, Respectability, and Work in the Antebellum City." *Journal of the Early Republic* 26 (Summer 2006): 173–219.

Marten, James. *Texas Divided: Loyalty and Dissent in the Lone Star State, 1856–1874*. Lexington: University Press of Kentucky, 1990.

Medford, Edna Greene. " 'I Was Always a Union Man': The Dilemma of Free Blacks in Confederate Virginia." *Slavery and Abolition* 15 (December 1994): 1–16.

Merrill, James M. "Confederate Shipbuilding at New Orleans." *Journal of Southern History* 28 (February 1962): 87–93.

Miller, Ilana D. *Reports from America: William Howard Russell and the Civil War*. Phoenix Mill, England: Sutton Publishing, 2001.

Moneyhon, Carl H. "Disloyalty and Class Consciousness in Southwestern Arkansas, 1862–1865." In *Civil War Arkansas: Beyond Battles and Leaders*, edited by Anne J. Bailey and Daniel E. Sutherland, 117–32. Fayetteville: University of Arkansas Press, 2000.

Moore, John Hammond. "Sherman's 'Fifth Column': A Guide to Unionist Activity in Georgia." *Georgia Historical Quarterly* 68 (Fall 1984): 382–409.

Mulkern, John R. *The Know-Nothing Party in Massachusetts: The Rise and Fall of a People's Movement*. Boston: Northeastern University Press, 1990.

Olsen, Christopher J. " 'Molly Pitcher' of the Mississippi Whigs: The Editorial Career of Mrs. Harriet N. Prewett." *Journal of Mississippi History* 58 (Fall 1996): 237–54.

Pace, Robert F. " 'It Was Bedlam Let Loose': The Louisiana Sugar Country and the Civil War." *Louisiana History* 39 (Fall 1998): 389–409.

Palladino, Grace. *Another Civil War: Labor, Capital, and the State in the Anthracite Regions of Pennsylvania, 1840–68*. Urbana: University of Illinois Press, 1990.

Paludan, Phillip Shaw. *Victims: A True Story of the Civil War*. Knoxville: University of Tennessee Press, 1981.

Pickering, David, and Judy Falls. *Brush Men and Vigilantes: Civil War Dissent in Texas*. College Station: Texas A&M University Press, 2000.

Pierson, Michael D. *Free Hearts and Free Homes: Gender and American Antislavery Politics*. Chapel Hill: University of North Carolina Press, 2003.

———. " 'He Helped the Poor and Snubbed the Rich': Benjamin F. Butler and Class Politics in Lowell and New Orleans." *Massachusetts Historical Review* 7 (2005): 36–68.

Piston, William Garrett, and Richard W. Hatcher III. *Wilson's Creek: The Second Battle of the Civil War and the Men Who Fought It*. Chapel Hill: University of North Carolina Press, 2000.

Powell, Lawrence N., and Michael S. Wayne. "Self-Interest and the Decline of Confederate Nationalism." In *The Old South in the Crucible of War*, edited by Harry P. Owens and James J. Cooke, 29–45. Jackson: University Press of Mississippi, 1983.

Prokopowicz, Gerald J. *All for the Regiment: The Army of the Ohio, 1861–1862*. Chapel Hill: University of North Carolina Press, 2001.

Quist, John W. *Restless Visionaries: The Social Roots of Antebellum Reform in Alabama and Michigan*. Baton Rouge: Louisiana State University Press, 1998.

Rable, George C. *The Confederate Republic: A Revolution against Politics*. Chapel Hill: University of North Carolina Press, 1994.

———. " 'Missing in Action': Women in the Confederacy." In *Divided Houses: Gender and the Civil War*, edited by Catherine Clinton and Nina Silber, 134–46. New York: Oxford University Press, 1992.

Radley, Kenneth. *Rebel Watchdog: The Confederate States Army Provost Guard.*
Baton Rouge: Louisiana State University Press, 1989.

Ripley, C. Peter. *Slaves and Freedmen in Civil War Louisiana.* Baton Rouge:
Louisiana State University Press, 1976.

Robinson, Armstead L. *Bitter Fruits of Bondage: The Demise of Slavery and the
Collapse of the Confederacy, 1861–1865.* Charlottesville: University of Virginia
Press, 2005.

Rockman, Seth. *Welfare Reform in the Early Republic: A Brief History with
Documents.* New York: Bedford/St. Martin's, 2003.

Roedigar, David R. *The Wages of Whiteness: Race and the Making of the American
Working Class.* London: Verso, 1991.

Rogers, William Warren, Jr. *Confederate Home Front: Montgomery during the Civil
War.* Tuscaloosa: University of Alabama Press, 1999.

Rousey, Dennis C. *Policing the Southern City: New Orleans, 1805–1889.* Baton
Rouge: Louisiana State University Press, 1996.

Rubin, Anne Sarah. *A Shattered Nation: The Rise and Fall of the Confederacy, 1861–
1868.* Chapel Hill: University of North Carolina Press, 2005.

Ryan, Mary P. *Women in Public: Between Banners and Ballots, 1825–1880.*
Baltimore: Johns Hopkins University Press, 1990.

Sacher, John M. *A Perfect War of Politics: Parties, Politicians, and Democracy
in Louisiana, 1824–1861.* Baton Rouge: Louisiana State University Press,
2003.

Schultz, Nancy Lusignan. *Fire and Roses: The Burning of the Charlestown Convent,
1834.* New York: Free Press, 2000.

Sewell, Richard H. *Ballots for Freedom: Antislavery Politics in the United States,
1837–1860.* New York: Oxford University Press, 1976.

Shugg, Roger W. *Origins of Class Struggle in Louisiana: A Social History of White
Farmers and Laborers during Slavery and After, 1840–1875.* Baton Rouge:
Louisiana State University Press, 1939.

Sifakis, Stewart. *Compendium of the Confederate Armies: Louisiana.* New York:
Facts on File, 1995.

Smelser, Marshall. *The Democratic Republic: 1801–1815.* New York: Harper & Row,
1968.

Smith, Leonard V. *Between Mutiny and Obedience: The Case of the French Fifth
Infantry Division during World War One.* Princeton, N.J.: Princeton University
Press, 1994.

Smyrl, Frank H. "Texans in the Union Army, 1861–1865." *Southwestern Historical
Quarterly* 65 (October 1961): 234–50.

Soulé, Leon Cyprian. *The Know Nothing Party in New Orleans: A Reappraisal.* Baton
Rouge: Louisiana Historical Association, 1961.

Stampp, Kenneth M. *The Imperiled Union: Essays on the Background of the Civil War*. New York: Oxford University Press, 1980.

Still, William N., Jr. *Confederate Shipbuilding*. Athens: University of Georgia Press, 1969.

Storey, Margaret M. *Loyalty and Loss: Alabama's Unionists in the Civil War and Reconstruction*. Baton Rouge: Louisiana State University Press, 2004.

Strong, Michael J. *Keystone Confederate: The Life and Times of General Johnson Kelly Duncan, CSA*. York, Pa.: Historical Society of York County, 1994.

Surdam, David G. "Union Military Superiority and New Orleans's Economic Value to the Confederacy." *Louisiana History* 38 (Fall 1997): 389–408.

Sutherland, Daniel E., ed. *Guerillas, Unionists, and Violence on the Confederate Home Front*. Fayetteville: University of Arkansas Press, 1999.

——. "Mansfield Lovell's Quest for Justice: Another Look at the Fall of New Orleans." *Louisiana History* 24 (Summer 1983): 233–59.

Tatum, Georgia Lee. *Disloyalty in the Confederacy*. Chapel Hill: University of North Carolina Press, 1934.

Taylor, Anne-Marie. *Young Charles Sumner and the Legacy of the American Enlightenment, 1811–1851*. Amherst: University of Massachusetts Press, 2001.

Towers, Frank. *The Urban South and the Coming of the Civil War*. Charlottesville: University of Virginia Press, 2004.

Trefousse, Hans L. *Butler: The South Called Him Beast*. New York: Twayne Publishers, 1957.

Varon, Elizabeth. *Southern Lady, Yankee Spy: The True Story of Elizabeth Van Lew, A Union Agent in the Heart of the Confederacy*. New York: Oxford University Press, 2003.

——. *We Mean to Be Counted: White Women and Politics in Antebellum Virginia*. Chapel Hill: University of North Carolina Press, 1998.

Voss-Hubbard, Mark. *Beyond Party: Cultures of Antipartisanship in Northern Politics before the Civil War*. Baltimore: Johns Hopkins University Press, 2002.

Wakelyn, Jon L. *Confederates against the Confederacy: Essays on Leadership and Loyalty*. Westport, Conn.: Praeger, 2002.

Way, Peter. *Common Labor: Workers and the Digging of North American Canals, 1780–1860*. Cambridge: Cambridge University Press, 1993.

Weinert, Richard P., Jr. *The Confederate Regular Army*. Shippensburg, Pa.: White Mane Publishing, 1991.

Williams, David. *Rich Man's War: Class, Caste, and Confederate Defeat in the Lower Chattahoochie Valley*. Athens: University of Georgia Press, 1998.

Winters, John D. *The Civil War in Louisiana*. Baton Rouge: Louisiana State University Press, 1963.

index

Index